THE LATER FICTION OF NADINE GORDIMER

Also by Bruce King

THREE INDIAN POETS: Ezekiel, Ramanujan and Moraes
MODERN INDIAN POETRY IN ENGLISH
THE NEW ENGLISH LITERATURES:
Cultural nationalism in a changing world
CORIOLANUS
HISTORY OF SEVENTEENTH-CENTURY ENGLISH
LITERATURE
MARVELL'S ALLEGORICAL POETRY
DRYDEN'S MAJOR PLAYS

Books edited by Bruce King

POST-COLONIAL ENGLISH DRAMA: Commonwealth
drama since 1960
THE COMMONWEALTH NOVEL SINCE 1960
WEST INDIAN LITERATURE
A CELEBRATION OF BLACK AND AFRICAN WRITING
LITERATURES OF THE WORLD IN ENGLISH
INTRODUCTION TO NIGERIAN LITERATURE
CONTEMPORARY AMERICAN THEATRE
DRYDEN'S MIND AND ART
TWENTIETH-CENTURY INTERPRETATIONS OF
ALL FOR LOVE: A collection of critical essays

Series editor

MODERN DRAMATISTS
ENGLISH DRAMATISTS

The Later Fiction of Nadine Gordimer

Edited by

Bruce King

St. Martin's Press   New York

823
G66 zk

First published in the United States of America in 1993

Printed in Hong Kong

ISBN 0–312–08534–6

Library of Congress Cataloging-in-Publication Data
The Later fiction of Nadine Gordimer / edited by Bruce King.
p.   cm.
Includes index.
ISBN 0–312–08534–6
1. Gordimer, Nadine—Criticism and interpretation.   2. South
Africa in literature.   I. King, Bruce Alvin.
PR9369.3.G6G76   1993
823—dc20   92–13518
                                                        CIP

This book is dedicated to the memory of Michael Wade who died, an exile from South Africa, in Jerusalem, September 1990. He was an excellent critic, author of three books about South African literature, a revolutionary and a friend. The essay included here was edited, with his wife's permission, from a longer version. B. K.

Contents

Notes on the Contributors   ix

Introduction: A Changing Face   1
Bruce King

Part I   General Essays
1   'Nobody's Children': Families in Gordimer's
    Later Novels   21
    John Cooke

2   Collector's Art, Collective Action: The Search for
    Commitment in Nadine Gordimer's Fiction   33
    Graham Huggan

3   Black and White in Grey: Irony and Judgement in
    Gordimer's Fiction   45
    Rowland Smith

4   Placing Spaces: Style and Ideology in Gordimer's
    Later Fiction   59
    Brian Macaskill

5   Landscape Iconography in the Novels of
    Nadine Gordimer   74
    Kathrin M. Wagner

Part II   The Novels
6   *The Conservationist* and the Political Uncanny   91
    Lars Engle

7   The Interregnum of Ownership in *July's People*   108
    Rosemarie Bodenheimer

8   The Politics of Place in *Burger's Daughter*   121
    Daphne Read

9   Making Metaphors/Moving On: *Burger's Daughter*
    and *A Sport of Nature*   140
    Susan Winnett

10   *A Sport of Nature*: Identity and Repression of the
      Jewish Subject   155
      Michael Wade

11   *A Sport of Nature* and the Boundaries of Fiction   173
      Stephen Clingman

12   *My Son's Story*: Drenching the Censors – the Dilemma
      of White Writing   191
      Susan M. Greenstein

Part III   The Shorter Fiction

13   Feminism as 'Piffling'? Ambiguities in Gordimer's
      Short Stories   213
      Karen Lazar

14   Once More into the Burrows: Gordimer's Later
      Short Fiction   228
      Alan R. Lomberg

15   Archive of Apartheid: Nadine Gordimer's Short
      Fiction at the End of the Interregnum   237
      Jeanne Colleran

Index   246

Notes on the Contributors

Rosemarie Bodenheimer is Professor of English at Boston College and author of *The Politics of Story in Victorian Social Fiction*.

Stephen Clingman, a South African, is Professor of English at the University of Massachusetts–Amherst. His publications include *The Novels of Nadine Gordimer: History from the Inside* and the editing of Gordimer's *The Essential Gesture: Writing, Politics and Places*

Jeanne Colleran teaches English at John Carroll University, Cleveland, Ohio. Her interests include drama, South African and Renaissance literature.

John Cooke is Professor of English at the University of New Orleans, author of *The Novels of Nadine Gordimer: Private Lives/Public Landscapes* and editor of the four volumes of *New Orleans Ethnic Cultures*.

Lars Engle is Assistant Professor of English at the University of Tulsa. He is the author of the forthcoming *Shakespearean Pragmatism* (Chicago, 1993), and numerous articles on Early English and recent South African literature.

Susan M. Greenstein taught English at Western Washington University and St Mary's College of Maryland, and currently is an administrator with the National Endowment for the Humanities. She often writes about South African and women authors.

Graham Huggan is English, studied for his doctorate in Canada and teaches English at Harvard University. He is editing a collection of essays on J. M. Coetzee to be published by Macmillan.

Bruce King is the author of *New English Literatures, Modern Indian Poetry in English, Three Indian Poets, Coriolanus* and other books. Among the books he has edited are *The Commonwealth Novel since 1960* and *Contemporary American Theatre*. He is editor of the English Dramatists series and co-editor of the Modern Dramatists series.

Karen Lazar is a South African who teaches English at the University of the Witwatersrand, Johannesburg.

Alan R. Lomberg is from South Africa, has taught at the University of Malawi and now teaches English at Algoma University College in Canada.

Brian Macaskill, from South Africa, teaches English at John Carroll University in Ohio. His interests are South African literature, the novel and theory.

Daphne Read wrote her doctoral thesis on Gordimer's *Burger's Daughter*. She teaches English at the University of Alberta, Edmonton, Canada.

Rowland Smith is McCulloch Professor in English at Dalhousie University, Nova Scotia, Canada, and Dean of Arts and Social Sciences. His publications include *The Literary Personality of Roy Campbell* and the editing of *Critical Essays on Nadine Gordimer* and *Exile and Tradition: Essays in African and Caribbean Literature*.

Michael Wade was Professor of English and African Studies at the Hebrew University, Jerusalem, Israel. He wrote the first books on Gordimer and Peter Abrahams. He lived in exile from South Africa after his involvement in revolutionary activities; he was wanted by the South African police and banned from entry into his native land.

Kathrin Wagner writes regularly on South African fiction. She is from Germany and Senior Lecturer in English at the University of the Witwatersrand, Johannesburg.

Susan Winnett teaches English and Comparative Literature at Columbia University, New York. Her *Terrible Sociability: The Text of Manners in Laclos, Goethe, and Henry James* was published by Stanford University Press.

Introduction:
A Changing Face
BRUCE KING

A book of essays about the later fiction of a highly productive, contemporary author at the peak of her powers is unusual; such specialized attention is normally reserved for the long-dead classics of our culture – the late works, say, of Shakespeare, Ibsen, Henry James. Nadine Gordimer, however, is an unusual writer; her recent fiction has evolved so rapidly in new directions that there is considerable puzzlement about what she is doing and why. Many readers feel her later fiction has a prominent place among the classics of our time; others do not like it or became lost along the way. While some object to her politics, more are confused by the rapid changes in the style, manner and form of her novels. What are the novels saying and why has she chosen these forms?

In Gordimer's fiction there are often tensions between the personal and the political and between the traditions of the European novel and the urgencies of African politics. In both spheres, the personal and artistic, there is a strongly-felt need to overcome feelings of being alienated and isolated by the burden of colonialism and to become part of the emerging new black-governed Africa and the political processes that are shaping her era. Her novels increasingly have central characters who are either revolutionaries or who offer alternative views of modernization and reform. But despite Gordimer's desire to transcend the limitations of a white writer in Africa, her fiction still has its origins in the opposition between the personal and political and between the art and concerns of the European novel and the need for political self-realization through commitment. While the white woman, especially the white female liberal, intellectual, artist, or activist, so prominent in Gordimer's fiction, is the perfect 'place' in which to examine the conflicts heightened in contemporary South Africa between the personal and public, she also must be seen as embodying the author's conflicting desires. The more public and seemingly objective the later fiction becomes, the more Gordimer self-consciously returns to the personal basis of her fiction – the instinctual, including sexuality, the effects of

1

family life, the role of family and society in creating conscience, the traditions of the European novel as expressions of the self, especially the self in times of conflict and crisis.

If her writing is highly self-conscious of craft and art, it is also self-conscious of two opposing polarities, each of which has its own contradictions. One tendency might be described as feminine (the instinctual, the personal, the socially and morally conscious). The other is masculine (public, rational, dominating, distinguishing between public politics and personal possessions). There is a desire in Gordimer's fiction to bring together these opposites into an existence that is both personal and communal, instinctual yet, through politics, publicly responsible. If the essential wish is to overcome the self's dual alienation from its desires and from others, the articulation of the psychology is shaped by an awareness that the tradition of the European novel concerns the crisis of conscience of the bourgeoisie and that in South Africa the white artist is faced by the prospect of becoming irrelevant, an historical embarrassment that will be forgotten. Hence her existential need to reassert herself in history as the white woman, the white bourgeois artist, aware of her dilemma and whose fiction mirrors both the major political changes of her time and her own attempts to adapt as a writer to a new historical situation.

Almost from the first Gordimer was recognized as a potentially major artist, a talented, serious and careful writer who treated important contemporary issues. She was the heir of the politically-conscious fiction of the thirties and forties, one of the first truly impressive novelists to appear in Africa, someone who could write sensitively about local life with complex consciousness. Her prose ranged in its manner according to what was being described or shown. She brought together the traditions of English and European fiction, while being at the forefront of those establishing new national English literatures in the former colonies. Although a realist concerned with detailing the manners, ideas and changes in her society, including its politics and racial injustices, she had, and still has, an unusual interest in the symbolic, the psychological as well as the art of fiction. For some critics her writing is even too consciously high art in its nuances, its increasingly elliptical conciseness, sense of multiple ironies and self-conscious awareness of the traditions of the novel.

While Gordimer seems better-read, more at home with, and more responsive to ideas, especially socialist and Marxist theory, than do most contemporary novelists, she also gives voice to the body and its desires, to the eye and mind's consciousness of surroundings and landscape, to the specifics of South African society and politics, especially as they influence personal relations. Her fiction seems personal, about rebellion from family, explorations of ways of living, attempts to bring together the truth of the body and the senses with the demands of the mind and moral consciousness in the confusing cultural and political variousness of South Africa. The novels evolve from the *bildungsroman*, although often written while still in the process of discovery, of exploration.

Her early novels appear to have originated in the lives of people she observed who had themselves engaged in such quests. As the novels probed the dilemmas of the liberal conscience in racially segregated South Africa, and the impossibility of total fulfilment, they paradoxically became both more significant yet more restricted and despairing, even depressing, seemingly a dead end. The mixture of the British fictional tradition, with its liberalism, individualism, social detail, and the European literary tradition of ideas and revolutionary demands, required new forms, new techniques, a new consciousness. The personal had to be more firmly anchored in the rapidly changing politics of black Africa. *The Late Bourgeois World*, with its main character's moral and political despair, appeared the end of a road, as if the South African novel about personal relations could go no further in the darkening climate of apartheid.

Since then Gordimer has tried to write the new novel of Africa while producing variations on the novel of the Interregnum. The form evolved to become increasingly 'post-modern' and multivoiced as the subject matter became the world of radicals, revolutionary situations, discussion of means and ends, commitments to the People – which represented the heightened tensions of contemporary Africa; yet her later novels remain focused on family relations, manners, morals and their effects on individual actions. In spite of their radicalism of form, subject matter, implied politics and desire to revise and go beyond the bourgeois novel, at their core is the *bildungsroman*. Even the questions raised about individual will versus biological, economic and social determinism are familiar from nineteenth-century Naturalism. It is possible to see *A Sport of Nature* as a self-conscious examination, even a parody, of the traditions from which Gordimer's writing has continued to develop.

John Cooke suggests that a new direction begins with *A Guest of Honour* with its larger, pan-African perspective. This novel introduces many of the concerns of the later fiction, such as awareness that black rule in independent Africa has not led to social or political justice; that a more humane and egalitarian black Africa requires a further revolution destroying the role of the white progressive in Africa.[1] *A Guest of Honour* foreshadows the novels which follow by assuming that the post-colonial in most of independent Africa is neo-colonial, a stage of contradictions in the march of history towards authentic independence and justice for the masses. Liberal values, such as personal freedom and interracial friendship, are likely to be found irrelevant as black leaders attempt to create their own version of a just society, need to consolidate power, or reward their followers. Although *Burger's Daughter*, *A Sport of Nature* and *My Son's Story* allude to specific historical situations, they develop insights already explored in the earlier novel.

The pan-African perspective of *A Guest of Honour*, like *A Sport of Nature*, has its South African significance. Besides mirroring what has been happening in many parts of post-colonial Africa, the novel reflects the increasing pressure in South Africa to go beyond liberalism towards radical political action. Although such issues were to be tackled explicitly in subsequent novels, Gordimer's imagination was already anticipating the adjustments required of the white liberal in a future black Africa. She felt that the political and economic culture was incapable of reform; something more extreme was needed. Where did she and those like her fit into the future?

Her stories imaginatively examine individual lives within a changing historical situation. The increasing mixture of politics, economics, sociology and psychology is indebted to Marxian theorizing; but the novels are too filled with the details of individual lives, too ironic, too aware of other realities, including personality and the instinctual, to be programmatic or primarily analytic. In Gordimer's fiction the sexual is a microcosm for or related to the political; the main character's political realignment in *A Guest of Honour* is paralleled by his leaving his English wife for a new woman. If a new politics means a new life and new sexual interests, something more fundamental is being examined with the political. As the political situation darkens, the tension between the personal and political sharpens. How to overcome feelings of being left behind by history? How to overcome ageing? Personal vitality seems to require political renewal.

The Conservationist and the short stories published at that time are usually felt to be Gordimer's entry into post-modernist fiction, a foreshadowing of the many voices, the confusion of facts with fantasies, the unreliable or dislocated multiple narration, found in such works as *Burger's Daughter* and *July's People*. Mehring in *The Conservationist* represents the progressive Afrikaner elite which has joined the late capitalist international order. His private environmentalism and conservationism is a form of private domination. The ending is ambiguous, facts and fears merge into an unreliable narrative, the subjectivity of the main character is invaded by the external world of politics and race; there is the eruption of what Freud called the uncanny. All this implies a recognition that the self-willed individual is a product of society, culture and economics, a repository of the past, situated in a precise historical context.

Mehring, however, cannot be reduced to an allegorization of the failure of the Afrikaners to reform themselves through modernization and the pressures of economic development, although that is certainly one theme of *The Conservationist*. I agree with Lars Engle's suggestion that critics have at times been too ready to dismiss Mehring. For all his faults and attitudes Mehring is often an attractive character; the method of narration ensures the reader's interest and grudging sympathy. Except for the dead black body there really is no one else in *The Conservationist* who is a focus of concern. The characters who hold all the politically correct attitudes are vague, unattractive, unsympathic. This is not just a matter of entrapping the reader, by offering a dominant, active, attractive Satanic centre of consciousness. There are enough examples in Gordimer's novels of energy, physical attraction, power, intelligence, strength of will, sexual desire, and other political irrelevances being fully appreciated, respected and understood.

Some of the power of this still underrated novel and of *Burger's Daughter* lies in their multiplicity of authorial sympathy, appreciation of the idealized organic community of the Afrikaner past, recognition of, and argument with, the Afrikaner progressives, and recognition of a sophisticated Afrikaner intelligentsia and business class. Gordimer understands that male sexual instinct is related to desires to build, control, dominate; the same inquisitiveness, energy and creativity which make Mehring a success in business drive him sexually and cause him to want a piece of rural Africa as his own. He embodies the paradoxical contradictions of modernity and liberal capitalism. If *The Conservationist* concludes by showing that no individual, regardless of how intelligent and powerful, is likely to escape from the injustices that are part of South African capitalism, the libido and its relationship to the ego are given their full due. As often in modern literature, psychology and politics are in conflict. And, of course, there is the question of what does occur at the end of the novel. Is Mehring entrapped by the police? Or is the scene an expression of his anxieties, an eruption of the fears brought about by racial guilt? Gordimer is already moving towards the kind of ambiguous, multi-perspectival novel which will be given a more formal, deconstructed form in *Burger's Daughter*.

Because of the increasing radicalism of Gordimer's later comments, her novels are often assumed to be a programme for the future rather than a mirror of what was happening and being said in Southern Africa at the time. *Burger's Daughter* examines, among other things, the history of the South African Communist Party, its need to adapt Marxist theory to local realities, and its resistance to white exploitation of blacks, and shows why it became influential within the ANC leadership until the rise of the Black Consciousness movement undermined what had been one of the few examples of whites and blacks successfully cooperating as equals. The novels test and revise ideas by actual historical experience. *A Sport of Nature* suggests that ends justify means, including the use of repression to better the conditions of the People; but as Lionel Abrahams has shown,[2] there are enough ironies to subvert such a reading for those *au courant* with its allusions to and parodies of contemporary African politics. *My Son's Story* questions whether the collapse of Communism in Eastern Europe does not suggest that the economic and political programmes of the South African revolutionary leadership are headed for disaster. If the later novels examine the lives of radicals and revolutionaries, what at first seems a fictional programme for revolutionary action is found to be loaded with ironies and grounded in the personal. Each time the form of the novel, however, is different, more radical than previously. Each of the novels also investigates the place of whites in contemporary black Africa.

With *Burger's Daughter* Gordimer supposedly became a postmodern writer. It might be said that the bourgeois novel — with its concern for individual will, personal narratives, and the relationship of self to conscience and social position – is undermined by a shift from the centrality of the subjective and individual to include South Africa in its various highly contested sets of relations, attitudes and voices. The many perspectives, the multiple voices, the inclusion of supposed police reports and of genuine black African student tracts, the mixing of the real with the imaginary, of the subjective with the objective, and the parallels to actual events and lives, creates a baroque formal structure in which, despite the focus on Rosa Burger's story, other stories, perspectives, voices and historical events intrude to disrupt and impinge on the narrative. While the novel has been the subject of much structural analysis, its formal innovations, like those of most post-colonial post-modernist novels, are parts of its politics rather than play and aestheticism. Rosa is a product of and is situated in a complex historical situation in which the personal cannot be separated from such other realities as the South African police state and the black African struggle. Whereas many novels of the late colonial or early post-colonial periods assert the communal, in *Burger's Daughter* fragmentation replaces unity of narrative, as the social order is itself in disarray and moral imperatives require its destruction.

To speak of moral imperatives is to recognize that even here there still is a version, an attempted revision, of *The Late Bourgeois World*. It is still Rosa's story and a story as much concerned with psychology, family, will and conscience as determined by material, social and political history. Gordimer has tried to incorporate communal, material history, to show how it influences, even partly determines, the personal; but the title *Burger's Daughter* announces that at the novel's core there is a Freudian family saga. At the novel's conclusion, Rosa's imprisonment seems as much determined by family history as by rational choice and political circumstances. The historical situation is the time and place in which the individual acts; but the actions may be as much influenced by the emotional as by the objective or material world. The ironies open and make ambiguous rather than close the significance of the narrative. A Gordimer trait is the ambiguous, possibly ironic, ending.

That Brian Macaskill and Stephen Clingman can reach such contrary interpretations of the novel's ending shows that the various levels, discourses, or themes remain unresolved. Indeed, the more Gordimer shifts the focus from inside the central character to outside influences, the less likely it is we will know what is the basis of Rosa's decisions. This narrative method is carried much further in *A Sport of Nature*. Such purposeful ambiguity is, as I understand it, the point of the technique, the reason for the baroque form of *Burger's Daughter*. Understanding Rosa is more difficult than understanding Hamlet, but for similar reasons. We are given an excess of information, a variety of interpretive perspectives, without being given any privileged insight into her decision-making at significant moments. The break in the narrative between her exile in Europe and her return to South Africa is similar to Hamlet's offstage voyage to and return from England, a decisive time about which we are uncertain what has really taken place.

Gordimer evolved a method similar to that found in Shakespeare's major tragedies in which characters offer contrasting interpretations of other characters, past and present events. The scenes contrast, each giving a different perspective, allowing a different voice. There is an excess of information and no guidance as to what might be correct. Often there are implied subtexts – such as those suggested by the lives of the women Rosa meets in Europe, or even by the paintings and architecture she views – which may or may not throw the story into another perspective and interpretation. In such works – Ibsen is another master of the technique – the linear narrative, the plot or story, is challenged and subverted by interruptions, digressions, contrasts, ambiguities, gaps. The story may seem a clothes-line on which to hang various contrasting materials which modify the significance of the narrative. Hence all the ironies, the differences of opinion between critics about what actually occurs at the end of a Gordimer novel.

Such self-consciousness about the nature of telling and portraying, about the essential nature and conventions of the art, develops in many of the best writers and artists, as well as being characteristic of new artistic periods and movements. Yet artists have their own ways of deconstructing their art and making it new. Gordimer has taken the classical bourgeois novel in its modern form, with its Freudianism, its irony, its symbolism, as well as its sense of cultural crisis, and enlarged it to include other elements such as post-modernist decentring, historical determinism and analysis of the effects of colonialism and decolonization in South Africa. But for all their post-modernism, her later novels are a contemporary version of the late bourgeois novel, especially if one keeps in mind the sense of radical irony at the heart of much nineteenth-century Continental fiction. Is *A Sport of Nature* a contemporary update of *A Hero of Our Time? A Heroine of Our Time?*

I suspect Gordimer's political sympathies and conscience inhibit the scepticism, the radical subversiveness, that is part of her imagination and at which her fiction hints; therefore she has to find other ways to wed the political with the appropriate form. No matter how much Gordimer suspects that the new Africa may be disillusioning, her moral and political commitments keep guard over such panic. Despite its ironies, *A Sport of Nature* takes the easy way out. By keeping the narration on the outside, by gliding over what is alluded to and cleverly parodied, Gordimer makes the blood of revolutionaries worth much more than that of those supposedly liberated. By avoiding realism the means justify the ends.

Both the equation of Gordimer's later fiction with the postmodern and indeterminate, and the alternative view which attempts to resolve her multiplicity into a political statement, are flawed. A little decentredness does not make a novel as unstable as the collage of images in T. S. Eliot's major poems. Gordimer's alternative visions are expressed through irony, ambiguity, stories ending in defeat. Gordimer aims at the impossibility of saying exactly what motivates her characters, the variety of influences on them, the recognition of the political situation as well as the psychological, the difficulty of 'reading' others. The politics of her novels are like their form, hovering on the edge of a radical leap, going a step further with each novel, but always holding back from taking that plunge.

In *July's People* the reader, like Maureen, knows little about July's world, his thoughts, his relationship to his wife and the woman with whom he lived, his society at home. Only short sections of the novel focus on his thoughts. Maureen's attempt to become part of the village community and to claim a special relationship with July is rebuffed and she remains an outsider. She is another version of that figure who recurs in Gordimer's fiction – Liz Van Den Sandt of *The Late Bourgeois World*; Rosa – the white woman who wants a place in the future black Africa, but who is excluded by skin colour, culture, historical guilt. What has she to offer but her property and sex? If Maureen's marriage dissolves with the loss of property and authority is transferred to July, the barriers still remain.

Other questions are raised. What is black culture? The chief to whom July owes allegiance? The black urban revolutionaries? Not being raised in the culture and society Maureen would always remain an outsider, an exile in black Africa, as Rosa was in Europe. The novel seems to imply that for those of the Interregnum there is no solution, as there is for Maureen's children who, still young, adapt to black rural culture.

At the conclusion of the novel Maureen 'runs: like a solitary animal at the season when animals neither seek a mate nor take care of young, existing only for their lone survival, the enemy of all that would make claims of responsibility' (p. 160). There is a shift from the analytical, social, political and psychological to basic, fundamental human instincts that are not constructed by society and culture.

A totally different discourse has entered the narrative, undermining the kinds of analysis that seemed to dominate the story. We might allegorize Maureen's story in terms of the improbability of the bourgeois white woman finding a suitable place in the new Africa; we could discuss the conclusion as a South African version of a middle-aged woman's revolt; as panic; as much else, including a critique of the kind of return to the primitive found in Margaret Atwood's *Surfacing*, and which was often seen as a necessary phase before renewal in many novels of the late sixties and early seventies. (The relationship between the fiction of Atwood and Gordimer needs more attention than it has received.) We do not know what is going on in Maureen's mind, or what Gordimer's attitude is towards Maureen's attempted escape. Is her flight a 'morbid' symptom, a refusal of collective responsibilities, or is it good to have such a sense of survival – a sense which her husband, Bam, lacks?

Such writing is often found in the novels and short stories of the period between *The Conservationist* and *July's People*. After that Gordimer moved on to other approaches in trying to portray the complexity of influences on people and our inability to separate the economic, social, political, psychological and animal. Her range of ways of seeing reality became too complex to fit into her desire for analysis. *A Sport of Nature* shuts out the inner life; *My Son's Story* offers an inner life but only as seen by a biased narrator, and shuts out most of the inner life of the other characters who are important to the story. Nothing seems satisfactory; there is no way to tell what needs to be told. Both novels are highly self-conscious works of fiction, calling attention to their models, to their artifice and through allusions suggesting self-parody. If the novels from *Burger's Daughter* to *My Son's Story* increasingly focus on revolution and revolutionaries and appear to affirm a new radicalism, they still are capable of being interpreted ironically, and as much concerned with the nature of political fiction as with politics.

In the early, or first phase of her later fiction, Gordimer attempts to undermine the Lockean notion of individual liberty based on personal property. Such a justification of personal rights would be against the interests of the majority of black South Africans and if seen as essential to liberty would exclude blacks from any real social justice for a long time to come. It is associated with the attempt to create a conservative black middle class. Personal rights must give way to the freedom struggle and to raising the standard of living of the masses. Gordimer's analysis of the relationship of property to class privilege is seen in *The Conservationist* and *July's People*. Yet as in most of Gordimer's writing the issues cannot be reduced merely to the political. We both sympathize with and are shocked by Maureen.

Criticism of modernization and capitalism often includes a romantic nostalgia for an idealized pastoral past, an unfallen home. In *Burger's Daughter* there is sympathy with the older, supposedly organic rural communities of the Afrikaners. While such emotions are appropriate to Rosa we might see this as lingering English liberal guilt about the British domination of the Boers; equally significant are Gordimer's own longings throughout her fiction for the organic, the primitive, the animal. The Afrikaner pastoral in *Burger's Daughter* is a past, a home which contrasts strongly with what is known about Gordimer's own background. While the attractive, caring Afrikaners of *Burger's Daughter* are part of Rosa's nostalgia they could be part of Gordimer's for a world unlike the one ruled by the British ways upon which her mother insisted. After all, Gordimer is the author of the novel's pastoral scenes.

If this myth of origins is fatally compromised by racial domination over blacks, Gordimer's distrust of the modern and of the world of business emerges through her fiction in various guises whether in the attractiveness of the hippie drop-out, July's community, or of living through the senses. Communalism, the instinctual, the unanalytical and the natural are often rejected as irresponsible, part of a passing order, or based on compromised rights; but their desirability is there and in *A Sport of Nature* appears again miraculously part of the new Africa. Here a white woman living through her senses, like an animal, manages to be free of guilt while politically correct. She progresses naturally from the instinctual to the analytical without effort or finding contradictions.

Gordimer's preoccupation with the white woman in Africa is personal, political and an extension of the concern of the traditional novel. *A Sport of Nature* might be regarded as an inversion of *Mansfield Park*, its opposite. Where Austen teaches caution, Gordimer sympathizes with the revolutionary, the liberating, the impoverished. In its concern with manners, morals, individual will, desire, social and psychological differences, the European novel often explores the ways individuals cross, or the reasons to avoid crossing, class, ethnic, religious or other boundaries. In South Africa the obvious subject is black–white relations in sex and marriage since, until recently, these were by law forbidden territory. Every Gordimer novel touches on such taboos. But it is the relationship between a black man and white woman which is usually the most forbidden – as female sexuality is the ultimate property, because the ultimate desire, of the dominating male. For the white woman, as for the black male, sex between the races becomes the symbol of rebellion, of liberation, of revolution.

In Gordimer's novels sexuality is associated with politics, one revolution being paralleled by the other – the classic modern mixture of Freud and Marx. If her early novels explore the liberal fringes outside racial boundaries through friendships, with sexuality always hovering, the later novels link sexual freedom to radical action. Although alluding to the need for women to have economic freedom, Gordimer's novels are not concerned with that and seem to assume that money is no real problem for whites. Perhaps, living in South Africa, she assumes that white women have too much money? While the financial problems of women are mentioned in *Burger's Daughter* and *A Sport of Nature* they are given far less attention than other questions. Although the novels are critical of bourgeois marriages, marriages seldom trap Gordimer's female characters; the bonds seem weak and women easily follow their interest in extra-marital sex and politics. But if women's liberation is seen in the free life of her body, such liberty becomes compromised in the grey areas of politics where ideals are not free from personal faults, feelings of guilt, manipulation by others for political ends and sacrifice of the self for causes. *The Sport of Nature* attempts to imagine a solution to the problems raised at the conclusion of *The Late Bourgeois World* by Liz's demoralized acceptance of radicalism and black leadership, when liberalism and its values seem at an end:

'A sympathetic white woman hasn't got anything to offer him – except the footing she keeps in the good old white Reserve of banks and privileges. And in return he comes with the smell of the smoke of braziers in his clothes. Oh yes, and it's quite possible he'll make love to me, next time or some time. That's part of the bargain. It's honest, too, like his vanity, his lies, his loans he doesn't pay back; it's all he's got to offer me. It would be better if I accepted gratefully, because then we shan't owe each other anything, each will have given what he has, and neither is to blame if one has more to give than the other. And in any case, perhaps I want it. I don't know. Perhaps it would be better than what I've had – or got.' (p. 94)

Liz's echo of Marx ('each will have given what he has') is ironic and defensive. Her re-entry into politics is disillusioned. That is Gordimer's point. In the late bourgeois world of South Africa at that time – after the failure of the Trotskyite bombings as represented by her first husband Max – what else is left to do but slide into being used by the shadowy world of black activist politics? This attitude also suits Liz's own psychological and sexual needs ('perhaps I want it'). Hillela is Gordimer's first female character who lives like an animal through her body and yet is politically correct; that is why she is a sport of nature.

The much-discussed question of Gordimer and feminism has been somewhat confused by her public statements, just as criticism of most of her imaginative writing has been plagued by the more limiting, more singleminded political concerns of many of her essays. Clingman, Karen Lazar and others have shown the relationship of the fiction to precise political situations in South Africa and explained how the fiction incorporates seeming contradictions. I think, however, that woman's liberation is another matter about which Gordimer's novels go their own way regardless of her declarations elsewhere. If intellectually Gordimer's overriding concerns are political, the body in her fiction has its own life, its own politics. It is often the sexual which is liberating to the women in the novels. The instinctual animal, sexual desire without responsibility, is the natural state to which desire aspires. Gordimer attempts to tame it, to make it politically correct, whether in Liz or Hillela, but it is always there, running contrary to the political, as can be seen in *My Son's Story*. But as that novel shows, people also need companionship and intimacy, so sexuality is bound to become complicated by other desires and politicized.

If the stories as ideological illustrations say we are trapped in our bodies, Gordimer's imagination subverts the political. The prose comes alive, it pants, when speaking of sexual desire and the joys of the body, even the comforts of intimacy, especially the possibilities of youth. Gordimer's later fiction often laments the passing of youth and failures to seize the day and make use of time. Yet she does not write about sexual experience as well as she does about other matters. There are no great scenes of sensuality, of romance, or love, of pleasure and orgasms in her novels. The few explicitly sexual scenes are shocking, vulgar. *A Sport of Nature* attempts to transcend the contradiction between the political and sexual, *My Son's Story* offers an analysis, but the contradictions remain. That is part of the interest of the novels.

Because there is no possible, no logical, resolution to such contradictions, Gordimer has, in such novels as *A Sport of Nature* and *My Son's Story*, entered still another phase where the central characters are seen from the outside or by others; or their lives are written by others, so we are given either no inner life or a suspect treatment of it. There is often a strong undertow of parody, an increasing use of literary allusion. Hillela's world of instinct cannot be known; we only see or hear about her actions and often at a distance. *My Son's Story* calls its own truthfulness into doubt throughout by the narrator's jealousy of his father, the filtering of the story through the son's narration and by the closing remark: 'I am a writer and this is my first book – that I can never publish.' (p. 277)

The more Gordimer tries to resolve the contradiction between the political and the sexual, the more she returns to the problems raised by the novel as a genre in its infancy. This can be seen in the use of the picaresque in *A Sport of Nature*, where Hillela is a female free spirit experiencing life without the conscience and psychological depth of the bourgeois novel; in *My Son's Story* Gordimer returns to the 'how this story came to be written and published' problem of the early eighteenth-century fictional autobiographies and with it the nature of bourgeois realism. No matter how far Gordimer criticizes, deconstructs and attempts to go beyond the bourgeois novel, she is still preoccupied with and writes a more contemporary version of it. I think that rather than being post-modern in the sense of recognizing no centres, no privileged vantage point, Gordimer's most recent novels – the second phase of her later fiction – might better be described as Brechtian. The subjective world is blocked off to avoid the reader's empathy, the story is distanced to permit objectivity and analysis of the characters, their histories, and the conventions of narrative. With hindsight we can see that such Brechtian distancing is the direction her fiction has been exploring since *July's People*, but if she wants to make her fiction political by objectivizing, there is a continuing impulse towards the personal and subjective. As in the nineteenth-century European novel, irony results from such a double perspective.

Gordimer's later fiction keeps mapping such new social territories as the Afrikaner progressive industrialist, the Afrikaner Communist leader as hero, the private lives of black revolutionaries. That Gordimer appears to have overcome, in *My Son's Story*, her reluctance to write about black lives – as an unknowable culture for a white writer; one which the white liberal should respect as different and not exploit – might distract attention from the novel's insistence on the Oedipal and the way family life determines much else. This is a novel about a brown family that lives like a white one in a white neighbourhood. They are also sports of nature, social mutants; of the people, revolutionaries, yet bourgeois. Like Hillela they symbolically bring together white liberal culture – including the nuclear family, a sexual double standard and knowledge of Shakespeare – with the black revolution. If Hillela represents the drop-out rescued for politics, Sonny is the political hero revealed as bourgeois father while Sonny's son (Gordimer plays games with the symbolic names of characters in her later fiction) is the Oedipally-crippled bourgeois youth who as artist will write about the family drama which is the hidden, the non-public, side of the revolution. In this revision of the classic bourgeois novel it is difficult to say where a reassessment of literary conventions stops and where parody begins. But, as in *A Sport of Nature*, Gordimer seems to be investigating the sources of her earlier fiction. If the modern novel has its dynamic in the crisis of conscience of the bourgeoisie then the revolutionary novel must analyze its origins.

Gordimer's early fiction often concerned youthful rebellion against the restrictions of family and the need to explore the world outside social boundaries. In *The Late Bourgeois World* Liz rejects the nuclear family as belonging to a dying social order. Subsequent novels glance with interest at other forms of family organization, extended families, African communities, the seeming casual relationships of convenience between urban Africans, and, in *The Sport of Nature*, the possible advantages of being without a close family life and its taboos. Yet as much as Gordimer wants to find an alternative to the Oedipal relations of the Western family, she sees it as central and determining, whether in *Burger's Daughter* or *My Son's Story*. *A Sport of Nature* is a sport in that it tries to imagine a situation outside the usual family relationships and how freedom from such a past might create a different individual, a more naturally spontaneous and instinctual person. Rosa Burger is introduced briefly into the story to provide a reminder of a contrasting history, a family-influenced history, of someone whose life may resemble Hillela's, but who because of her past is driven by guilt, conscience, examples, and cannot be a free spirit. Hillela takes up the drop-out character, the apolitical free spirit, toyed with but rejected in other novels, such as *Burger's Daughter*, and tries to see what might be done to make it political and responsible while still instinctual. But even Hillela can be 'read' as inheriting the ways of her mother and relatives, although she goes beyond them to combine ideally the instinctual and political.

In both *Burger's Daughter* and *My Son's Story*, there is a celebration of family which, although strongly tinged with irony, recognizes that a sense of guilt is necessary to develop conscience and the desire for justice for others. These two novels and, paradoxically, *A Sport of Nature*, can be understood as attempts to extend, and thus rescue, the bourgeois family story that was so often treated unfavourably in the early modernist novel and show how political conscience is formed. The recognition that the events in Eastern Europe and the failure of Communism may put into doubt many of the orthodoxies that seemed required as part of the South African freedom struggle may, in these recent novels, have influenced Gordimer's own evaluation of the family. But, as John Cooke shows, Gordimer has also become increasingly aware of how much she is a product of her past, a past which she is now willing to examine and yet, as Michael Wade suggests, continues to reject and hide. Gordimer's recent novels, it seems to me, reveal an acceptance that the novel of new Africa may be a more self-conscious, more theorized, analytical revision of its origins in European bourgeois fiction and its discontents.

I have not tried to explain Gordimer's later fiction through a new interpretation, theory or by claiming a correct reading. Details will undermine any claims to an authoritative statement about what the novels intend or show. Their interest is in part that they cannot be explained by any single interpretation, no matter how sophisticated and complex the reading or theory. There are continuing preoccupations which keep being probed in new ways; there is an evolving concern with the right form. The variety of approaches, insights, claims, readings and opinions in the following chapters reveal some of Gordimer's changing faces.

Notes

1. Besides the essays to which my Introduction alludes, I want to thank the following for their comments on an early version of it: Denis Hirson, Ruth Morse, Anne Thieulle, Charlotte Sturgess, David Coad. The idea to commission this book originated from a December 1989 MLA Convention Division 33 panel on politics in Gordimer's fiction, which I chaired and in which Rowland Smith, Michael Wade, Stephen Clingman and Lars Engle participated.
2. 'Revolution, Style and Morality', *Sesame* 12, 1989, pp. 27–30.

Part I
General Essays

1

'Nobody's Children': Families in Gordimer's Later Novels

JOHN COOKE

I

Except for Henry James, we rarely speak of the late period of a novelist's work. In 1969, Gordimer claimed that her own work might not fracture well into periods when she wrote that 'we all write one book', that 'in the end, for a writer, your work is your life and it's a totality'.[1] Still, Gordimer's fiction was to change markedly in the second half of the 1970s as she found resolutions to the two obsessive concerns of her fiction. The key events leading to her later fiction occurred in 1976. One was public: the Soweto children's uprising, which would usher in the close of *Burger's Daughter*. There, for the first time in Gordimer's novels, one of her White South African protagonists finds a way to identify with the African world. In *The Lying Days* Helen Shaw ends by leaving for Europe; in *Occasion for Loving* Jessie Stilwell ends lamenting white privilege, 'a silver spoon clamped between your jaws'; in *The Conservationist* Mehring withdraws into a paranoid fantasy prompted by his covert desire to sleep with a black woman.[2] By contrast, Rosa Burger ends in a prison with black and white women where, she says, 'My sense of sorority was clear.'

The other event was private: the death of Gordimer's mother, who had been unusually protective of her daughter. From the outset of *The Lying Days*, when Helen Shaw stands outside the mine-compound feeling 'the tingling fascination of the gingerbread house before Hansel and Gretel, anonymous, nobody's children, in the woods', Gordimer's dominant private theme had been the need for children to escape domineering parents. But only after the death of her mother does Gordimer create novels that take as their starting-

21

point what it takes even Rosa an entire novel to understand: that she is of value simply as Rosa Burger, not as Burger's daughter. *July's People* (1981) and *A Sport of Nature* (1987) offer two very different options for those who have escaped from their parents, become 'nobody's children'. *My Son's Story* (1990) offers a third option. While the narrative is about a son's breaking free from his father's influence – in this sense it a masculine counterpart to *Burger's Daughter* – its structure finally reveals that the son is free from parental dominance throughout.

Only in a 1976 interview with Melvyn Bragg did Gordimer speak publicly of the most significant event of her childhood:

> *Bragg*: When did you start writing?
> *Gordimer*: When I was about nine. I wanted to be a dancer, and I went to dancing class like all little girls. I was an acrobatic dancer. Then I got some strange heart ailment, and had to stop dancing, and it was about then that I began to write. I time it to this illness, you see. Otherwise I wouldn't know so precisely.
> *Bragg*: It's unusual to remember so clearly, and start so young.
> *Gordimer*: Well, I had a very strange childhood, because from that age I really didn't go to school. This mysterious ailment is something I can talk about now, because my mother's dead; as long as she lived, I couldn't. I realized after I grew up that it was something to do with my mother's attitude towards me, that she fostered what was probably quite a simple passing thing and made a long-term illness out of it, in order to keep me at home, and to keep with her.[3]

Gordimer's few earlier autobiographical fragments make no mention of this event. Even in the 1963 'Leaving School – II', which covers her life from roughly 8 to 22, she avoids the incident.

In interviews conducted in 1979 and 1980, which appeared in the summer 1983 *Paris Review*, Gordimer returns at greater length, and with greater emotion, to her 'very strange childhood'. Dancing was, she says here, 'my passion, from the age of about four to ten' and, after the heart ailment was uncovered, 'the dancing stopped like that, which was a terrible deprivation for me'.[4] Moreover, Gordimer's mother took her out of school and arranged for a tutor to visit three hours a day. This arrangement which, Gordimer says, 'changed my whole character', was 'a terrible thing to do to a child':

I spent my whole life, from eleven to sixteen, with older people, with people of my mother's generation. She carted me around to tea parties – I simply lived her life. . . . I got to the stage where I could really hardly talk to other children. I was a little old woman.

In this interview Gordimer twice calls this event terrible, as well she might: a 'whole character' was changed; an 'acrobatic dancer' became 'a little old woman'.

This event impelled a series of novels in which the protagonists are all intent on escaping from mothers who would 'live their lives'. In *The Lying Days* Mrs Shaw's success in maintaining control over her daughter Helen is reflected in the action which gives the narrative its shape, Helen's compulsion to return repeatedly to her mother's house. In *Occasion for Loving* the autobiographical basis is more evident; Jessie Stilwell struggles to keep from acting like 'her mother [who] had sucked from her the delicious nectar she had never known she had' by using the pretext of a heart ailment to prolong Jessie's dependence (p. 45). Mrs Burger usurps Rosa's early years by using her relentlessly in the service of her political goals; Rosa is even persuaded to feign engagement to a political prisoner in order to smuggle messages into prison. Where these earlier novels take as their focus the attempts of daughters to break free of the mother's control and, more broadly, of parental domination, *July's People* and *A Sport of Nature* begin when the parental power is almost entirely eroded. They deal with opportunities open to those who are 'nobody's children'. In both cases the escape from parental bonds is a precondition for a change in political allegiances. As Gordimer told John Barkham in 1963, 'First, you know, you leave your mother's house, and later you leave the house of the white race.'[5] By Gordimer's later novels these two leave-takings are one.

II

In the opening days of the Smales' sojourn in July's village, Maureen and Bam Smales remain confident in the power their parental roles have always conferred. When Victor, the oldest of their three children, wants to show his racing-car set to the village children, Maureen responds:

– To whom? –

The black children who watched the hut from afar and scut-
tled, as if her glance were a stone thrown among them, re-formed
a little way off.

– But tell them they mustn't touch it. I don't want my things
messed up and broken. You must tell them. –

She laughed as adults did, in the power they refuse to use. – I
tell them? They don't understand our language. –

The boy said nothing but kicked steadily at the dented, rusted
bath used for their ablutions.

– Don't. D'you hear me? That's July's. –[6]

The family unit is very much as it was in Johannesburg. Maureen is
secure in the adult power she really doesn't refuse to use; she pro-
tects adults' possessions, like July's tub here. Victor and the black
children contest this power by withdrawing and sulking. In the
novel the parental and racial boundaries are equated. Those black
children flee as much from the white as the adult presence, and
while Victor has the desire to mix with them, he still wants the white
prerogatives to which he is accustomed to be enforced by his mother.
Indeed, Victor's concern with the racing-car set is a clear sign of his
identification with the white order, for Maureen and Bam fix on their
vehicle as the symbol of their power which had gone unquestioned
'back there' in Johannesburg.

This old order is quickly undermined along both generational
and racial lines. In their new surroundings, the Smales children soon
begin to equate their parents' treatment of the Africans and themselves. During an early quarrel between the parents and their sister
Gina, the two Smales boys observe 'their parents closing in one of
their own kind' (p. 42). The phrase echoes the language used to
designate Africans, as in the novel's opening, when 'July began the
day for them as his kind has always done for their kind.' We also
look from the children's perspective when Bam patronizes a man,
whose orange sack the children had used, by patting him on the
back; then Victor is aware that 'his father laid the same calming hand
on him' (p. 86). A counter-process is already under way, for in his
homeland July naturally becomes the provider. He has begun to
patronize Bam, for instance, in his comments to the children about
Bam's small contribution to the village of a tank to catch rain water:
'You lucky, you know your father he's very, very clever man. Is
coming plenty rain, now everybody can be happy with that tank, is

nice easy, isn't it: You see, your father he make everyone – everyone to be pleased' (p. 63). But as both July and the children know, July is the clever man here, for he gets food from the neighbouring town and instructs the children in the ways of the village.

The merging of the children into the life of the village is not due so much to these perceptions of their parents' attitude toward them or of the changed power structure. The children change simply because they are young enough not to have been completely formed by the world of 'back there' as their parents have. Gina, the youngest, adapts most quickly; within a few days of the Smales' arrival, she enters their hut carrying an African baby on her back 'with the old woman's sciatic gait of black children who carry brothers and sisters almost as big as they are' (p. 41). The two boys, about 6 and 9, change more slowly, but by the time Bam's gun disappears – only a few weeks after their arrival – they observe his distress as the African children would. Bam seems to sense their greater allegiance to the village world when he accuses the boys of having divulged the hiding place of the gun; for their part, 'neither would dare risk telling their father everybody knew it was there, every chicken that scratched, every child whose eyes went round the interior of the hut, *mhani* Tsatswani's hut, where the white people stayed' (p. 144). The boys clearly see the hut with the eyes of the African children, and Victor at once pinches his brother's leg to keep him from implicating their sister and mocks his father by advising, 'You c'n tell the police, dad' (p. 145). Victor knows, of course, that the police are only 'back there' and that his parents have become powerless, as the contrast of this scene with the early racing car scene indicates. Indeed, Victor's ability to put that car aside, where his parents remain preoccupied with their vehicle, is a clear sign of his greater acceptance of village life.

The Smales may continue to speak 'in the sub-language of hints and private significance foreign to children', but by the novel's close it is not that sub-language which figures most in the children's lives (p. 67). The language of the village becomes less and less 'foreign' to them; when the *gumba-gumba*, a musical sound system from the city, arrives, it is 'something for which Victor, Gina, and Royce knew the name in the village people's language but not in their own' (p. 40). The children are becoming truly bi-lingual; they don't try – in one of the most loaded words in the novel – to 'translate' from one culture to another as their parents do. They are not preoccupied with new contexts, with comparisons with 'back there', with the different life they might have led had the family run from South Africa in time. The last image of them is of the eldest unselfconsciously receiving a gift from July in the traditional African way: 'Victor is seen to clap his hands, sticky with mealie-*pap*, softly, gravely together and bob obeisance, receiving the gift with cupped palms' (p. 157). Throughout the novel, for something to 'be seen' is for it to be experienced, taken into oneself – the landscape around the village is 'not seen' by Maureen as the city is 'never seen' by Martha, July's wife. The authenticity of Victor's response is emphasized by its juxtaposition with a picturesque view typical of European photographs, a panorama of the African village 'held in the pantheistic hand' (p. 156). Victor, unlike photographers who create such scenes, does not view the village from afar; his hands are smeared with mealie-*pap*.

July's People, then, offers an escape from the European family into an alternative family, an African family. The entire Smales family is offered this prospect – they have all perforce become 'July's Children', in an early title of the work – but only the Smales children can accept the offer. They are more likely to flourish there than in their previous home. In *The Black Interpreters*, Gordimer had contrasted the unhealthy Western mother–son relationship, as is seen in the fiction of the 'mother-fixated Proust' and the 'terrible burden' of a mother's love in *Sons and Lovers*, with the relationship depicted in African fiction, in which 'there is never any suggestion that mother love can be warping'.[7] The Smales children, all younger than the age when Gordimer was forced to 'lead her mother's life', are suddenly offered an alternative life: July, the former 'boy', becomes the father, and the Smales children enter his African house.

III

Maureen's fate might remain obscure at the novel's close, but her desire to be rid of her children is clear; she runs 'like a solitary animal at the season when animals neither seek a mate nor take care of young'. Where this novel ends, *A Sport of Nature* begins, with the renunciation of a mother's role by Ruthie, who is Hillela's mother only in a biological sense. For the first time in Gordimer's fiction, the protagonist grows up unfettered by parents. Hillela's relations are not called 'mother' or 'father'. Only 'Ruthie' and 'Len', with whom she lives only briefly in her early life. Hillela does experience some pain because of Ruthie's absence, particularly when she comes across her love-letters to the man with whom she ran off to Mozambique, but Hillela does not think of herself as anyone's daughter. Of one aunt she lives with, for instance, she will say, 'I'm like the daughter she didn't have', not that the aunt is like the mother she herself never had.[8] In the novel Hillela's parentless state is not a detriment but a rare blessing. Her cousin Sasha says, you seem so free' because Hillela has escaped what Gordimer calls all the 'predications' advanced by parents, such as their absently-put questions about what children want to be when they grow up (p. 87). The relationships of parents and children are universally debilitating; only Hillela, because of 'the abstract relations of her own childhood . . . was free of the patricidal and infanticidal loves between parents and children' (p. 296). From early in the novel, when a pregnant girl commits suicide because 'Her terror of her parents had been greater than her fear of death', until near the close when Sasha writes from prison that communicating with his mother is 'like being thrust up back again into the womb', it is clear that Hillela is blessed by being, as Sasha calls her, 'a lucky orphan' (pp. 102, 328).

The solution of *July's People* – the African family in which the mother's love can never be warping – is pointedly denied in *A Sport of Nature* in two ways. One is through the development of Hillela's only child, by Whaila, who works for the African National Congress in exile. Hillela names their only child Nomzano, after Winnie Mandela. Nomzamo does not follow in the path her name predicates; she becomes a fashion-model known, as is the custom, by 'a single name – hers is Nomo – easily pronounceable by French, Italian, German, American and English couturiers and readers of fashion journals. An international model does not hamper her image with national politics; to the rich people who buy the clothes she displays or the luxuries her face and body promote, she is a symbol of Africa, anyway . . . ' (p. 202). As the novel progresses, the non-political creature's name becomes ironic. 'The namesake, who looks out from magazine covers, unsmiling with charming haughtiness, nostrils dilated, is [Hillela's] only child, her daughter' (p. 224).

To Hillela's credit, the naming is her only attempt to determine Nomo's life. Hillela let her go, most pointedly when she meets Ruthie in Luanda by chance late in the novel. Even Ruthie still has the need for a sense of family, for she asks Hillela for a photo of her granddaughter. Hillela has two photos in her room: the one of Nomo she gives to Ruthie; the other of Whaila, herself, and their baby Nomo she puts away in a drawer. Hillela dismantles her vestigial family album, giving up her daughter's picture as easily as she had refused a picture of her mother at the novel's outset. Hillela is troubled by Ruthie's presence, but not because it calls up Ruthie's early disappearance from her life or Hillela's separation from her own daughter. Hillela mourns, rather, the end of her marriage, not her loss of a mother or a daughter. When Ruthie arrives, Hillela is reminded of another departure – Whaila's when he was murdered by anti-ANC forces. She recalls the visit of men who don't give their names when Ruthie, a lady that won't give her name, calls; and 'the room lurched in tears' around her when she puts Whaila's picture in the drawer.

The alternative of the African family is denied in a second, more pointed way when the general with whom Hillela is living wants Ruthie to come and live with them. Hillela tells him that Ruthie, a person she has never lived with, means nothing to her: 'This had no significance for the General. Among his people most children were brought up by grandmothers or other kin as well as or in place of their mothers – anyone who performed the function shared the title: the mother remained the mother' (p. 308). Not for Hillela, who suggests that, if they really need to do something, they might get Ruthie 'a cheap ticket to Europe'.

The consequences of being in a family are foregrounded in the final scene of the novel, the installation of a majority-ruled government in South Africa. Hillela alone is present of the aunts, uncles, and cousins among whom she was raised. Both sons of one aunt have positions in the new government, but neither, Gordimer observes, is in the crowd. The other aunt, a supporter of the ANC during the 1950s and 1960s, is also absent, as is her son Sasha, who had been detained for his political activities, for 'His Dutch wife has twins and she is nervous of going to an unfamiliar country with small children' (p. 353). Sasha and his mother 'have been unable not to resume their own congenital war' (p. 353). Set against them is a different family – 'the living mass' of blacks and whites at the celebration, the family of 'Whaila's country' in the title of the novel's final part. Hillela had drawn the contrast between the two types of families when she listed those 'who have given up being white': 'Bram Fischer, the Weinbergs, Slovos, Christa, Arnold. And there are others . . . another kind. I knew them, I was in a family . . . they wanted to but they didn't seem to know how?' (p. 193). The pointed absence of those who remain 'in a family', the presence only of

Hillela at the celebration, suggest that getting out of the family is a necessary condition to participation in the new South African world.

Hillela is there as 'a sport of nature', defined in the epigraph as 'a departure from the parent stock or type'. If the departure is from the parent type of the race, it is also from biological parents. Gordimer's dedication of the novel allows for this departure. It is to her children, but they are not identified as such. The inscription reads: 'For Orlane and Hugo'.

IV

While Gordimer has concentrated on the 'terrible burden' imposed by mothers on daughters, she has also dealt with the conflicts of fathers and sons. In *The Conservationist*, the failed relationship of Mehring and his son seemed so important in the novel to Christopher Ricks that he titled his review 'Fathers and Children'. In the masculine version of parental dominance, as in the feminine, Gordimer has been drawn to the most extreme conflicts. Indeed, she researched one of the most tortured of those publicized in modern literature to write the 1984 'Letter from His Father', an imagined rejoinder from the grave by Kafka's father to his son's bitter 'Letter to His Father'. *My Son's Story* is a kind of conflation of such a correspondence, as sections providing the first-person account of the son alternate with the third-person account of the father's life.

Until the novel's final sections, *My Son's Story* appears to be an account of the bondage of the son Will to his father. In fact, the very names of the main characters – the father is named Sonny, his daughter Baby – imply that a life-long imprisonment in a child's world controlled by adults is a general condition. The very title of the novel suggests that Will is defined by his role of son: this is not 'Will's Story' but a son's story: and the epigraph from Shakespeare's Sonnet XIII – 'You had a Father, let your son say so' – sets the son's role as purveyor of his father's story.

The narrative centres on how the son's obsession with his father's life has stultified him. The novel opens with Will finding his father, a man of mixed race, leaving a cinema with a blonde white woman. For Will, his learning of their affair undercuts his father's role as an opponent of apartheid; his father might have served time in detention and have given his life to political change, but in his son's eyes he is still oppressed in spirit, being conditioned to lust after white women. This chance meeting arrests Will's development; he will get a job selling tickets in a movie theatre, and he repeatedly fantasizes about his father's relationship with the white woman.

Moreover, with his father away on political missions and, Will assumes, keeping assignations with the white woman, Will feels bound to provide his mother Aila with the attention that should naturally fall to the father. Even when his mother is detained, Will's world must still remain his father's house: 'I can't leave my mother alone, and because my mother counts on me to be there with him when she's away, I can't leave him.'[9] He is forced to be, as he says repeatedly, 'always there at home, her boy, mother's boy' (p. 222). The feeling, as Will says repeatedly, is that 'There's no air in my life' (p. 245).

Will finds himself in the typical place of Gordimer's children, locked in his parent's house. The end of his bondage is heralded by the burning of that house near the narrative's close. Will protests that the arson was committed by the white neighbours by asserting. *'This is my father's house'*, as they watch it burn; but he welcomes the destruction of his house. He says simply, 'I was glad to see it go', for the smell of smoke destroys the smell of the white woman his father brought into it (p. 274). What Will wants, however, is not simply the removal of the father but dominance over him. He wants the power his sister Baby exercised over their mother when Baby's political activity led Aila to become politically involved; as Will understands, 'Baby has made her what Baby wanted *her* to be' (p. 232).

Will had begun to claim this power by operating in a political role near the novel's close when it was he who discovered that the police had planted weapons in the house as a means to secure Aila's imprisonment. He contrasts this experience with his complicity in his father's affair through refusing to inform his mother of it. Now, Will feels, 'I was at its centre for this, the only time. I was nobody's conspirator. I had found my own point of reference through my own experience' (p. 249). Will is 'at the centre' in a more important way, as a consequence of the state his father has bequeathed him: 'I'm the man who's likely to be around at home in my room because I've begun a project – call it that – that needs solitude. I've found a use for the state, compromised and deserted, he dumped me in when he walked off so calmly with his blonde after an afternoon at the cinema' (p. 196). This project, the final section of *My Son's Story* reveals, is the novel itself, and in the novel Will has complete control. While the novel's title and the epigraph suggest that the father is dominant, the son has actually fashioned the narrative according to his own needs. As Will observes, 'All the details about Sonny and his women? – oh, those I've taken from the women I've known' (p. 276). The son's perfect revenge is to have recast his father's life.

But *My Son's Story* suggests more of an accommodation of parent and child than Gordimer's other later novels. Twice in the novel Gordimer alludes to what were termed in *A Sport of Nature* the 'predications', those questions that parents pose to children about what they want to do when they grow up, without caring about the response (pp. 36, 250). Will (named after Shakespeare) does become what his father wanted him to be, a writer, but in doing so he establishes his own view of the world, the view given in the novel. If, to return to the title and the epigraph, the focus in the novel is the father, the purveyor of the story is the son. Will ends by lamenting that 'this is my first book – that I can never publish', partly because of its intensely personal nature, partly because of its compromising political information. But it is still only his 'first book'; the next will more emphatically be Will's own story. Speaking of his parents, Will claims that it is now 'My time that's coming with politics. I was excluded from that, it didn't suit them for me to have any function within it' (p. 276). Having worked free of his parents' control – of the stories they made for him – Will is poised to act in his own right; only by having become nobody's child is he free to act in the political world as all Gordimer's adult protagonists must.

Notes

1. 'Nadine Gordimer Talks to Andrew Salkey', *The Listener*, 7 August 1969, p. 185.
2. *Occasion for Loving* (London: Jonathan Cape, 1978), p. 279; *Burger's Daughter* (New York: Viking, 1979), p. 356.
3. 'The Solitude of a White Writer', *The Listener*, 21 October 1976, p. 514.
4. Jannika Hurwitt, 'The Art of Fiction LXXVII: Nadine Gordimer', *Paris Review*, LXXXVIII (Summer 1983), pp. 89–90.
5. John Barkham, 'South Africa: Perplexities, Brutalities, Absurdities', *Saturday Review*, 12 January 1963, p. 63.
6. *July's People* (New York: Viking, 1981), p. 14. Subsequent references in the text are to this edition.
7. *The Black Interpreters: Notes on African Writing* (Johannesburg, 1973),

p. 12. For a later expression of the same view, see 'The Child is the Man', her review of Wole Soyinka's *Ake: The Years of Childhood*, *New York Review of Books*, 21 October 1982, pp. 2–6.

8.   *A Sport of Nature* (New York: Penguin, 1987), p. 9. Subsequent references in the text are to this edition.

9.   *My Son's Story* (New York: Farrar Straus Giroux, 1990), p. 185. Subsequent references in the text are to this edition.

2

Collector's Art, Collective Action: The Search for Commitment in Nadine Gordimer's Fiction

GRAHAM HUGGAN

The work of Nadine Gordimer constitutes a sustained debate on the nature of the South African writer's commitment. Commitment: the word harks back to the *littérature engagée* of Sartre, and there are certainly echoes in Gordimer of Sartre's now-famous definition of writing as 'a certain way of wanting freedom' (p. 1068). But while the context for Gordimer's own defence of freedom is clear – struggle for black liberation in South Africa – the dilemma it raises for a white South African writer caught between her desire to participate in that struggle and the awareness of her own – at least partial – detachment from it is far from resolved. The crux of the problem is again revealed in Sartre:

> Writing is a certain way of wanting freedom; once you have begun, you are committed. . . . Committed to what? Defending freedom? That's easy to say. Is it a matter of acting as a guardian of ideal values . . . or is it concrete everyday freedom which must be protected by our taking sides in political and social struggles? The question is tied up with another one . . . for whom does one write? (p. 1068)

For whom, then, does Gordimer write? Gordimer perhaps comes closest to answering in her essay 'The Essential Gesture' (1984), when she declares that to be a white South African writer is 'to be presented with a political responsibility to raise the consciousness of white people who, unlike himself, have not woken up' (p. 293). Gordimer's commitment to the struggle for black liberation has not blinded her, then, from the realization that her primary responsibility as a writer is towards a predominantly white, middle-class readership, in her own country and elsewhere, whose complacency has insulated them from the daily realities of oppression under the apartheid system. Nor is it sufficient to register the shock-waves of liberal sympathy. Far from 'preaching to the converted', Gordimer persistently challenges an international readership whose progressive views may well have attracted them to her work in the first place, but who find themselves in turn the subjects of Gordimer's withering critical scrutiny. Indeed, Gordimer suggests throughout her work that liberal philanthropy may be considered a form of false consciousness which is ultimately as likely to impede the march towards human liberation as it is to sustain it.

Implicit in Gordimer's critique of liberalism, and in her uncompromising analysis of the limitations of her own position as a dissident South African writer, is the notion of possessive individualism.[1] A cornerstone of liberal political philosophy, possessive individualism has its basis in the protection of individual human rights; but it can also easily be manipulated to serve a free-market economy which thrives on the exchange and accumulation of private property. Although Gordimer's left-wing politics is clearly at odds with the ideology of possessive individualism, she remains aware of the tensions arising in her work between political and artistic praxis, tensions registered in the dual – potentially competing – responsibilities of the artist towards society at large and towards his/her own work:

> The writer is eternally in search of entelechy in his relation to society. Everywhere in the world, he needs to be left alone and at the same time to have a vital connection with others; needs artistic freedom and knows it cannot exist without its wider context; feels the two presences within – creative self-absorption and conscionable awareness – and must resolve whether these are locked in death struggle, or are really foetuses in a twinship of fecundity. Will the world let him, and will he know how to be the ideal of the writer as a social being, Walter Benjamin's storyteller, the one 'who could let the wick of his life be consumed completely by the gentle flame of his story?' (pp. 299–300)

The issue of possessive individualism thus raises a series of questions which are fundamental not only to Gordimer's work but to all supposedly committed art. To whom does the committed work of art belong? Can one distinguish between its aesthetic and its social function? To what extent is its political effectiveness compromised by its dependence on a Western market in which the 'use-value' of art has been largely replaced by its 'exchange-value' as a cultural commodity? Can (Western) art transcend its debased status as a collector's item to stimulate the desire for collective action? And if so, can it produce social change, or is it rather, as Herbert Marcuse has said, that 'art cannot change the world, but it can contribute to changing the consciousness and drives of the men and women who could change the world'? (pp. 32–3).

These questions are at the heart of the Marxist aesthetic that informs much of Gordimer's work. Adorno's formulation comes readily to mind: 'Committed art, necessarily detached as art from reality, cancels the distance between the two. "Art for art's sake" denies by its absolute claims that ineradicable connection with reality which is the . . . a priori of the attempt to make art autonomous from the real. Between these two poles the tensions in which art has lived in every age till now are dissolved' (p. 178). A more obvious influence on Gordimer, however, is the work of Ernst Fischer. For Fischer, the 'essential function of art' is to 'enlighten and stimulate action' (p. 14). Art is necessary 'in order that man should be able to recognize and change the world' (p. 14); but it is also necessary in order to defamiliarize the world of everyday experience. The dialectical contradictions of art thus emerge from tensions generated by the *derivation* of art 'from an intense experience of reality' (p. 9) and by the *reconstruction* of alternative (or 'substitute') realities by art. Gordimer's fiction is fraught with such contradictions, her self-consciousness as an artist deriving in large part from the dialogue in her work between an art which, turning out to the world, seeks to 'enlighten and stimulate action' and one which, turning in on itself, contemplates its own (illusory) self-sufficiency.

Few of Gordimer's commentators have discussed the profound implications of Fischer's aesthetic theory for her own work. One who has, Judie Newman, illustrates how Fischer's *The Necessity of Art* functions as an intertext to Gordimer's novel *The Late Bourgeois World* (1966).[2] 'Something of an aesthetic manifesto' (Newman, p. 35), the novel investigates the questionable role played by art in 'late bourgeois' society. 'In a decaying society', says Fischer, 'art . . . must also reflect decay . . . [it] must show the world as changeable. And help to change it' (p. 48). Gordimer targets the complacent aestheticism of Liz Van den Sandt's lover Graham, for whom 'there is nothing moral about beauty' (p. 109), for her critique of the static, mystificatory aesthetics of 'late bourgeois' art. Following Fischer, the novel moves towards the promulgation of a socialist aesthetic in which art, recovering its capacity to unite 'the individual with communal existence' (Newman, p. 36), projects a more hopeful – if hardly Utopian – view of the future.

If *The Late Bourgeois World* can be considered as Gordimer's aesthetic manifesto, her later novels test this manifesto to the limits. *Burger's Daughter* (1978) and *A Sport of Nature* (1987) provide Gordimer's most detailed analyses of a 'late bourgeois world' in which art is frequently reduced to the status of collector's item, and in which the fetishism of the art lover is seen as the pathological symptom of a society's unwillingness to transform itself. Ironically, however, in neither novel does it seem to be possible to envisage the future in other than aestheticist terms: the attempt to replace a decadent bourgeois aesthetics with the social dynamic of committed art results in a wry awareness not only of the limited capacity of art to change the world but of the apparent opportunity provided by art to escape from it.

The social and moral irresponsibilities of aestheticism are most clearly shown in *Burger's Daughter* and *A Sport of Nature* in Gordimer's heavily ironic treatment of the artistic patronage of Brandt Vermeulen (in the former novel) and Hillela's Aunt Olga (in the latter). Vermeulen's sophisticated defence of white suprematism – he is an Afrikaner nationalist – stands in ironic counterpoint to his championing of modern art. A connoisseur, 'a patron of the painter' (*BD*, p. 181), Vermeulen undoubtedly has taste but, as Rosa Burger discovers when he escorts her around his luxurious house, he lives in an atmosphere of decadent, even brutal eroticism. At the poolside, 'white wooden chaises-longues on wheels were splattered with purple droppings from the cape thrushes who were feeding their young on the dangling bunches of grapes' (*BD*, p. 180). And inside the house, underneath a series of oil paintings 'composed radially from figures which seemed flung down in the centre of the canvas from a height, spread like a suicide on a pavement, or backed against a wall, seen from the sight of the firing squad', stands a 'life-size plastic female torso, divided down the middle . . . with its vaginal labia placed horizontally across the outside of its pubis, like the lips of a mouth' (*BD*, p. 181). Paraded among Vermeulen's assembled masterpieces from Europe, America and Africa, Rosa finds herself reduced like them to the fetishistic status of a collector's item. The revolutionary potential of Vermeulen's art is defused by his self-serving patronage. His love of the 'modern' clashes sharply with his adherence to antiquated nationalist sentiments, so that the slick iconoclast is eventually revealed to be a dangerous reactionary. Vermeulen's art collection may be removed from its social and cultural context, but its scarcely concealed violence issues a grotesque reminder of his links with the outside world.

An unlikely counterpart to Vermeulen in *Burger's Daughter* is Hillela's arch-conservative Aunt Olga in *A Sport of Nature*. Another self-styled 'patron of the arts' (*ASN*, p. 24), Aunt Olga is an enthusiastic collector of valuable antiques and *objets d'art* whose 'selection from the past only of what is beautiful [is] lifted cleanly from the context of its bloody revolutions' (*ASN*, p. 324). Unlike Vermeulen, Aunt Olga makes no pretensions to cultivating a modern sensibility; but like him, what she fears most is change. Aunt Olga's collection symbolizes her desire to escape into a past which provides illusory refuge from the horrors of the world that surrounds her. She conveniently forgets, however, that their 'historic value' is determined by the present; their 'timelessness' is contradicted by the shockingly immediate link between the 'context of bloody revolution' from which they have been lifted and the current atrocities of the apartheid state. Gordimer uses the technique of ironic juxtaposition here to bring out the absurdity of artistic pretensions to 'neutrality'. Scandalized by the bedroom antics of Hillela and her cousin Sasha, Olga remains blind to the implications of a 'forbidden' alliance in her own room between a Carpeaux *Reclining Nude* and a 'gilt-turbaned Blackamoor holding up a lamp' (*ASN*, p. 113). The disinterested pleasure Olga claims to take in the fine arts is now forcibly – even farcically – set against the contemporary context of apartheid: Olga's claim to escape from the battleground of South African politics into a free zone of depoliticized art, where designer catalogues offer comforting evidence of 'the survival of rare and beautiful objects' (*ASN*, p. 75), only testifies to the reprehensibility of her own instinct for survival.

Through her ironic treatment of the two art collectors, Brandt Vermeulen and Aunt Olga, Gordimer shows that the opposition between the rarefied world of art and the everyday world of social praxis is based on false consciousness; for if the production and consumption of art are inescapably political, then the 'choice' Hillela is supposed to make, between Olga's world of aesthetic pleasure and (her other aunt) Pauline's world of social commitment, is really no choice at all. Nor is Pauline's position invulnerable. Although she and her civil rights lawyer husband Joe believe that they are 'healthily engaged with the realities of the country' (*ASN*, p. 56–7), they seem unaware of the contradictions inherent in their position as political activists. These contradictions are explicitly revealed in the sexual taboos surrounding Sasha's 'incest', but they are also implied in the social taboos that surround his revolutionary activities. The philanthropy of Pauline and Joe is eventually shown to disguise a deeper desire for social conformism. They may believe that they are sacrificing the 'idle pastime' of collecting art to the pressing demands of collective action, but the newspapers, files and pamphlets which litter their house are like those in so many other 'shabby-affluent living room[s]' where liberal do-gooders or leftist intellectuals gather to congratulate each other on the strength of their social consciences (*ASN*, p. 229).

Pauline and Joe are not alone; for Fischer's belief that the necessity of art lies in its capacity to 'enlighten and stimulate action' is adopted by many of the supposed freethinkers in Gordimer's fiction as a slogan which smacks less of the desire to engineer social change than of the wish to appear politically 'correct'. Included among these freethinkers are armchair activists such as Rosa Burger's lover, trendy academic Bernard Chabalier. Chabalier claims glibly that the shock-events which 'change the consciousness of the world . . . [are] register[ed] seismographically in movements of art' (*BD*, p. 291), but it is obvious that he is much happier observing these events than participating in them. For Chabalier, leftist politics and modern art coalesce in the glittering but ultimately empty rhetoric of radical chic: 'activism' becomes one buzzword among others in the pretentious vocabulary of (Parisian) café philosophy. Opposed to Chabalier, but indirectly linked with him, are genuinely active intellectuals such as Dr Leonie Adlestrop, the 'new white hunter' of *A Sport of Nature*. Adlestrop is a voracious opportunist. While she works untiringly to help the dispossessed, her efforts also go towards furthering her own career: her 'hunter's trophies' are the political refugees whom she duly parades at wealthy American universities to 'prove' the liberalism of the latter while handily enhancing her own reputation. Less ostensibly than Vermeulen or Aunt Olga, Chabalier and Adlestrop are also collectors, high-profile individualists whose 'correct' views and praiseworthy actions are conscripted into the service of academic success. While Gordimer's ambivalent portrayal of characters such as Chabalier and Adlestrop contributes to the critique of political tokenism to be found throughout her fiction, it also points to the more fundamental tensions in her work between theory and praxis, the formulation of ideas and the eventual uses to which those ideas are put. In both *Burger's Daughter* and *A Sport of Nature*, these tensions are explored in a false opposition between the intellectual satisfactions afforded by 'art' and the physical attractions offered by 'nature'. On the one hand, Gordimer's protagonists, Rosa and Hillela, are perceived as instinctive creatures acting on (predominantly sexual) impulses, on the other hand as aesthetic objects for the delectation of a number of (usually male) admirers. But it is clear that these perceptions are linked: the idea of 'instinct', like that of 'beauty', is manipulated by the interests of a patriarchal society which has naturalized the commodification of the female body.

Two further connections are worth pursuing here. The first is between the construction of Rosa and Hillela as aesthetic objects and the creation of a series of aesthetic environments in both novels. The second is between the voyeuristic appeal of erotic art and the lure of exotic worlds whose 'otherness' diverts attention away from the responsibilities of daily praxis. These connections are made most explicit in Gordimer's multi-faceted portrayal of Hillela in *A Sport of Nature*. Hillela is viewed almost exclusively in the novel as the object of other people's desires and voyeuristic fantasies: she is the quarry of 'white hunters' such as Leonie Adlestrop and Bradley Burns or, closer to home, her aunts Olga and Pauline, who would capture her and mould her to their own expectations; she is that coveted collector's piece, a 'genuine' South African political refugee (for export only); and she is the star attraction in 'old hand' Archie Harper's African Arts Atrium, where her sensuous curves nicely offset the 'leopard skins mounted on scalloped green felt, [the] dead snakes converted into briefcases, [and the] elephants turned into ivory filigree carvings' (*ASN*, p. 182).

Later in the novel there is an ironic parallel between the African Arts Atrium and the President's State House, whose collection of votive offerings includes 'the toadying gifts of white visiting artists or the multinational firms who commission them – heroic animals . . . leopards, elephants, lions – paintings as subconsciously representing the white man's yearning for Africa to be a picture-book bestiary instead of the continent of black humans ruling themselves' (*ASN*, p. 355). An equally hyperbolic comparison in the novel is that between Ibn Sulaiman's fake palace (where Udi Stück indulges his fantasy of Hillela as an Oriental hetaira) and the Belgian embassy (*ASN*, p. 194). A characteristically brilliant exposure of the pretensions of international diplomacy, these ironic comparisons also remind us of the economic underpinnings of colonialism and of the continuing subjection of Africa to the expansionist designs of multinational capitalism. Posing in the Art's Atrium, the 'sport of nature' is converted into big-game trophy, emporium curio: all to satisfy the 'white man's yearning', but also to prove that (South) Africa *sells*. Gordimer drives the point home with a further ironic parallel. Hillela's subsequent career as a fashionable dissident – much sought-after on the American university circuit – is compared with that of her daughter Nomzamo, an international model whose exotic image is carefully protected from the potentially disruptive influence of national politics, but who is all the rage at parties and rallies as the 'fashion-show benefit for a [liberal] cause' (*ASN*, p. 227).

　　Hillela's uncertain progress towards a revolutionary consciousness, like Rosa Burger's, is continually hindered by 'promoters' who parade her South-Africanness for their own benefit and by 'protectors' who offer her an illusory escape from the social and political battleground of her own country by spiriting her into a deodorized world of *haute couture*/culture in which South Africa provides a fashionable talking-point in cocktail-party conversations and South African art is reduced to a series of 'interchangeable airport gifts' (*BD*, p. 228). In *Burger's Daughter*, this privileged world is represented by Europe: a place of exile for Rosa, but above all a place of escape where she can indulge in the easy pleasures of the Mediterranean beaches, the flamboyance of Parisian café culture, or the cosy domesticity of a London impressionistically rendered in 'tiers of shade down the sunny street, the shy white feet of people who have taken off shoes and socks to feel the grass, the sun wriggling across the paths of pleasure boats on the ancient river; where people sit on benches drinking outside pubs, the girls preening their flashing hair through their fingers' (*BD*, p. 324). Gordimer contrasts the harsh environment of Rosa's native land with the 'harmless European jungle[s]' (*BD*, p. 261) through which she is conducted by a succession of wealthy suitors and protectrices. 'Nature' here is made to seem indistinguishable from 'art'. Chabalier, escorting the mesmerized Rosa through the galleries and museums of Paris, implicitly likens her to the sultry girl in Bonnard's exoticist painting (*BD*, pp. 286–7). Rosa's perception of the South of France is no less exotic. Like Bonnard's canvas, the Midi conjures up images of an invented paradise; the soft features of the Mediterranean landscape assume the qualities of an impressionist painting, a delicately erotic haze of colours with subtle effects of chiaroscuro (*BD*, p. 226).

Rosa's identification of a Europe that, like Aunt Olga, she has 'lifted cleanly from the context of its bloody revolutions,' is epitomized in her dreamy appreciation of a medieval tapestry at the Musée de Cluny. To Rosa, the tapestry evokes 'an old and lovely world, gardens and gentle beauties among gentle breasts . . . such harmony and sensual peace in the age of the thumbscrew and dungeon . . . ' (*BD*, p. 341). Just as Hillela is fascinated by the garish splendour of Ibn Sulaiman's fake palace, so Rosa finds herself irresistibly drawn, through art, to a world that never was. Clearly, the temptations of 'pure' art – its fork-tongued promises of a world untrammelled by conflict or violence – are not necessarily diminished by the progress of Gordimer's two protagonists towards political commitment. Indeed, the search for commitment which unconsciously shapes the lives of Rosa and Hillela remains ambivalent to the last. A similar argument can be made for Gordimer's work, which is better seen as a search for, rather than a statement of, commitment. Gordimer's inquiry into the meaning of committed art is driven both by the continuing restrictions placed upon artistic production in a country where censorship is commonplace and by the hypocritical promotion of 'universal' aesthetic values which disguise the commercial viability of South African art on the international market. But her attempt in novels such as *Burger's Daughter* and *A Sport of Nature* to bridge the gap between collector's art and collective action – between art as a commodity for private consumption and art as a stimulant to social change – brings no easy solutions.

For Fischer, 'late bourgeois' art lacks a vision of the future. Despite Gordimer's indebtedness to Fischer, it is debatable whether the endings of *Burger's Daughter* and *A Sport of Nature* provide the hopeful view of the future that Fischer's version of committed art prescribes. In *Burger's Daughter*, Rosa's erstwhile protectrice, Madame (Katya) Bagnelli receives a letter from prison in which Rosa refers disingenuously to the 'comforts of a cell as if describing the features of a tourist hotel that wasn't quite what the brochure might have suggested' (*BD*, p. 361). Such apparently innocuous aestheticism is permitted by the prison authorities; but an indirect reference to Rosa's father, Party stalwart Lionel Burger, has previously been spotted by the censor and erased. For the prison authorities, 'art' is allowed, 'politics' is not; Gordimer challenges the distinction, however, and in so doing also challenges those, like Madame Bagnelli, who are unwilling to read between the lines of letters such as Rosa's, which must conceal their meaning if they are to communicate with the outside world. But how effective is Rosa's final communiqué? Whatever hidden message it might have is certainly lost on Madame Bagnelli; the revolutionary potential of prison writing is defused by its failure to reach its target audience.

'Prison literature', 'political manifesto', the documentary modes of 'socialist realism': these three strands of committed art are woven into the texture of *Burger's Daughter* and *A Sport of Nature*. But Gordimer's subtle manipulation of mode and genre in these, her two most ostensibly 'political', as well as her two most consciously 'literary' novels, is consistently underscored with a wry irony. The ending of *A Sport of Nature* is a case in point. An apparently joyous prefiguration of the birth of a new South African Republic under a black president – Hillela's second husband, Reuel – the final scene is undoubtedly Utopian; but it is also suspiciously contrived. Even in a novel which repeatedly flaunts its own artifice, this final spectacle seems unduly cosmetic. Fischer himself could not have hoped for a more hopeful view of the future, but that view is granted at the expense of parody: the socialist Utopia is shown to be another 'invented paradise', the synthetic creation of an ideal society.

At a conference on the modern writer in Africa in 1967, Albert Memmi expressed the view that 'the true commitment of the writer does not . . . consist in signing manifestos, deciding whether or not to vote, but in daring to depict reality as it really is'.[3] Gordimer's fiction demonstrates the impossibility of ever achieving that goal. While art is incapable of 'depicting reality as it really is', it *is* capable of showing a variety of new perspectives on reality. Here Gordimer would agree with Memmi: the nature of committed art does not consist in its unswerving allegiance to political causes but in its ability to *transform* experience. Yet do the transformations produced by art engender social change, or is their effect merely stylistic? Does the defamiliarization that might produce new perspectives on reality serve a social function, or just an aesthetic one? I have suggested in this essay that Gordimer's poetics calls such divisions between the 'social' and the 'aesthetic' functions of art into question. The modernist techniques of her fiction – its complicated shifts in voice and perspective, for instance – are clearly designed to jolt her readers into an awareness not only of alternative ways of *looking* at society, but also of alternative *societies*. Yet these techniques also afford the opportunity for multiple ironies. It seems significant that, in later fictions such as *A Sport of Nature*, Gordimer has created a (post-) modernist pastiche which cuts through the illusions of attempting to 'transform the world through style' while perpetuating those self-same illusions. The options appear limited. On the one hand, Gordimer critiques the facile slogans of agitprop but, on the other, she exposes the facticity of a self-conscious art which threatens to degenerate into a random play of aesthetic substitutions. In *A Sport of Nature*, the dialectic between art and action in Gordimer's fiction is less resolved than ever. The search for commitment must go on; but Gordimer has never lost faith in its basic premise: that artists are not responsible to themselves alone, but also to their society.

Notes

1.   The term is C. B. MacPherson's. For MacPherson, the central difficulty of modern liberal-democratic theory can be traced back to seven-teenth-century conceptions of the individual 'as essentially the propri-etor of his own person or capacities, owing nothing to society for him'. The individual was thus seen 'neither as a moral whole, nor as part of a larger social whole, but as an owner of himself' (p. 3). James Clifford has recently used MacPherson's notion to suggest that 'in the west . . . *collecting* has long been a strategy for the deployment of a pos-sessive self' (p. 218, my emphasis). Gordimer's critique of liberalism in *Burger's Daughter* and *A Sport of Nature* focuses on the figure of the collector as 'possessive individualist'.
2.   See Newman's succinct analysis of *The Late Bourgeois World* in her survey *Nadine Gordimer* (London: Routledge, 1988), pp. 35–9.
3.   Per Wästberg (ed.), *The Writer in Modern Africa* (Uppsala: Scandinavian Institute of African Studies, 1968), p. 83.

Works Cited

Adams, Hazard (ed.), *Critical Theory Since Plato* (New York: Harcourt, Brace, Jovanovich, 1971).

Adorno, Theodor, 'Commitment', in Ronald Taylor (ed.), *Aesthetics and Politics* (London: Verso, 1980), pp. 177–95.

Alvarez-Péreyre, Jacques, *The Poetry of Commitment in South Africa*, trans. C. Wake (London: Heinemann, 1984).

Clifford, James, *The Predicament of Culture* (Cambridge: Harvard University Press, 1988).

Fischer, Ernst, *The Necessity of Art*, trans A. Bostock (Harmondsworth: Penguin, 1963).

Gordimer, Nadine, *Burger's Daughter* (London: Jonathan Cape, 1979).

——— , *The Essential Gesture: Writing, Politics and Places*, ed. S. Clingman (Harmondsworth: Penguin, 1989).

——— , *The Late Bourgeois World* (London: Viking, 1966).

——— , *A Sport of Nature* (London: Jonathan Cape, 1987).

MacPherson, C. B., *The Political Theory of Possessive Individualism* (Oxford: Oxford University Press, 1962).

Marcuse, Herbert, *The Aesthetic Dimension: Toward a Critique of Marxist Aesthetics* (Boston: Beacon Press, 1978).

Newman, Judie, *Nadine Gordimer* (London: Routledge, 1988).

Sartre, Jean-Paul, 'Why Write?', in Hazard Adams (ed.), *Critical Theory Since Plato* (New York: Harcourt, Brace, Jovanovich, 1971): pp. 1059–1068.

Taylor, Ronald (ed.), *Aesthetics and Politics* (London: Verso, 1980).

Wästberg, Per (ed.), *The Writer in Modern Africa* (Uppsala: Scandinavian Institute of African Studies, 1968).

3

Black and White in Grey:
Irony and Judgement in
Gordimer's Fiction
ROWLAND SMITH

Those who dislike Nadine Gordimer's work usually complain implicitly or explicitly about her tone. And those who dislike her fiction come from both the right and the left. To conservative white South Africans she can appear self-righteous and hectoring;[1] to those committed to political change in South Africa, her fiction can seem to be indulgent in its absence of political message or programme. To such latter, committed critics, the nuances in Gordimer's depiction of the South African scene, including its revolutionary elements, are too ambiguous, too elusive, in a context in which there can be no deviation from service in the cause of liberation.[2]

In each case the disapproval is a result of Gordimer's constant use of irony. Even when she does make ex-cathedra statements in her fiction, particularly summatory statements like those that conclude *The Conservationist* or *Occasion For Living* or 'Something Out There', there is an irony of situation underlying the statement itself and giving it its particular bite.[3] In *The Conservationist* the anonymous dead black man who has haunted the white protagonist's 'property' is finally buried by the ragged, black farm labourers in the land that is now inalienably his: 'There was no child of his present but their children were there to live after him. They had put him away to rest, at last; he had come back. He took possession of this earth, theirs; one of them' (p. 252). In *Occasion For Loving* the drunken comment ('White bitch – get away') of former black friend, Gideon, to white protagonist, Jessie, epitomizes the rent in their relationship even though he has forgotten the incident: 'the sense of his place in the Stilwells' life and theirs in his that she felt that night never came again. So long as Gideon did not remember, Jessie could not forget'

(p. 288). In 'Something Out There' the team of of black and white saboteurs who have hidden in what is assumed to be a disused turn-of-the-century mine-working are finally placed by the author in indigenous authenticity: 'centuries before time was measured, here, in such units, there was an ancient mine-working out there, and metals precious to men were discovered, dug and smelted, for themselves, by black men' (p. 203).

These concluding moments are simultaneously resonant and oblique. The ironic juxtaposition of present dispossession with the legitimate assumption of land in both past and future is at the heart of the first and last passages quoted, while the searing simultaneity of social friendship and subconscious hatred offers a decorously ironic view into racial horror in the second passage. For all their understatement, however, they are authorial interventions, and their authority is unquestioned.

In the body of her texts Gordimer is seldom as explicit as this. She more frequently builds up a pattern of responses and reactions to her characters by a series of deadpan depictions of behaviour or speech. The absence of authorial comment in such passages enables her constantly to make judgements without being judgemental. And here she can confuse her readers. Some are not sure who is being got at. Because Gordimer's depiction of the minutiae of the local scene is so accurate, the rhythms and diction of her dialogue so familiar, the 'rightness' in the presentation of her characters is disturbingly at odds with the 'wrongness' of their behaviour and understanding. It is the jarring wrongness of situation that so much of Gordimer's fiction investigates, and that aura of a world amiss is strikingly counterpointed – *sans* authorial comment – with the simultaneous aura of a world known and recognized intimately.

White South African mores are so constantly served up whole in Gordimer's work, and the external viewpoint is so frequently her lens on to that society, that its foibles become the norm. In particular, the blandness of white response to black anguish or fury is a consistent element in the fiction. And when blandness is what is most startlingly inappropriate in a fictional situation, the absence of explicit authorial comment on that inappropriateness confuses those readers without a sense of irony.

Those who do read ironically are seldom confused about the way Gordimer's white characters are presented, but reaction to her black characters is more complicated. Because blacks are the victims of the South African regime, disregarded by frequently myopic whites, there is an instinctive assumption on the part of many readers that black characters are to be taken at face value in fiction that sets out to depict the convolutions of their plight. While it is natural in such fictional circumstances to react to the ironies of white duplicity or self-deception, the irony with which black posturing is revealed is less predictable. And yet in Gordimer's work little is presented without an ironic tinge. Presentation of the surface is both her great strength and her method of comment. The surface is created with extraordinary verisimilitude, and what that surface reflects or reveals – often by what is not shown or what is not acknowledged – provides the moral edge to the scene.

The contrast between two members of underground resistance movements in *The Late Bourgeois World* is essential to that novel. The ineffectual white saboteur, the news of whose suicide opens the book, is as central a character as is his divorced wife, through whose understanding the action unfolds. The member of the black resistance who visits her in the closing section of the novel, with his terrifyingly viable plan for her to use her white privilege and act as a banker for his group, is necessarily a less rounded character. The fact that we understand so much about the motives and foibles of Max, trapped in his lethal white heritage, and know so little about Luke who arrives out of nowhere and departs similarly, is part of the claustrophobic over-elaboration in Gordimer's depiction of the static white bourgeois world. Even the luxury of its analyzable 'personal relations' – in the Forsterian sense – emphasizes a contrast with the stark realpolitik of the ultimately inaccessible black one. So far so good, but what do we make of Luke himself, apart from the obvious difference between his low-key effectiveness and Max's approval-seeking ineffectiveness?

The irony of Max's failure as a white revolutionary is never in doubt: 'He is dead now. He didn't die for them – the people, but perhaps he did more than that. In his attempts to love he lost even his self-respect, in betrayal. He risked everything for them and lost everything' (p. 93). And the tainted need at the heart of Max's activities is also beyond doubt:

he hovered irresistibly towards what could never be got down, what Spears [his black co-activist] didn't need to get down because it was his – an identity with millions like him, an abundance chartered by the deprivation of all that Max had had heaped upon himself. Some of the white people I know want the blacks' innocence; that innocence, even in corruption, of the status of victim; but not Max. . . . He wanted to come close; and in this country the people – with all the huddled warmth of the phrase – are black. (pp. 80–1)

While establishing Max's hopeless predicament, the passage also hints at a corruption possible in the black status of victim, and it is that potential for corruption and unscrupulousness that hovers around the presentation of Luke.

Luke is ultimately incomprehensible in a 'white', bourgeois sense. That is the point of his presentation. But the affable surface of that presentation is as menace-filled as is the demand he makes of Liz. His impenetrability of manner is a mixture of the false and the warm. It is a moot point which predominates at any moment. Liz likes him, but her description of his antics leaves in doubt the degree to which the reader likes him. The flippancy of their banter is too studied, the tone of their exchanges ultimately non-comprehending. The woodenness of Liz's narration is part of the non-communication embodied in the scene. There is nothing but surface in her depiction of Luke's arrival: 'It was a game; he gave me a little appraising lift, with the heel of the hand, on the outer sides of my breasts, as one says, 'There!', and we went into the living-room' (p. 127). The sexual innuendo is more pronouncedly false in the dialogue that follows. Without the tension of the politics in the scene – if both characters were suburban whites, for instance – the exchange would be a depiction of banal role-playing:

> He heard me clattering about in there and when I came out with the tray, I said to his broad smile, 'What is it now?' and he said, 'That's what I like about white girls, so efficient. Everything goes just-like-that.'
> 'Oh, I'm making a special effort,' I said, putting the bread and salad and butter on the table.
> 'Oh I'm appreciative,' he came back. (p. 129)

The non-communication in the scene is not gratuitous. On Luke's unexpected visits, Liz is always uncertain – until he comes out with the request that has occasioned the visit – what it is he wants her to do, and in the context of his underground activity those requests entail varying degrees of risk. The sexual small talk is a screen for the serious business yet to come, but even in that light, the opacity in their chatter is all-pervasive: 'I said *to his broad smile.*'

Luke's mixture of assurance and gall is what makes him effective. Not needing approval in anything like the way poor, dead Max did, Luke can be almost appropriately wrong, so intent is he on the ultimate, political purpose of his socializing. Even his impenetrability is unimportant – part of the surface of his presence; his falsity is trivial alongside his singlemindedness. What is absent in Liz's reaction to him is both an understanding of his 'real' reactions to their present social fencing and – more important – the 'real' point of the visit. Both these absences contribute significantly to the extraordinary ripples of tension under the surface of the text. 'I don't know whether he's professionally affable or if he really experiences the airy, immediate response to his surroundings', comments Liz. She continues: 'Much of his small talk is in the style of American films he has seen, but it fits quite naturally, just as the rather too hairy, too tweedy jacket he wore was all right, on him' (pp. 129–30). The fact that assumed styles fit 'quite naturally' when Luke makes his potentially painful appearances is one of the many elements that contribute to the cumulatively terrifying mood of impotence and entrapment with which *The Late Bourgeois World* ends. All the characters in the fiction have contributed to that mood. None has been exempted from the author's ironic treatment.

Luke is one in a series of black characters in Gordimer's fiction who act as reflectors to white protagonists: Rosa Burger and Baasie/ Zwelinzima, Maureen Smales and July, Jessie Stilwell and Gideon. In their reactions to the demands presented by such characters the white protagonists come to an understanding of themselves and their situations that would be impossible without the traumatic clash of cultural claim and counterclaim embodied in a personal confrontation that alters everything. Because the focus of interest in these revelatory encounters is on the protagonist and on the change worked in her by what she gathers from the encounter, it is easy to overlook the subtlety with which Gordimer has set up the collision. Never simplistic, always many-sided, the moments of confrontation are so peculiarly shattering because the black catalyst in the process of revelation is frequently depicted as self-interested, victimizing as well as victimized, and ultimately beyond the emotional reach of the protagonist. And the ironic result of such a clash – which can involve moral blackmail among all its other unstated goals and suppressed motives – is that it changes utterly the protagonist's perception of herself and her world.

In *The Conservationist* the protagonist is male, and the confrontation that alters his confidence is not with a single, living black catalyst, but rather with a series of recollections. The black corpse discovered, buried, washed up and buried again on 'his' – Mehring's – farm does provoke Mehring into many forms of reverie, not least of which is his non-rational physical sympathy with the dead man; he instinctively imagines, through his senses rather than his thoughts, his own body experiencing the physical proximity to earth, reeds and mud that the black corpse manifests. Since the inauthentic relation to the land he owns but cannot possess is part of Mehring's crisis of consciousness, this surreptitious sabotage by his sensory imagination is itself a crucial irony in the novel. But the dialogic component in his debate with the circumstances of his life comes from white, not black disapproval of his ways and values. It is with the liberal disdain of his ex-mistress, Antonia, and with the well-meaning, if half-baked, social conscience of his son that Mehring carries on his endless, ultimately destabilizing internal debates.

Once again the text of *The Conservationist* reveals a constant clash of cultural claim and counterclaim in a personal confrontation – this time internal and imagined – that alters the protagonist's perception of himself. Once again the 'opponents' in the revelatory debate are self-interested. Once again an unstated and implicit inappropriateness of reaction is a constant element in Gordimer's ironic presentation of moral jockeying for position. Unlike black catalysts in other novels, however, the white catalysts in Mehring's continual debate with his memories occupy moral high ground only in their posturing. Antonia and Terry are not in a situation in which their actions, like Luke's in *The Late Bourgeois World*, inevitably have some claim on the reader's and protagonist's sympathy. Their actions are minimal, as is their effectiveness, and they cannot themselves be seen as special victims of the regime or of circumstance.

The aridity and shallowness of Antonia's self-righteousness (much more marked than the puniness of Terry's nascent social conscience) are part of the dead-end in the debate between 'liberalism' and 'realism' that preoccupies Mehring. The non-viability of either position as expounded by Mehring and his imagined or remembered opponents is a feature of *The Conservationist* that makes it as claustrophobic in its own way as any of Gordimer's mid-career texts. Obsessed by irrational fears, Mehring flees at the end of the novel from both his imagined Afrikaans-mine-police-or-white-thug observer (in headlong Mercedes-driven panic) and from the oppressive tenor of his daily existence (in jet-travel to distant places). Without the ironic counter-presence of the autochthonous black corpse and motley black farm-dwellers, the reader would also need to flee the circular smugness of the endless debate among those wanting to justify their different forms of *status quo*. What opens up the text are the lyrical descriptions of the land itself, often coinciding with an evocation of the black body's merging with it, and the non-articulate (or at least non-wordy) ethos of shared consciousness and resolve in the overlooked and misunderstood black world on 'Mehring's' land.

The debate in *The Conservationist* is thus threefold. There is a constant dialogue between Mehring, the realist, and all his liberal, bleeding-heart critics epitomized by the safely-departed Antonia. The thematic counterpoint to this sneering, white clash of words and attitudes forms the third element in the debate: the black scene and its closeness to the natural world, fused in the dead man's taking possession of 'this earth' in the last line of the novel. That leitmotif offers a continual, ironic comment on the skirmishing that preoccupies Mehring and – in retrospect – his Antonia.

Mehring's confident ripostes frequently show Antonia's self-righteous scorn for this world to be superficial; situation and narrative tone often reveal his worldly wisdom to be smug and sentimental in its own way; the deadpan juxtaposition of the blacks' instinctive sense of community and their easy assimilation of and into the terrain provides an overwhelming judgement of the ultimate triviality and superficiality of white concerns and of their temporary occupation of the land.

The point of moral balance is typically elusive in a post-coital argument with Antonia over Mehring's feeling for the land he has bought:

> Women expect something then – a caress, an endearment – they often don't seem to know what. You were like the others, although you were going on about my 'historical destiny.' I don't have anyone hanging around here, thank God, if you walk about this place on your own, I can tell you, you see things you'd never see otherwise. Birds and animals – everything accepts you. But if you have people trampling all over the place – (p. 167)

The irony at this point is working against Mehring: the fog-like obtuseness of his characterization of all women and their foibles, particularly from the perspective of one who is all-experienced in such matters, is of a piece with the false-assertiveness of 'I can tell you', which adds a note of vulgarity that Mehring usually manages to avoid. At the same time, however, as a counter to Antonia's equally all-knowing tone about industrial male chauvinists – with one of whom, as Mehring frequently points out, she chooses to fornicate – there is in spite of themselves a refreshingly non-introspective aura to Mehring's clichés and assertions. The text supports Mehring's summation that Antonia would have become (is?): 'A bore in the end, . . . Ingesting, digesting and excreting moral problems clearly as a see-through gheko' (p. 170).

What is most obtuse about Mehring's assertion that he is accepted by 'this place' is not his attitude to Antonia and through her to all women, but his blinkered understanding of his situation on the farm, on which he is seldom really alone. The people with whom he shares the space are black and therefore invisible to him. When the viewpoint shifts to that of those blacks themselves, the non-'acceptance' of Mehring's presence in that context – its irrelevance to the permanently present black peasantry and proletariat – is an integral part of the narrative perspective. It is within those passages in which the viewpoint is not Mehring's that the ephemeral nature of his occupation of the land – birds, plants, dust and all – is at the ironic centre of the text.

Antonia herself – naked in bed – shows scorn for Mehring's just-quoted assertion of his sense of union with his 'place'. Her disdain is based on an assertion of the transitoriness of his 'belonging', but the sarcasm of her knee-jerk is unappealing and false in spite of the ultimate correctness of her deductions:

> All to yourself. You've bought what's not for sale: the final big deal. The rains that will come in their own time, etcetera. The passing seasons. It's so corny, Mehring. I thought you had more to you than that. I'll bet you'll end up wanting to be buried there, won't you? Down there under your willow trees, very simply, sleeping forever with your birds singing to you and Swart Gevaar tending your grave. O Mehring! – hiking herself up from the bed on one elbow, the way she did, so that her brown breasts swung like weights in a sling – O Mehring – her laugh – you are a hundred years too late for that end! (pp. 167–8)

Those pendulous breasts are the clinching, external factor in the general impression of indelicacy in the exchange. Of course they can be explained away as part of Mehring's recollected viewpoint and therefore informed by his basically misogynous (women are only good for one thing) outlook. But even without their undignified swaying across the scene, their owner's condescension is too studied, too rhetorical ('O Mehring!'); even the superior Antonia cannot escape the coy vulgarity of 'I thought you had more to you than that.'

Once again, then, the wrongness in the passage is one of tone, of appropriateness. Correct as Antonia's comments are (and they do offer a choric prescience of both Mehring's obsessive identification with the black corpse and its triumphant repossession of the land in the final paragraph) they are part of her aura of wrongness and falsity.

In contrast, the depiction of two farm-children walking back each day from the variety and excitement of the 'location' where they go to school, places Mehring's relation to them, the land and the enduring life of the 'place' (Mehring's own word) with a marvellously chilling externality:

> Walking home after school from the location, the dirt road gathered itself ahead or behind, rolling up its surface into a great charge of dust coming at them; there was a moment when they saw a car and a face or faces at the fuming centre, and then they were whipped into turmoil, it lashed round them a furry tongue of fiery soft dust spitting stinging chips of stone. When they could breathe and see again, the fury was already gathering up the road on the other side, smoking against the sun and blocking the other horizon. Sometimes it was Mehring whom they found in that split second when they saw into the core of the storm. (p. 80)

The point of view here is that of the children, although the narrative voice is authorial. The detachment of that voice, with its combination of vivid immediate detail and cosmic distance, informs the whole passage with a sense of the abiding verities of life for the indigenous children at the same time as it places the clouded turmoil of Mehring's temporary and disturbing presence as something alien and bemusing. The detachment itself contrasts ironically with the intimate mode of Mehring's never-ending internal debates, and the sudden awareness of distance and perspective created by the scene places Mehring's obsessions as absurdly self-centred and indulgent.

The use of the words 'they' and 'their' is part of the narrative irony throughout *The Conservationist*. In the schoolchildren-passage just quoted the children are constantly referred-to as 'they'. This is in keeping with the externality of the narrative voice at that point, but in no way distances the children. Their perceptions and their sensuous world are intimately experienced for an instant even though they are anonymously perceived and understood. When the voice is authorial in *The Conservationist*, the words 'they' and 'their' frequently suggest both the non-individualistic, group-ethos of the black world depicted and its closely-woven community of interest and identity. This narrative feature is at its most resonant in the celebrated closing lines describing the final burial of the nameless corpse, already quoted as an example of Gordimer's *ex-cathedra* manner:

> The one whom the farm received had no name. He had no family but their women wept a little for him. There was no child of his present but their children were there to live after him. They had put him away to rest, at last; he had come back. He took possession of this earth, theirs; one of them. (p. 252)

When the narrative voice is Mehring's, on the other hand, the words 'they' and 'their' reflect opacity, paranoia and the impenetrable otherness of all the human elements natural to his 'place'. In unease at his compromised situation with his dubious female passenger-pick-up in a disused mine property at the end of the book, Mehring's musings on the people of his farm reflect his own uncontrollable alienation, the temporary nature of any occupation he can muster, and the chasm of incomprehension separating him from all of 'them':

> Perhaps they thought I was dead; they know another one will always come. They would take off their hats at the graveside as they'd take them off to greet the new one. – We think something is to happen. – But it can only happen to me. They have been there all the time and they will continue to be there. They have nothing and they have nothing to lose. (pp. 245–6)

This is the closest Mehring gets to understanding his relation to the land and its people. What he says here is, in paraphrasable content, very similar to the author's closing comments on the dead man's 'coming back'. The shattering difference between the two passages is entirely one of tone and perspective, and the resonance of each extract is typical of the textural subtlety inherent in Gordimer's ironic narrative manner.

The Conservationist is a closely-worked novel that moves inexorably to its summatory closure. As a result, its ironies, both of situation and tone, are cumulative and coherent. Although moral balance shifts throughout the narrative, its direction is never confused or obscure.

The ironies in *A Sport of Nature* are more elusive. 'Wrongness' in that late novel is easily understood in the depiction of the two Johannesburg aunts who attempt to bring up its freakish protagonist. Liberal Aunt Pauline and materialistic Aunt Olga represent the familiar Scylla and Charybdis of the Johannesburg white suburbs, and the ironic presentation of their self-satisfied world is similar to that in other Gordimer fiction. The hedonistic protagonist herself, and the sanctity of her cause, pose problems, however.

Hillela is different from other whites. Her guiltless identification with the black cause is beyond the capabilities of others, and represents a new element in Gordimer's fiction: the imagined qualities needed to break out of white cultural, social and emotional limitations and 'join hands' both with black individuals and with their group needs.[4] Gordimer has to create a freak to do this. The bonds of both white materialism and white liberalism are too strong for representatives of those dominant cultural spheres to achieve anything like the physical (with two black husbands) and political union achieved by Hillela.

The irrelevance of Forsterian values in the South African context is often the target of Gordimer's irony, yet life without Forsterian sensibility does produce a wrongness of manner in *A Sport of Nature*. Hillela's self-centredness is described ironically even when her overall objectives are correct. The feature of so much Gordimer irony in other texts – a wrongness or inappropriateness of tone reflecting a wrongness of situation – is inverted in *Sport*. In it, wry comments on Hillela's singlemindedness are coupled with a sense of the overriding correctness of her politics. Her opportunism works. The often-repeated comment, 'Trust Hillela', sums up both this irony and the central role she plays. In the text the words are used in varying contexts and from many points of view, but they usually reflect all the varieties of tone imaginable: from the sarcastic and exasperated to the admiring.

The early pages build up the differences between Hillela and her world with all the ironic subtlety of Gordimer's other books. When morally superior Aunt Pauline cannot cope with the young Hillela's freedom from the code of the family, the point of view is hers: 'it was simply that she seemed not to notice all that Pauline and Joe had to offer that was worthwhile. . . . To resist Pauline would at least have meant to have belonged with Olga; why didn't Hillela understand that was the choice? The only choice. . . . – She's a-moral. I mean, in the sense of the morality of this country' (p. 56). Such an ironic slash at the limitations of Pauline's self-righteous understanding is typical of all Gordimer's depictions of white complacency.

But the tone in a detached authorial comment towards the end of the book on the successful Hillela's marriage to her African General-President is less easily assimilated. The reader has earlier been informed that the 'charming children' of the presidential household, 'probably have been born to the President since his third marriage [Hillela], by the second wife' (p. 360): 'theirs appears to be what is called a happy marriage. Which surely, in the curiously mysterious while too public sense of the relationship between symbolic figures, means a good combination of accommodation' (p. 386). There is no point of rest in this series of oblique ('appears to be', 'what is called') comments on an (admirably?) 'good combination of accommodation'.

Hillela achieves union – physical and political – with the black cause, and this is an ideal that has constantly eluded whites in all Gordimer's fiction. In presenting her cultural background, an ironic narrative mode captures all the nuances of the moral and emotional white quagmire that the protagonist avoids. The liberation of South Africa, in which Hillela and her President-husband play a subsidiary role, is a goal presupposed to be desirable throughout the text. It is in these circumstances that Gordimer's deadpan irony is a surprisingly constant feature of *Sport*.

The rightness of outcome is accompanied by an insistent wrongness of tone. White 'accommodation' to the changes of the times is presented with the familiarly 'neutral' voice of Gordimer's ironic manner. Olga's entrepreneurial sons are promised advisory positions in the new revolutionary regime, and make a good profit on the side with liberation T-shirts. They are not at the liberation ceremony in Cape Town: 'they wouldn't get mixed up in any mob. The struggle was not their struggle. The celebration is not their celebration' (p. 395).

But even in describing those for whom the celebration is 'theirs', the text presents an irony of situation and language. Explicable as the needs for authoritative control in such a situation are, the keeping out of a huge crowd does suggest a figuratively ominous limitation of 'room within' the new regime: 'A cordon of police and the liberation army keeps out the huge crowd for whom there is not room enough within [the stadium]' (p. 393).

The ambiguous way in which Luke is presented in *The Late Bourgeois World* is part of the stifling total effect in that novel. *A Sport of Nature* ends in an ostensibly celebratory scene, in which a victorious conclusion to the South African struggle has been reached. This positive outcome does not readily admit the kind of ironic presentation that Gordimer has constantly used in all her fiction. The deadpan externality of point of view in the final section of the late novel leaves the ironic moments as part of a detached scepticism about the human agents carrying out the longed-for and welcome change of affairs. The inevitability of such a change has been the subject of much of Gordimer's later fiction, and seldom has she investigated without irony the human interests entangled in that struggle.

Notes

1. Two very different examples of white unease indicate the wide range of response from those reacting negatively to what they take to be self-righteousness. The South African writer Christopher Hope made this comment in 1975: 'At best there is her admirable fidelity to the landscapes she describes, at worst she drives home her points, tediously and sententiously, leaving nothing to the imagination.' ['Out of the Picture: The Novels of Nadine Gordimer', *London Magazine* (April/ May 1975), p. 53.] A less sophisticated letter-writer to the Johannesburg *Star* is more forthright: 'It's listening to Miss Gordimer's self-satisfaction being trumpeted whenever the occasion presents itself that makes me ask her to turn down the volume a bit.' (S. M., 'Gordimer Trumpets Her Own Virtues', *Star*, 23 November 1982, p. 16.)
2. A classic statement of the committed position is found in a review of *Burger's Daughter* published in *African Communist*: '"Burger's Daughter" is the third novel of Nadine Gordimer's to have been banned. In a way this is a tribute to be valued more highly than the Herzog or CNA prizes, even though, if, like the authorities, one is searching for revolutionary content one might feel it is undeserved.' [Z. N., 'The Politics of Commitment', *African Communist* 80 (1st Quarter, 1980), p. 101.]
3. In an interview published in 1981, Gordimer has this to say about her use of irony: 'My method has so often been irony. I find irony very attractive in other writers, and I find life full of irony, my own life and

everybody else's; somehow one of the secret locks of the personality lies in what is ironic in us.' [Susan Gardner, '"A Story for This Place and Time": An Interview with Nadine Gordimer about *Burger's Daughter*, *Kunapipi* 3 (Fall 1981), p. 110; republished in Nancy Topping Bazin and Marilyn Dallmin Seymour (eds), *Conversations with Nadine Gordimer* (Jackson and London: University Press of Mississippi, 1990), p. 172.]

4.	Hillela's cousin Sasha uses the word 'utopian' to describe the difference between the impetus behind her kind of action and that of ineffective 'reformers' like her Aunt Pauline. He comments on Pauline's reaction ('It solves nothing') to the news of Hillela's marriage to a black man: 'She's jealous. Saturday classes for kids. Reformers are (take pride in being) totally rational, but the dynamic of real change is always utopian. The original impetus may get modified – even messed up – in the result, but it has to be there no matter how far from utopia that result may be' (p. 217).

Works Cited

Gordimer, Nadine, *The Conservationist* (1974; New York: Viking, 1975).
_____ , *The Late Bourgeois World* (1966; London: Jonathan Cape, 1976).
_____ , *Occasion For Loving* (1963; London: Jonathan Cape, 1978).
_____ , *Something Out There* (London: Jonathan Cape, 1984).
_____ , *A Sport of Nature* (London: Jonathan Cape, 1987).

4

Placing Spaces: Style and Ideology in Gordimer's Later Fiction
BRIAN MACASKILL

Across one of the pages that precedes our acquaintance with Lionel Burger's daughter occurs a solitary inscription from Claude Lévi-Strauss: 'I am the place in which something has occurred.' Indeed, much has occurred – both outside and inside Gordimer's writing – since those early stories in which she first began to express a critical love for the place about which she writes: South Africa, its placement of her as a white woman, and her placement of it as a writer – one who rearranges worlds in the spacing of words. Much has changed since one of the earliest stories, 'Is There Nowhere Else Where We Can Meet?' was written in 1945. In that story, written before the word *apartheid* had been minted as official currency,[1] there seemed 'Nowhere Else' than the arena of violence for white to meet black, though a desire on Gordimer's part for there to be some other place is palpably present; she has since sought to create such a place in and through her writing.

In the same year *Burger's Daughter* first saw publication, 34 years after she wrote the story in which 'Nowhere Else' seemed available, Gordimer could insist that 'South African literature . . . should have a potential greater than that of Latin American Literatures' and that 'whites could have a unique opportunity to make . . . a vital instead of predatory connection with a post-apartheid indigenous culture' ('From Apartheid to Afrocentrism', p. 47). Now she could conceive of a cultural space brought about and distinguished by literature in which 'whites could enter with blacks into the discovery of truly African ideas, related to this continent and away from ties with other continents' (p. 47). In an uncommonly personal interview with Stephen Gray a year later, she reflects on some of the changes that have accompanied apartheid and its opposition *as stylistic effects within her writing.* She points out, for instance, that the Soweto revolt 'overtook' the writing of *Burger's Daughter* (p. 269), and that the more equivocal mediation of her novels from *The Conservationist* onwards is an attempt to convey 'a constant shifting of foothold' amongst whites 'on very uncertain and uneven ground' in South Africa, where 'you are either running away from your inevitable place, or you are taking it on' (pp. 265, 267). 'By place', Gordimer adds, 'I don't mean a predetermined place; your place depends on the role you take in society' (p. 267).

What Gordimer sees in her later novels when she looks back at her earlier work is the manifestation of changes in her sense of Africa's 'articulated consciousness', which it is the novelist's duty to provide ('An Interview', p. 270). Much later in the text prefaced by Lévi-Strauss's cryptic comment on place, Rosa Burger finds herself amongst the 'family, relatives, friends and furniture' crowded into a house whose township dimensions are familiar to her, and what *she* sees is that 'this commonplace of any black township became to me what it is: ' "place"; a position whose contradictions those who impose them don't see, and from which will come a resolution they haven't provided for' (pp. 150–1). In this essay I argue that Gordimer's later work – from the appearance of *The Conservationist* onwards – responds to changes of ideological placement within the 'external' space of South Africa by reconfiguring the stylistics 'internal' to her writing, and that the stylistic reconfigurations in turn bear upon the ideological shape of the future.

I

Gordimer's later works create a space for negotiation between a moribund order of white supremacy and a new order waiting to be born. They seek to open and fill a space advertised in the epigraph to *July's People*, again by quotation from an influential cultural theorist, this time Antonio Gramsci: 'The old is dying and the new cannot be born; in this interregnum there arises a great diversity of morbid symptoms.'[2] Itself implicated within the 'morbid symptoms' amidst which it struggles to be born – including the rejection of radical white participation in a new South Africa by the Black Consciousness movement and the revolt by Soweto schoolchildren – the reconfiguration Gordimer seeks through her fiction must thus oppose the currently white-dominated space of South Africa, and must draw instead on blackness, for 'through blackness is revealed the way to the future' (*BD*, p. 135).[3] According to the alternate hegemonics of Black Consciousness concurrent with the writing and publication of this novel, however, Gordimer's fiction has no voice to give the future and no say in how that future will take place. Writing thus from a marginalized position and apparently overtaken by history, Gordimer seeks 'The comfort of black' (*BD*, p. 143), filling white pages with black markings that refuse to be relegated to the margins. The ideological course projected in the later fiction relies on Gordimer's defiant act of placing herself within projections of the future, on the contribution her fiction may make towards that future – on the placement, that is, of these works within the Gordimer *oeuvre* and its milieu – and is most compelling negotiated in practical terms as the increased attention paid in these works to what I shall call the stylistics of placement.

The sense of 'place' that Rosa Burger comes to in the previously mentioned party at a house in Soweto makes her realize that she understands place – even this acronym, So(uth)We(stern)To(wnships) – and the propositions of the Communist Party faithful 'in a way theory doesn't explain' (*BD*, p. 151). Like Rosa Burger, and like Hillela Capran from *Sport of Nature*, Gordimer is a practitioner whose credentials rely more on intimacy than on abstraction. It is not *immediately* to theoretical questions of focalization or point of view, or voice or power that we must turn, then, in order to understand the significance of this unpredictable placement of Hillela or of Gordimer in that unpredictable place which they inhabit and which is taken up in such innovative ways by the later novels. Neither the acronyms nor the jargon out of which the political activist or the literary critic may build a career will initially be of much help, though *'a career can be built out of acronyms'* (*SON*, p. 250). Instead, it is to the more minute particularity with which *'the child plays with alphabetical blocks on the floor, builds houses with them'* that we must turn our attention (*SON*, p. 250). Or, to abandon the conceit of this bit of italicized text without leaving its *slant*, we must turn to the placement of verbal blocks in Gordimer's textual building. We must pause, and start, with placement as style: the scaffolding for getting from here to somewhere else.

II

Shortly after Maureen and Bamford Smales arrive among July's people, they are introduced to July's mother. Accordingly, on the last three lines of page 15, July interprets for the Smales and for the reader that which his mother has said:

> She say, she can be very pleased you are in her house. She can be
> very glad to see you, long time now, July's people –

But on the very next line, the first line over the page, on the line that begins a new page and is further distanced by the blank gap that signifies a new paragraph, on this line thus simultaneously distanced and foregrounded, we read: 'But she had said nothing' (p. 16).[4]

Surely this configuration is the inverse of *coincidence*: not a coming together, but a setting apart – yet still an attribute of placement. While it might simply be the case that the type runs across the page-break fortuitously, by coincidence, there remains no way of getting around this coincidence without turning the page; there is no escaping that (a) the paragraph-break calls attention to a block of text that undermines its predecessor; that (b) by virtue of placement, a dialogue is here established between two paragraphs and their constituent words; and that (c) such acts of placement become significantly pervasive – and incrementally so – in Gordimer's later fiction. The value of this unobtrusively introduced dialogue is that it underscores the increased attention Gordimer pays in her later fiction to the *value* of words (in the term's structuralist sense) and of their placement and replacement: their weight, counterpoint, and revision, a rhetoric in turn translatable into the political domain of assertion, negation, and reformulation.

In an innovative departure from the stylistics of Gordimer's earlier novels, *The Conservationist* had already inaugurated a self-conscious programme of dialogic interruption by means of which the impressions filtered through the initially dominant consciousness of the white protagonist, Mehring, are challenged by a revolutionary collaboration of image and style that gradually becomes more powerful as the novel progresses. The collaboration between image and stylistic interruption in this text literally constitutes an 'underground' movement that derives from the figure of an unidentified black man shallowly buried on Mehring's farm. The 'underground' politics of this image are extended further by means of an affiliation Gordimer creates between the corpse and unknown black ancestors, an affiliation she achieves through the stylistic irruption into the text of quotations from Henry Callaway's *The Religious System of the Amazulu*, an account of the *Amatongo*, or spirits of the dead: *'they who are beneath'* (*C*, p. 163). The first quotation from Callaway calls attention to its alien origin by interruptively appearing, without announcement, as italicized script on an otherwise unoccupied and unpaginated page itself preceded by a completely blank page: *'I pray for corn, that many people may come to this village of yours and make a noise, and glorify you.'* While she herself refrains in this text from speaking openly and in her own voice on behalf of black aspirations – a reverse to which the mute presence of the corpse bears silently eloquent testimony – Gordimer allows the italicized extracts from Callaway to speak for the dispossessed and to intimate an 'underground' tradition of socio-political organization and possession of the land that is utterly different from the 'legal' and 'above ground' conquest of the land familiar to the lineage of white colonizers from whom Mehring is descended and whose conquests he seeks to conserve. Near the end of the novel, the corpse is finally washed out in a violent storm; it comes above ground to supplement the challenge inaugurated by the extracts from Callaway's informants quoted throughout the text. Together, in an interruptive amalgam of style and image I have elsewhere studied in some detail, the quotations and this corpse displace Mehring's authority and replace it with their own claim to the land.[5]

With *The Conservationist* Gordimer critically calls for the coming of a consciousness whose historical advent would shortly overtake the production of *Burger's Daughter* and occasion there a surprisingly difficulty for the writer who had so presciently anticipated its arrival. In *Burger's Daughter* the thematic and structural play between above and below so fundamental to *The Conservationist* is transformed into a slippage between outside and inside. In the early pages of the novel, whose opening sequence describes Rosa and others waiting outside the prison doors to visit relatives inside, the prison and its environs are evoked as a place of viewing and of feeling to which the narrative periodically returns.[6] This opening sequence, in which Rosa's waiting is presented in various degrees of intimacy and distance, motivates the subsequent oscillation in the book's narrative presentation: sometimes we are offered a first-person account originating from Rosa Burger, while at other times the presentation of narrative authority is located at a position that allows Rosa to be observed 'historically', as it were, from the outside. In its opening pages the novel takes in those intimate observations of a Rosa construed within the circle of people who knew she *'could be counted on in this family totally united in and dedicated to the struggle'* (p. 12). But, like a yo-yo spinning and gliding from the grasp of a hand to the farthest reach of its string, the narrative takes in and gives out more than this, affording also a view of Rosa as she might have been seen by an outsider in a passing bus: 'Imagine, a schoolgirl: she must have somebody inside. Who are all those people, anyway?' (p. 9)

The coming and going of words here seems again to turn on a sentence wilfully isolated and inscribed on a page of its own, thereby constituting a 'chapter' all to itself: *'When they saw me outside the prison, what did they see?'* (p. 13) The way this sentence is placed – isolated from its neighbours and set apart by italics – emphasizes that its origin is curiously obscure. Its origin is not the same as that of the response immediately presented – both right away and with less mediation – over the page: 'I shall never know' (unequivocally attributable to Rosa). Nor yet does this sentence originate from the authority that picks up the narrative three pages later with the utterance, 'After the death of her father . . . ' (p. 17). Instead, it comes from some other place. Here, one might say, *something has happened*, something akin to the work accomplished by that equivocal pronoun in the epigraph which insists of itself 'I am the place in which something has occurred', and to whose uncertain antecedent the italicized sentence seems to relate itself, iteratively suggesting that it does not come from an omniscient narrator outside this fictional world, nor yet exactly from a character within called Rosa Burger. The situation of this italicized sentence, the way it is itself located, situates us as distant readers (are we not analogous to the 'ordinary people' looking down from a bus?) But its mediation also gives us immediate access to Rosa Burger in the first person. It is this shifting presentation that in turn reveals Rosa's figural status as a conduit between inside and outside: 'I just knew that my mother, inside, would know, when she got the things I was holding, that I had been outside; we were connected' (p. 15). And the body of this text similarly connects together geographical and political outsides to the most intimate inside tissue of its interior stylistics, the body – mental, physical, and politic – of Rosa Burger.

No longer knowing 'how to live in Lionel's country' (p. 210), wanting instead *'to know somewhere else'* (p. 185) and 'to know how to defect from' Lionel Burger (p. 264), Rosa leaves for Europe, where she hopes to find what Katya had found, the ' "whole world" outside what [Lionel] lived for' (p. 264). In the exotic geography of that other place, however, Rosa finally finds it impossible to escape the politics of Lionel Burger – 'his spirit was everywhere' she hears at a meeting in London (p. 313) – and she returns home in the final pages of the novel to pick up the 'connection' she had earlier lost with the world of Burger's burghers (p. 172). The annunciation of Rosa's reconnection has already been prepared for by those early pages which describe her as an adolescent outside the prison who becomes aware of her first menstrual bleeding – 'that monthly crisis of destruction, the purging, tearing, draining of [her] own structure' – which there, 'outside the prison', turns 'the internal landscape of [her] mysterious body inside out' (pp. 15–16). By the end of the novel this annunciation of an inseparable linkage between inside and outside – between Rosa and her place of birth, between Rosa and her parentage, and between this adolescent and that prison – has run its course.

The closing pages of the novel locate Rosa in prison. According to Flora Donaldson, who gets permission to visit her there, she ' "hadn't changed much" ' and 'looked like a little girl . . . About fourteen . . .' (p. 360). Rosa seems to be back where she started, over three hundred pages ago. But of course she is not. Replaced by the text that positions her, a text which has itself been 'overtaken' by the historical occurrences that mark Rosa's return to father and fatherland as ironic in some senses,[7] Rosa and this text constitute equally 'the place in which something has occurred', and promise equally the engendering of further but as yet unspecified occurrence. Despite their whiteness, and in response to the overturnings of history effected by black agency, Rosa and this text ask for a role in a future they stand ready to serve.

It is precisely to the reconfiguration of roles that Gordimer's following novel turns. Readjustments in *July's People* are brought on by disruptions of time and place, and presented as the effects of a changed present still contaminated by the past, but in ways now different from those contaminations recorded in *The Conservationist*. Woken up to unfamiliarity in a hut among July's people by the familiar ritual of July serving early-morning tea, Maureen Smales becomes aware that she will have to learn a new language with which to situate her new role in these paradoxical circumstances of change and sameness.

Not surprisingly, then, with *July's People* Gordimer turns again to what had for her been a dominant concern in the production of *The Conservationist*: the difficulties of speaking on behalf of blackness. Gordimer here seeks what *for her* constitutes a renegotiation of narrative placements – a new language, a fiction that will compete with the paperback that had somehow accompanied the white family's flight from the city and which Maureen now finds herself too displaced to read (p. 29). Under circumstances in which all is under revision, Gordimer revises her earlier reluctance to speak on behalf of blacks and their blackness, as she does even more emphatically in her most recent novel, *My Son's Story*, which is presented as the literary product of Will, the 'Coloured' son indicated by the novel's title (p. 277).

In the first 'chapter' fragment specifically set aside for the perceptions of July and his people, July becomes aware of 'something he had not known' before about white people: 'They can't do anything. Nothing to us any more. . . . Here they haven't got anything – just like us' (pp. 21–2). Shortly after another such chapter, strategically placed halfway through the text (pp. 81–4), July and Maureen fight for psychological purchase of ground, and the scene is presented as a meditation on time and place. July is attempting with Daniel's help a minor repair to the yellow pick-up truck. Upon Maureen's arrival, work ceases, Daniel is sent off, and an exchange strained by the past and complicated by the present ensues, during which July resists Maureen's involvement in the daily work of the black women: ' – The women have their work. They must do it. This is their place, we are always living here and they are doing all things, all things how it must be. You don't need work for them in their place' (pp. 96–7). Having long since abandoned her attempt to read the paperback – but determined to try to read her new circumstances – Maureen tries to interpret: 'He might mean "place" in the sense of role, or might be implying she must remember she had no claim to the earth – "place" as territory' (p. 97). In the verbal struggle that follows, Maureen for the first time feels fear: 'She had never been afraid of a man. Now comes fear, on top of everything else' (p. 98). The chapter that delivers this exchange ends by describing Maureen as she leaves, 'unsteady with something that was not anger but a struggle: her inability to enter into a relation of subservience with [July] that she had never had with Bam' (p. 101), and thus reinforces our growing appreciation that the exchange has been shaped not only by habits of racial negotiation but also by those of gender.

Yet a third occasion of a chapter narrated as if from within July's world substantiates our appreciation of gender complicities within and between the older order and the new. This chapter – which presents a 'his' and 'her' version of the domestic and economic life shared by July and Martha, his wife (130–7) – again serves as a prelude to an encounter between July and Maureen, and the encounter again takes place in the 'place of ruin' that conceals the pick-up truck, where July and Maureen's words now sink 'into the broken clay walls like spilt blood' (p. 153). In the 'incredible tenderness of the evening' that surrounds them 'as if mistaking them for lovers' (p. 153), Maureen flaunts her sexuality in a 'death's harpy image' which means nothing to July, 'who had never been to a motor show complete with provocative girls' (p. 153), but which prefigures her triumphant submission – that can no longer be construed as submission, the word's value having been revised – to the mythological Zeus-helicopter towards which Maureen runs at the novel's close. '[T]rusting herself with all the suppressed trust of a lifetime, alert, like a solitary animal at the season when animals neither seek a mate nor take care of young, existing only for their lone survival' (p. 160), Maureen runs past her husband and children and 'under the beating wings' of the helicopter's noise, to where the helicopter, 'jigging in its monstrous orgasm', is opening its landing gear 'like spread legs' and 'battling the air with whirling scythes' (p. 158).[8]

The coincidence of sexuality and knowledge, which here come together and set Maureen apart from July and Bamford – and which converge again in *Sport of Nature*'s Hillela Capran – is also that which sets Hillela apart, which confirms her as the *lusus naturae* defined by quotation from the *Oxford English Dictionary* in the epigraph to this text: '*A plant, animal, etc., which exhibits abnormal variation or a departure from the parent stock or type . . . a spontaneous mutation; a new variety produced in this way.*' Hillela early demonstrates herself, to borrow an expression from her Aunt Pauline, as 'a-moral . . . in the sense of the morality of this country,' the place of her childhood (p. 44). Despite her tender years and her 'a-morality' (which Pauline tries to ascribe to innocence), Hillela demonstrates a concomitant *knowledge* that unsettles Pauline (p. 47). Although Hillela's behaviour is sometimes 'a-moral' in Pauline's terms rather than in those 'of this country' – as when she spends time '"with her friends"' instead of accompanying Pauline and Carole to protest meetings (p. 52) – she more intimately knows a world that Pauline imagines herself serving, for the parties '"with her friends"' take Hillela to 'areas Pauline had never taken her to *because the people who lived there were not white and had no vote to canvas*' (p. 53; italics added).

Above all, Hillela knows her body (p. 138), and her body, she learns, is '*a form of power*' (p. 198). Drawing 'upon the surety of her sexuality as the bread of her being' (p. 283), Hillela crosses the world from East to West and South to North, steadfastly maintaining herself – despite her apparent dependence on masculine figures[9] – as that mutant form she has invented herself as, or has been invented as, 'the non-matrilineal centre' that 'no-one has known could exist' (p. 310). And so too *Sport of Nature* comes to constitute a *lusus naturae* within Gordimer's *oeuvre*, and plots a mutant space for itself.

Nevertheless, and however much an initial reading of this picaresque and at times sensationalist novel might strike the reader as '*a departure from the parent stock*' of the novels immediately preceding it, however much it might initially remind the reader of a historiographic fantasy fathered by, say, André Brink rather than mothered by Nadine Gordimer, the 'Sport' played out by this text should prompt a consideration of what 'new variety' of Gordimer novel has been 'produced in this way'. While *Sport of Nature* might well represent a *lusus naturae* in the context of the later Gordimer works, it is hardly the 'spontaneous mutation' of the *OED* definition, but a carefully contrived and not entirely surprising aberration from its less flamboyant predecessors, those quieter in style and more proper in politics: its aberrant behaviour rests again on stylistic building-blocks familiar from the preceding texts and akin to the '*alphabetical blocks*' with which '*the child plays*' in this text (p. 250). The stylistic disruptions in *Sport of Nature* are once again the product of blocks of text – sometimes italicized or otherwise signalling their marginal origin – being placed in such a manner as to complicate our reading of other passages with which they participate in the kind of dialogic relationship described by Mikhail Bakhtin.

It is not always possible unequivocally to locate an origin for various passages of this narrative. When we read that 'Hillela could have been like anyone else', for instance (p. 57): are we getting this information from the 'omniscient' historian who also all-but-omnisciently informs the reader that there are gaps in the narrative – periods not documented 'in anyone's memory, even it seems, Hillela's own' (p. 100)?; or is this information focalized through Pauline, since the passage in question later and clearly occupies Pauline's perspective? 'It is easy', the text quizzically informs at one point, 'to confuse Hillela with someone else' (p. 197). To whom should we attribute the italicized utterance that sometimes constitutes a chapter or interchapter all of its own? Sometimes these interchapters embody Hillela's point of view; more frequently, however, they do not.

The fluctuation of voice and authority and the display of irony that this strategy of placement engenders – narrative lapses, lacunae, and admissions of unreliability included – serve to complicate any crippling reduction of the text as belonging to the category of, say, the novel of consciousness, or the picaresque adventure, or the feminist *bildungsroman*. Like Hillela, for whom 'Categories were never relevant to her ordering of life' (p. 108), *Sport of Nature* resists categorization as forcefully as Hillela herself does. Hardly recognizable in any sense as a feminist, Hillela nevertheless wields a power and knowledge – engendered as unequivocally female by this text – that allows her to place herself at the centre and dispose otherness around her: 'Hers is the non-matrilineal centre that no-one resents because no-one has known it could exist. She has invented it' (p. 310). As itself a mutation from the aesthetics of a historical materialism more at home in Gordimer's preceding novels – and yet keeping its distance from the post-modern fiction of J. M. Coetzee, say – *Sport of Nature* takes its place within South African literature by occupying a non-Lukácsian, non-Black Consciousness, and non-postmodern space of political aesthetics that it has invented for itself.

III

If the preceding commentary on placement in the later Gordimer novels has happened to focus more on matters of style than on ideology, it has done so only for methodological reasons.[10] The putative division between stylistic work and the ideological work stylistics undertakes may now be abandoned. Let it be replaced in these terms: the text, literary or otherwise, is a production of ideology and is produced in response to ideological configurations which preexist it and participate in its birth, but to which it also adds – explaining, perhaps, or contributing towards, or resisting against. '[T]he problem-solving process of the text', writes Eagleton, is 'a matter of the "ideological" presenting itself in the form of the "aesthetic" and *vice versa* – of an "aesthetic" solution to ideological conflict producing in its turn an aesthetic problem which demands ideological resolution, and so on' (p. 88). The stylistics of placement earlier described must now be emphasized as a series of aesthetic solutions to ideological conflict, most notably Gordimer's perception of the marginal status occupied by radical white belief.

Gordimer refuses to give in to marginalization, and instead crucially deploys the stylistic margins of her texts as loci of ideological utterance, especially in the epigraphs, quotations and other often-italicized narrative supplements described in the preceding analysis. Far from being mere idiosyncracies of Gordimer's narrative style – or coincidental markers of literary indulgence and detachment – the marginal supplements described above themselves describe a coincidence of style and ideology achieved through judicious placement. In its refusal to accept the marginal as redundant, Gordimer's stylistics can thus be specified as a series of ideological resolutions towards which the always temporary placement of aesthetic solutions incrementally struggles. In an attack levelled from the narrative margins of *The Conservationist* – by the strategically placed quotation of 'documentary' material from Callaway and by the figural recalcitrance of a corpse – Gordimer confronts the efficacy of shallow conservation, reveals the inadequacy of such conservation, dissociates herself from the conservatism of its once-dominant protagonist, and critically looks forward to a new order.[11] Despite the extent to which the historical heralding of this new order by Black Consciousness and the children's revolt further marginalizes the conceivable efficacy of radical white contributions to history, *Burger's Daughter* will not give up its marginal utterance. Stylistically turning itself inside out, *Burger's Daughter* projects from its transgressive margins a scene of transitive address put into place by Rosa's gradual acceptance of Lionel Burger's conviction that the 'conduit towards meaning' posits a life 'outside self', whose efficacy mediates the tension between 'the present and [the] creation of something called the future' (p. 86).[12] Situated within the Interregnum preceding this future, *July's People* responds to the challenge of depicting social reconfigurations, and tries to negotiate transformative redrawings of boundaries and margins without abandoning the belief that the white voice will have and must have a place in the future. In *Sport of Nature*, Gordimer's affirmation of this future place extends beyond Maureen's equivocally presented gesture at the end of *July's People* and – despite the apparently post-modern character of some of its strategies of mediation and textual deconstructions of narrative origin – actually returns again in some central senses to the transitive address of *Burger's Daughter*. Describing Hillela watching the flag unfurl over an unnamed new South Africa for the first time, the text supplies a coda: 'If it is true that the voice of a life is always addressing someone . . . there is a stage in middle life, if that life is fully engaged with the world and the present, when there is no space or need for reflection. The past is not a haunting, but was a preparation, put into use.' (p. 341). Placing ideology by means of style and vice versa – placing style by means of ideology – Gordimer's later fiction has tried to put its words and its past – along with past words and passwords of a South Africa it has intimately known – 'into use', for the future.

Notes

I wish to thank Jeanne Colleran for her valuable reading of an earlier version of this essay.

1. 'Apartheid' was apparently first used in print in 1943, but came into parliamentary and general usage only later (see Bunting). Gordimer provides the date of composition for 'Is There Nowhere Else' in her introduction to *Some Monday for Sure*.
2. See also Gordimer's 'Living in the Interregnum'.
3. These abbreviations will be used when appropriate: *Burger's Daughter (BD), The Conservationist (C), July's People (JP), Sport of Nature (SON)*.
4. The page-break does not occur at the same place in the uncorrected proofs of the novel, which divide pages at the words 'your are in her', and 'house. She can be . . . '. However, the configuration of placement I describe holds for all final versions of the text: the London edition of Jonathan Cape, the Johannesburg printing from Ravan Press, and the UK/US editions from Penguin and Viking Penguin. Furthermore, the following considerations are pertinent: firstly, Gordimer devotes scrupulous attention to the final placement of text on the printed page, and exacts from printers a faithful attention to her desires for textual arrangement; secondly, a perusal of the uncorrected proofs establishes that Gordimer required extensive changes in spacing for the final plates.
5. Macaskill, 'Interrupting the Hegemonic' and 'Figuring Rupture'.
6. The narrative returns to this scene on pp. 62, 81, 173 and 357.
7. In the interview with Gray, Gordimer points out that the Soweto revolt came 'not from the fathers of the people but from their children. Which is also, of course, a kind of reversal of what has happened to [Rosa]' (p. 269).
8. See Visser's discussion of this ending.
9. Hillela allows herself to be treated as an 'honorary man' (p. 175), sees herself as 'unfinished', needing the fulfilment of a man (pp. 177–9), and is surrounded by male 'protectors' (p. 180).

10.   I follow Eagleton, who argues at length that 'The distinction between "aesthetic" and "ideological" elements of the text . . . is methodological rather than real' (p. 178).

11.   The black labourers on Mehring's farm, who had previously disowned the corpse, finally give him a proper burial. In the last two sentences of the novel, strategically so placed, we read: 'They had put him away to rest, at last; he had come back. He took possession of this earth, theirs; one of them' (p. 267). The expression 'he had come back' evokes the ANC slogan, 'Afrika, Mayibuye' ('Africa, May it come back'), and thereby associates this text with the coming of a new order. For Gordimer's criticism of black apathy in this novel and on the affirmation of its ending see Macaskill; also see Gordimer's interview with Gray, in which she comments on her use of the ANC phrase (p. 268).

12.   Rosa insists that 'always one is addressed to someone' (p. 16); Rosa's discourse is addressed first to Conrad, later to Katya, and finally to Lionel himself. Like the frontispiece photograph of Lionel Burger's biography that shows Burger as if 'speaking to a crowd not shown but whose presence is in his eyes' (p. 116), *Burger's Daughter* is framed inside and out by transitive address: Rosa's address to Conrad, Katya, and Lionel; Gordimer's address to South Africa and the world.

Works Cited

Bakhtin, Mikhail, *The Dialogic Imagination: Four Essays*, trans. Caryl Emerson and Michael Holquist (Austin: University of Texas Press, 1981).

Bunting, Brian, 'The Origins of Apartheid', *Apartheid: A Collection of Writings on South African Racism by South Africans*, ed. Alex La Guma (New York: International, 1971).

Eagleton, Terry, *Criticism and Ideology: A Study in Marxist Literary Theory* (London: Verso, 1978).

Gordimer, Nadine, *Burger's Daughter* (New York: Penguin, 1978).

_____ , *The Conservationist*. (1974; Harmondsworth: Penguin, 1978).

_____ , 'From Apartheid to Afrocentrism', *English in Africa* (1980): pp. 45–50.

_____ , 'Is There Nowhere Else Where We Can Meet?' *The Soft Voice of the Serpent* (London: Gollancz, 1953), rpt in *Some Monday For Sure* (London: Heinemann, 1976).

_____ , *July's People* (1981; New York: Penguin, 1982).

_____ , *My Son's Story* (New York: Farrar, 1990).

_____ , *Sport of Nature* (New York: Knopf, 1987).

_____ , 'Living in the Interregnum', *New York Review of Books*. 20 January 1983: pp. 21–9, rpt. in *The Essential Gesture*, ed. Stephen Clingman (New York: Knopf, 1988).

Gray, Stephen, 'An Interview with Nadine Gordimer', *Contemporary Literature* 22 (1981): pp. 263–71.

Macaskill, Brian, 'Figuring Rupture: Iconology, Politics, and the Image',

Image and Ideology in Modern/Postmodern Discourse, ed. David Downing and Susan Bazargan (Albany: State University of New York Press, 1991).

_____ , 'Interrupting the Hegemonic: Textual Critique and Mythological Recuperation from the White Margins of South African Writing', *Novel* 23 (1990): pp. 156–81.

Visser, Nicholas, 'Beyond the Interregnum: A Note on the Ending of *July's People*', *Rendering Things Visible: Essays on South African Literary Culture of the 1970s and 1980s*, ed. Martin Trump (Johannesburg: Ravan Press, 1990), pp. 61–7.

5

Landscape Iconography in the Novels of Nadine Gordimer

KATHRIN M. WAGNER

> Ah, what an Age it is
> When to speak of trees is almost a crime
> For it is a kind of silence about injustice.
> *Bertolt Brecht*[1]

Nadine Gordimer's extraordinarily evocative depictions of the African landscape have attracted both considerable admiration and the most dismissive scorn as mere 'verbal photography' and 'local colour'.[2] However, the extent to which such descriptive passages both reflect a firmly established though barely acknowledged tradition of landscape representation within South African English-language fiction as a whole, and also express the particular dimensions of her own unique experience of the South African landscape as first apprehended in childhood, and then transformed by the imperatives of her political and ideological project in the novels, has barely been examined.[3]

On a more general level, however, a number of critics have gone some way towards revealing the ambiguously constructed elements of a uniquely South African landscape iconology[4] which has foregrounded the vast harshness and bleak aridity of the Cape Karoo landscapes over those of the lusher coastal areas and eastern mountain regions, in order to provide the literature with compelling metaphors of white settler exile and alienation, and of the withering impact of racist ideologies upon the human spirit. The relative emptiness of the interior in such early writings may indeed be read, as Coetzee has provocatively suggested, as a justification of the imperialist thrust into a hinterland conveniently conceived of as a vacuum inviting penetration and colonization.[5] An alternative construction of Africa as the exotic 'Other' to the metropolitan centre found expression in the mixture of attraction and repulsion, swaggering and fear, encoded in the ambiguous details of such constitutive myths of those of Adamastor and the Hottentot Eve;[6] while the imposition upon the African landscape of a familiar tradition of European Darwinian, Romantic, picturesque, or pastoral perspectives has been identified as serving to assist in the imaginative appropriation of an environment recurrently experienced as disturbingly alien.[7] What is largely absent from white English-language South African fiction, however, has been that mythologizing thrust which, within a similar time-span, made of the New World of America an Edenic landscape, an earthly Paradise which offered its colonizers the profound possibility of a redemptive regeneration. For complex political and socio-economic reasons, the southern African experience was metaphorized, instead, in terms of that Manichaean opposition between good and evil invested in the construction of an unbridgeable divide between self and other which lies at the core of the racist ideologies which have shaped South Africa's political realities.

Gordimer's awareness of the distorting power of such ideologies expressed itself in an early resistance to some of the stereotypes which have pervaded fiction about Africa. In particular, she was initially concerned to counter that image of the continent as simply 'exotic' which informed its representation in the fantasies of Buchan, Rider Haggard, and innumerable *Boy's Own* adventure stories. In *The Lying Days* (1953), Helen Shaw earnestly explains that life on the mines of the East Rand where Gordimer herself grew up was not

> even anything like the life of Africa, the continent, as described in books about Africa; perhaps further from this than from any. What did the great rivers, the savage tribes, the jungles and the hunt for huge palm-eared elephants have to do with the sixty miles of Witwatersrand veld that was our Africa?[8]

And, a year later, Gordimer observes to the British readers of *London Magazine* that

> I suppose it is a pity that as children we did not know what people like to talk of as 'the real Africa' – the Africa of proud black warriors and great jungle rivers and enormous silent nights, that

anachronism of a country belonging to its own birds and beasts and savages which rouses such nostalgia in the citified, a neighbour-jostled heart, and out of which a mystique has been created by writers and film directors. The fact of the matter is that this noble paradise of 'the real Africa' is, as far as the Union of South Africa is concerned, an anachronism. . . .[9]

Gordimer takes pains to set against such images the sober realities of the urban and industrialized landscapes of *A World of Strangers*, in which African exoticism is reduced to the frantic, unromantic boredom of a woman trapped on a bleak bushveld farm, or to the superficial and decaying tourist pleasures of a Mombasa seen from the perspective of an unthinking, pompous, self-righteous, and doomed colonialism. In the same novel, the hunter's world of *Boy's Own* stories is explicitly stripped of its residual mystique in Gordimer's contemptuous dissection of the guinea-fowl hunt in the Bushveld which Toby is invited to join, and in which the hostile, thorny landscape yields chiefly death: the death of the birds and of the faithful dog, Gracie, on the hunt itself; the collapse of his relationship with Cecil Rowe during his absence; and the final climactic discovery of the death in a meaningless accident of his friend, Stephen Sithole.

Yet Toby's decision at the end of the novel to remain in Africa rather than take the opportunity to return to England is highly significant in the fictional development of Gordimer's representation of place, for it is an expression of something more than his attraction to the vibrancy of Stephen's township world, or of his loyalty to Stephen's memory and to his new-found black friends. While temporarily lost in the Bushveld on the apparently inauspicious hunting-trip and forced to sit still and absorb what is actually around him, Toby has, in fact, found himself unexpectedly overwhelmed by an unmediated African landscape present to his senses as simply a series of natural phenomena in a way he has never before experienced: in an epiphanic moment it induces in him 'that sudden intense sense of [his] own existence that is all [he has] ever known of a state of grace'.[10] The deployment of the concept of 'grace' here alerts us to those unique spiritual dimensions of Gordimer's own apprehension of the continent which she articulates in a revealing passage published three years later, in 1961:

the problem of Africa, the idea of Africa and what she stands for imaginatively; the mixture of the old legendary continent and the new one drawing its first breath when the rest of the world is tired – this abstract Africa is becoming an element of the spiritual consciousness of the peoples of the modern world. As Donne could write of his mistress – 'O my America, my Newfoundland', so, today, the European or American can conceive of his Africa – not a physical concept of jungles and desert and wild beasts and black men, but *a state of regeneration, an untapped source* in himself to which he wants to find the dangerous way back; another chance for, perhaps, another, other civilisation that draws its sustenance from *very deep, very far back*. This Africa is a fearful place, but in the danger lies the hope of virtue. This Africa is, of course, really only a new name for an old idea – man's deep feeling that he must lose himself in order to find himself (my italics).[11]

In such passages we may discern an attempt, coloured by Gordimer's characteristic note of defiance, to appropriate for Africa some of that significance hitherto attached almost exclusively to North American iconography. Such a desire to invest the colonial landscape with redemptive, Edenic and Utopian qualities should, however, be read as another version of the rejected 'exotic'; not surprisingly, it is a perspective which is beset with difficulties in Gordimer's work, and is progressively transformed as her increasing politicization is reflected in her work. She begins with what are simply her own deeply experienced sensory connections with the South African landscape, which express themselves in her early sensitive evocations of the colour and atmosphere of both the Transvaal Highveld in which she grew up, and of the coastal landscapes of Natal where she spent her childhood holidays and which she contrasts to the bleaker Reef environments. In fact, having grown up on and been profoundly influenced by the classics of the Leavisite Great Tradition,[12] Gordimer felt her initial project to be that of 'giving a voice' to this African experience by imaginatively reflecting and illuminating the unsung reality about her through the transformative power of art, which alone could give it substance and significance.[13] Although, like Doris Lessing,[14] she suffered from the sense that 'there were no books about the world I knew';[15] she drew inspiration from such writers as Proust and Lawrence in her attempt to construct images of the African reality: of the latter she said in an autobiographical sketch written in 1954 that 'his sensuousness dilated my senses and brought up close to me rocks, petals, and the fur of animals around me'.[16] This early debt is demonstrated in such typical passages as the one below, in which she attempts to evoke the dimensions of her early response to the Natal South Coast landscape:

> the beach – ah, the beach lay gleaming, silent, mile after mile, looping over flower-strewn rocks; there were indeed many beaches, and always one where for the whole day there would be no footprints in the sand but my sister's and mine. In fine weather, the village was, I suppose, a paradise of sorts. In front of the little hotel was the warm, bright sea, and curving around behind it, hill after hill, covered with the improbable sheen of sugar-cane, which, moving in breeze, softened every contour like some rich pile, or like that heavy bloom of pollen which makes hazy the inner convolution of certain flowers. Streams oozed down from the hills and could be discovered by the ear only. . . .[17]

But powerfully complicating factors soon interposed themselves between Gordimer and the early, simple, sensory immediacy of her apprehension of landscape. She found herself exceptionally sensitive to the contrast between the bleak reaches of a mining world whose spiritually barren ordinariness was, she felt, aptly represented by the arid flat stretches of the Reef landscape, and the green fecundity of Natal. The family lived near perpetually smouldering coal dumps which aroused in the young child 'the idea of Hades', and she wrote that, as children, she and her sister 'simply took it for granted that beauty – hills, trees, buildings of elegance – was not a thing to be expected of ordinary life'.[18] We may speculate that, perhaps, for her, as for her protagonist Anna Louw, the activist lawyer of *A World of Strangers*, the revolt against her narrowly provincial and racist inheritance may well have begun as an aesthetic 'revolt of taste'.[19] The child appears to have decided that by definition 'reality' was harsh and ugly; beauty was a transient phenomenon and (in accordance with an archetypal colonial paradigm) something to be found and enjoyed *elsewhere* – away from the sterner contexts of home.

The formative effect of this perception on Gordimer's metaphoric construction of landscape in the fiction can hardly be overestimated. Very early on, her antipathy to the human ugliness of a society in thrall to a hegemonic racist ideology, whose dimensions she first came to comprehend within the physical bleakness of the urban environments of the Reef, expressed itself in her presentation of that landscape as a metaphor for the effects of collusion with such a system on the individual. In effect she reinscribes the earlier Karoo iconography of isolation, exile and alienation within the parameters of the Witwatersrand environment, but with the emphasis on an *internal* exile from sources of spiritual and emotional regeneration from which only a form of apocalypse can release the wilting victim. The moral impotence, pervasive hypocrisy, failed relationships, and corruption with which she characterizes white society is emblematized, for example, in the winter landscapes of *The Late Bourgeois World*. Gordimer, thus, early develops an iconography which makes of the Transvaal landscape a metaphor of that 'felt state of zombiehood'[20] which Gray identifies as the characteristic condition of the English-speaking South African colonial in English South African fiction: a state which she mercilessly dissects in her critique of an impotent and failed liberalism which is characteristically located within the parameters of the Johannesburg environment.

It is not surprising that, given such a context, the fiction should be dotted with attempts to escape: if all fullness of life and beauty is to be understood to be located elsewhere, in a world conceptualized through her reading and her experience of Natal as characterized by the emblematic green of the English countryside 'back home', the temptation to flee must, at one level, be by definition a self-protective, self-nurturing, and entirely natural impulse. It is one which consequently besets almost every one of Gordimer's protagonists, from Helen Shaw to Rosa Burger and finally to Hillela herself.

Gordimer is, however, remarkably consistent in either denying her characters this option or repeatedly returning them to South Africa and the Reef: a fundamental theme of the novels is that the desire to escape is one that must be resisted. The reasons for this are complex, and rooted in that intense, sensory identification with the South African landscape which is so powerful a presence in the early fiction. In imaginatively appropriating this landscape, it is clear that Gordimer was flouting those colonial values (including her own) which found the source of all aesthetic standards in an external, metropolitan centre; and her sense of the extent to which an identification with the African reality constituted a transgression of boundaries is sensitively inscribed in the account given of Helen's visit to the Concession stores in *The Lying Days*: her tentative defiance introduces the theme of rebellion which remains a constant in the fiction. Eventually, of course, Gordimer will reverse the concepts of 'inside' and 'outside', as her growing politicization gives a peculiarly South African twist to the symbolic resonances of this opposition. Helen moves from 'inside' the colonial mining world into the larger African contexts 'outside': from province to city and from fantasy to engagement. Later protagonists, however, find themselves uncomfortably kept on the 'outside' of the mainstream of African psychic life by virtue of their white skins. Thus, at a subtextual level, 'inside' comes to represent a condemnation to a form of imprisonment in whiteness which the spirit resists in vain; while 'outside' beckons as an alluring alternative to a burdensome daily reality. Finally, 'inside' will become the world to which first Rosa and then Hillela will *earn* their admission, both in the ironic metaphor of the actual prison Rosa is consigned to, and in the triumphant final image of Hillela's position at the heart of the Independence celebrations at the close of *A Sport of Nature*.

The tension between the need to engage in meaningful ways with the bleak realities of the South African situation, and the concomitant temptation to flee that imperative, betrays itself most clearly throughout the fiction in the extraordinary and probably unconscious relaxation in the style when the narrative moves outside the apartheid-dominated contexts of the protagonists' daily lives. Only when the narrative voice leaves the Witwatersrand – the symbolic heart of alienation and *anomie* – do colour, light, spontaneity, ease and gaiety reemerge as qualities warming the lives of Gordimer's characters. Such sidelong glances at the luxuriant possibilities for a fullness of life *outside* South Africa's arid contexts are a recurrent phenomenon in the novels: perhaps most powerfully inscribed in *Burger's Daughter*, it is the allure of the 'outside' world (in this case of the French Riviera) whose appeal is paradoxically most difficult to resist by the imprisoned and beleaguered imagination.

That this is so suggests a degree of repression and redirection of Gordimer's spontaneous response to the African landscape which attests to the strength of her need to subordinate its representation to her ideological concerns. The process of repression in fact operates on a number of levels in the novels: most significantly, perhaps in Gordimer's insistence that her characters signal their acceptance of their moral responsibilities by *refusing* the option of a retreat or flight to more hospitable contexts elsewhere. Gordimer attempted to justify this perspective in a 1980 essay in which she argued that the impulse to flee uncomfortable South African realities by opting for voluntary exile in 'the mother country' was itself a quintessential expression of that colonial mentality from which such cultural refugees were ostensibly in flight: writing in particular of Olive Schreiner, she condemned those who attempted to settle overseas on the basis that their 'motive generally was [not only]

> a deep sense of deprivation, that living in South Africa they were cut off from the world of ideas, [but also] underlying this . . . was another reason . . . the *real* source of their alienation . . .: that the act of taking the Union Castle mailship to what was the only cultural 'home' they could conceive of, much as they all repudiated jingoism, was itself part of the philistinism they wanted to put at an ocean's distance from them.[21]

We may identify in Gordimer's work a puritanism born, perhaps, of the spiritual aridity and isolation of her early years, which consigns her later protagonists to an indefinite sentence of spiritual and actual exile from beauty until such a time as the millennium which *A Sport of Nature* depicts may be achieved.

Within this general paradigm, Gordimer's work develops in revealing ways. In particular, a pattern of meaning accretes around the imagery of water, lake and sea which runs as a *leitmotif* throughout the novels and inscribes the complex tensions between the temptations of the private life and the imperative of public action through a sharply focused series of metaphors. Her own early connection of the sea with a sensory and sexual awakening, as most clearly delineated in *The Lying Days*, makes of it a continuing and powerful image of the mysterious and irreducible reaches of that private life which ideology demands must be subordinated to public and political ends. The vastness of the sea and the rich vegetation of the coastal dunes suggest, in the early fiction an Edenic landscape of a primal innocence as yet uncolonized: at this level, the sea and the natural world in general represent throughout Gordimer's work not only 'the oceanic'[22] – the power of the unconscious, the instinctual, and the sensual – but also and simultaneously an archetypal site of withdrawal and self-discovery. Yet, given Gordimer's larger ideological thrust, sea and water must be presented as only a *temporary* refuge; and in so far as such a retreat represents, as Ward suggests, 'the wish-fulfilment of a desire to evade human complexity', and symbolizes 'the attractions of a defection from humanity',[23] its temptations must characteristically be rejected or enjoyed only briefly.

There is, however, another significant dimension to images of the sea and of water in general in the novels: lake and sea also represent that ancient African world of archetypal Conradian indifference to and independence of human affairs, a world both of complex order, and of immutable 'otherness', unresponsive to imported aesthetic standards and entirely self-absorbed in its own processes. In such images the African continent itself is emblematized as existing beyond the puny reach of its temporary invaders; and in such passages as those describing Roly Dando's garden and the fig-tree Bray works under in *A Guest of Honour*, a vaguely threatening quality warns off the presumptuous intruder into this ancient world:

> coarse and florid shrubs, hibiscus with its big flowers sluttish with pollen and ants and poinsettia oozing milk secretion, bloomed, giving a show of fecundity to the red, poor soil running baked bald under the grass, beaten slimy by the rains under the trees, and friable only where the ants had digested it and made little crusty tunnels. A rich stink of dead animal rose self-dispersed like a gas . . . it was the smell of growth . . . the process of decay and regeneration so accelerated, brought so close together that it produced the reek of death-and-life, all at once.[24]

There is an uncompromising self-containment here, and a defiance of accepted aesthetic standards of beauty, which attest to the extent to which Gordimer had, by this stage, moved away from her earlier attempts at an 'innocent' representation of the sensory impact of the landscape upon the observer. Here thematic intention directs the eye in richly subtle ways to suggest that the colonial invasion has not only placed 'Africa' in its multiple levels of signification under siege, but has made its essence inaccessible, even invisible, to those who remain trapped in colonialist perspectives. In fact, through such images, Gordimer ironically reverses the issue of integration by suggesting that it is the white man who must find a way to meld with Africa and not the black man who must struggle for acceptance in white society. By implication it is suggested that the process of white integration must *begin* with a sensitivity to the land and its unique sensory impact; that is, the senses and the emotions must be 'Africanized' before the intellect can respond positively to the political and ideological demands Africa makes upon it.

Indeed, as a corollary to Gordimer's insistence on the irresponsibility of the attempt to escape, the novels suggest that the very idea of the possibility of refuge is illusory. In *Occasion for Loving* it is, significantly enough, landscape representation which carries the

burden of communicating this perspective. Jessie discovers no retreat is safe from invasion: upon her return from the store in which
she has heard talk of plans to introduce beach apartheid in the
village, she goes out on to the terrace and stands

> looking with a kind of disbelief at the wild, innocent landscape;
> the rain-calmed sea, the slashed heads of strelitzia above the bush
> almost translucent green with the rush of sap. The sun put a
> warm hand on her head. But nothing was innocent, not even here.
> There was no corner of the whole country that was without ugli-
> ness. It was no good thinking you could ever get out of the way of
> that.[25]

As a significant corollary to this bleak insight the landscape correspondingly loses its power to comfort and reassure; the absence of a
significant Lawrentian perspective in a later novel such as *July's
People*, despite the fact that it is set almost wholly within a rural
environment which Maureen and Bam reluctantly experience as a
refuge from the war raging in the urban centres, expresses this
insight with some power.

Nowhere is the irresponsibility of the desire to defect more clearly
inscribed than in the ironic treatment of the pastoral theme at
the core of *The Conservationist*. Mehring's initial delight in the land
as 'innocent' becomes increasingly an index of a deliberate self-
delusion.[26] The land in fact escapes his notion that it requires protection or conservation – both essentially paternalistic responses – from
him; as it endlessly, and seemingly effortlessly, renews itself after
the devastations of drought, fire, and flood in its own time, so it
typically shows itself to be entirely independent of and indifferent to
both Mehring's needs and his efforts on its behalf. In a significant
parallel, the farm labourers also, in their own fashion, draw upon
their particular ancestral sources of spiritual regeneration and en-
sure their survival, however under siege they are by white colonization. Mehring, relegated to the status of mere observer of these
processes, finds himself as dispensable and ultimately irrelevant as
the oaks and chestnuts he begins to plant and which, he understands, will fall to the axes of those of the meek who will inherit his
earth: 'I'm planting European chestnuts', he imagines himself saying
to Antonia, 'for the blacks to use as firewood after they've taken
over'.[27] Mehring's grasp of the land's 'indifference', however, is, as
Antonia points out to him, misguided and superficial: 'the famous

indifference of nature really sends you, doesn't it?', she mocks; 'it's the romanticism of *realpolitik*, the sentimentalism of cut-throat competition'.[28] She is suggesting that the capitalist mentality will naturally welcome a philosophy premised on the maxim of the survival of the fittest; but Gordimer both queries Mehring's assessment of the nature of fitness, and offers an alternative view of nature-as-life-force which avoids the privileging of hierarchy implicit in this conceptualization of evolutionary theory.

Mehring's conception of himself as a 'conservationist' is revealed as irremediably arrogant within this paradigm, and the bizarre nature of his tenancy of the land is aptly symbolized in the image of his early-morning walk into his dew-drenched fields, incongruously dressed for a day in the city in his business suit, and glorying in the full, sensuous beauty of this 'fair and lovely place'.[29] This richly evocative passage is symbolically bracketed by the description of the ragged 'army' of labourers which accosts him as he leaves the house, and by his cynical, self-seeking insensitivity towards his old servant, Alina, upon his return. Nowhere does Gordimer more forcefully suggest by a careful juxtaposition of imagery the essential immorality of such an indulgence in the private pleasures of a sensory immersion in the natural world: in a reverse movement, Mehring's delight in nature has the effect of radically diminishing his moral status rather than functioning as an index of his possible redemption.

In *The Conservationist* Gordimer's assessment of the nature of the white man's options in South Africa is brutal in its implications: she presents us with a vision in which it is assumed that it is inevitable that history will pass the unregenerate white man by as he fails to realize that the colonial era has already come to an end, and as the black masses, phoenix-like, resume control of their land. A fresh version of the myth of Adamastor is in effect offered in her vision of the black man as rooted in the land as no coloniser-exploiter can ever be, drawing from it a renewed strength and resilience, and finally triumphing over the multiple effects of detribalization, colonization and spiritual fragmentation. Africa will rise again to take back its own, in a clear parallel between the land's regenerative powers and Gordimer's prophetic vision of the black future. Yet in the development of such a paradigm Gordimer's landscape iconography is clearly connected to a larger South African iconology identified by Christie as one in which the landscape is 'seen as a moral agent that destroys the weak and wicked [white] but purifies and nurtures the good and strong [black] in the beauties of its bosom'.[30]

Gordimer's Eurocentric literary and philosophical heritage, which gave her not only a respect for genuine liberal values but internalized pastoral and Romantic attitudes to nature, survives in her novels not only by the anger which informs her dissection of the degraded and impotent liberalism of ostensibly anti-racist white South Africans, but also in her refusal to allow such pastoral and Romantic perspectives to provide that refuge and solace to the bruised spirit that tradition has assigned them. Although the pastoral idyll is presented as increasingly untenable within a context in which institutionalized racism is found to be the root of all evil, the thrust of the fiction implies that the revolutionary millenium will restore those pastoral pleasures which have had to be deferred until a more just dispensation has been achieved. Indeed, by the time Gordimer comes to write *The Conservationist*, it is precisely her acute sensitivity to place and its centrality in her own subjective and emotional life which determines her decision to make a misdirected pastoralism the ultimate symbol of white capitalist corruption and alienation. Within this paradigm it is not the hostility of the African landscape which makes what Christopher Hope calls 'the shapely categories of European pastoralism and romanticism'[31] invalid in the work, but the hostility of the political dispensation to the realization of such yearnings.

Thus, in Gordimer's work, the process whereby, as Gullon argues, 'the treatment of space [is linked] to the formation of an ideology'[32] is quite clearly evident. To summarize: she begins, as we have seen, by *documenting* with enormous evocative skill the sheer sensory impact of her world for both herself and a reader who is very early conceived of as likely to be non-South African. Her own powerful identification with the land typically expresses itself in her inscription of her early protagonists' responsiveness to landscape as an indicator of their potential for redemption: it becomes a symbol of their search for an inner wholeness and integration with Africa which will prepare the way for a regenerative political commitment. Thus, paradoxically, the foundation of an African identity for the white man is to be found rooted in the strength of a private sensory and emotional sensitivity to the land. As, however, the hope of integration comes to appear less and less tenable, Gordimer is caught up in conflicting responses: on the one hand, the original innocence of response can no longer be sustained as awareness broadens; and on the other hand the enjoyment of such subjective delights comes to appear increasingly suspect and inappropriate. Thus, in the later fiction, the relative decline of landscape as a private 'icon' is inevitable; whereas in the early novels landscape has the force of a vast presence, penetrating, diverting and healing consciousness, by the time we come to *July's People* it has been reduced to mere scaffolding, simply sketched in as a symbolically-laden backdrop in a narrative in which the political theme shapes and directs every detail. 'Place' survives only in so far as it can be made to take on an overtly symbolic function, and landscape description in general is both annexed to and attenuated by the ideological programme.

In conclusion, I would argue that nowhere, perhaps, is the extent to which European and African influences inextricably interpenetrate and permeate each other more evident than in Gordimer's landscape iconography: her work is firmly linked into both metropolitan and colonial iconologies which she modifies and varies rather than abandons entirely. Although European pastoral and Romantic impulses are ironized in their overt manifestations, they survive both in the early emphasis on the redemptive potential of sensitivity to the natural world, and in the use Gordimer makes of the typically pastoral opposition between the country and the city. Gordimer may, in fact, be seen as caught up in complex tensions between that immediacy of experience which negates stereotypes and those inherited conventions and traditions which help to shape and organize inchoate experience. In a final irony, her insistence that Africa 'belongs' to its indigenous black inhabitants may itself be seen as an expression of a version of the old stereotype of exoticism which she is at pains to counter in its cruder and more overt manifestations. The essential romanticism lurking behind the ideological thrust is perhaps most clearly evident in *A Sport of Nature*, in which alienation and spiritual exile are shown to be at last resolved in the transformative thrust of that Utopian vision of an ultimate acceptance by and integration into 'the beloved country' which the novel celebrates. In the hopeful naivety of this final triumphant articulation of her hopes for the future, Gordimer does not so much lay to rest the ghost of colonialism as demonstrate the extent to which she has remained in thrall to its residual stereotypes, and which it is the task of the post-colonial literature she has inaugurated in South Africa to move away from.

Notes

1. Bertolt Brecht, from 'To Posterity'. Translated from 'An die Nachgeboren', in Peter Suhrkamp (ed.), *Bertolt Brechts Gedichte und Lieder* (Berlin/Frankfurt am Main: Surkamp Verlag, 1958), p. 158.

2. Quoted in John Cooke, *The Novels of Nadine Gordimer*, unpublished PhD thesis, Northwestern University, 1976; pp. 75, 80.

3. See, however, John Cooke, 'The African Landscapes of Nadine Gordimer', in *World Literature Today* 52 (4), 1978.

4. Giulio Argan ('Ideology and Iconology', in *Critical Inquiry*, Winter 1975), following Erwin Panovsky, *Meaning in the Visual Arts* (1957); Harmondsworth: Penguin, 1970), develops the concept of an iconology.

5. See John Coetzee, *White Writing* (Sandton, South Africa: Radix; Century Hutchinson, 1988).

6. See Stephen Gray, *Southern African Literature: An Introduction* (Cape Town: David Philip, 1979).

7. See Paul Rich, 'Landscape, Social Darwinism, and the Cultural Roots of South Africa's Racial Ideology', unpublished paper, University of London, 1982.

8. Nadine Gordimer, *The Lying Days* (1953) (London: Virago, 1983), pp. 96–7.

9. Nadine Gordimer, 'A South African Childhood: Allusions in a Landscape', in *The New Yorker* (30), 16 October 1954; pp. 128–9.

10. Nadine Gordimer, *A World of Strangers* (1958; Harmondsworth: Penguin, 1962).

11. Nadine Gordimer, 'The Novel and the Nation in South Africa' (1961) in G. Killam (ed.), *African Writers on African Writing* (London: Heinemann, 1973) p. 38.

12. See, for example, Nadine Gordimer, 'Notes of an Expropriator', *The Times Literary Supplement*, 4 June 1964, p. 482.

13. See Jessie in *The Lying Days*, who says that, 'as [she] stood in this unfamiliar part of [her] own world, [she knew] and flatly [accepted] it as the real world because it was ugly and did not exist in books' (p. 21).

14. See, for example, Doris Lessing's short story, 'The Old Chief Mhlangu' in *African Stories* (New York: Simon and Schuster, 1981).

15. Nadine Gordimer, 'Leaving School – II', in *The London Magazine*, May 1963, p. 61; see also 'The Novel and the Nation', pp. 36–7, and *The Lying Days*, pp. 96–7.

16. Nadine Gordimer, 'A Writer in South Africa', in *The London Magazine* May 1965, pp. 21–8; see also 'Notes of an Expropriator'.

17. Gordimer, 'A South African Childhood', p. 118.

18. Ibid., p. 115.

19. *A World of Strangers*, p. 181.

20. Stephen Gray, p. 154.

21. Nadine Gordimer, 'The Prison-house of Colonialism' (1980), in C. Barasch (ed.), *An Olive Schreiner Reader* (London: Routledge and Kegan Paul, 1987), p. 224.

22. See David Ward, *Chronicles of Darkness* (London: Routledge, 1989), p. 118.
23. Ibid., pp. 118, 119.
24. Nadine Gordimer, *A Guest of Honour* (1970; Harmondsworth: Penguin, 1973), p. 18.
25. Nadine Gordimer, *Occasion for Loving* (1963; London: Virago, 1983).
26. Nadine Gordimer, *The Conservationist* (1974; Harmondsworth: Penguin, 1978), p. 199.
27. Ibid., p. 223.
28. Ibid., p. 200.
29. Ibid., p. 183.
30. S. Christie, in S. Christie, G. Hutchings and D. MacLennan, *Perspectives on South African Fiction* (Johannesburg: Ad. Donker, 1980), p. 184.
31. Christopher Hope, reviewing J. M. Coetzee, *White Writing*, in *The Weekly Mail*, 22–28 July 1988, p. 15.
32. Ricardo Gullon, 'On Space in the Novel', in *Critical Inquiry*, Autumn 1975, p. 15.

Part II
The Novels

6

The Conservationist and the Political Uncanny

LARS ENGLE

Albie Sachs, a writer and lawyer in exile with the ANC who lost an arm to a South African bomb, returned to South Africa in 1990; his position paper on aesthetic policy, 'Preparing ourselves for freedom,' aroused enormous interest there. It proposes that the activity of writers and artists be less politically focused, and less limited to the politically correct, than has hitherto been ANC policy; in perhaps its most polemical moment, the paper calls for a five-year moratorium on the phrase 'culture is a weapon of struggle'.

> If we [in the ANC and the liberation struggle generally] had the imagination of a Sholokhov, and one of us wrote: And Quiet Flows the Tugela, the central figure would not be a member of UDF or Cosatu, but would be aligned to Inkatha, resisting change, yet feeling oppression, thrown this way and that by conflicting emotions, and through his or her struggles and torments and moments of joy, the reader would be thrust into the whole drama of the struggle for a new South Africa. Instead . . . we line up our good people on the one side and the bad ones on the other . . .
>
> In the case of a real instrument of struggle, there is no room for ambiguity: a gun is a gun is a gun, and if it were full of contradictions, it would fire in all sorts of directions and be useless for its purpose. But the power of art lies precisely in its capacity to expose contradictions and reveal hidden tensions – hence the danger of viewing it as if it were just another kind of missile-firing apparatus.[1]

I will be discussing Nadine Gordimer's *The Conservationist* in terms suggested by this passage. I will point out difficulties in interpretations of the novel which see it as an opposition between good and bad, authentic and inauthentic, black and white. The novel has a

91

complex and in an odd way generous tendency to deconstruct the oppositions it examines, and I will suggest that it anticipates the kind of writing Sachs calls for, writing which explores with sympathy the experience of someone on the wrong side of a struggle. This approach to the novel will highlight the variety of attitudes, tensions, ambiguities, and contradiction in *The Conservationist*'s representation of industrial capitalism and possessive individualism.

Published in 1974, near the end of a periodic political lull in overt resistance to white rule in South Africa, *The Conservationist* has an honoured place among Gordimer's novels. It may be her best. She herself, asked about her preferences among her works, acknowledged it with pride as a thing well done in a 1984 interview.[2] Critics making general claims tend to praise it in terms dictated by what they think Gordimer is up to. Thus in 1978 Michael Wade saw the novel's protagonist, Mehring, as a mechanism trapped in a grid, and contrasted Mehring's dessicated life, devoted to Apollonian order-systems, unfavourably with the more romantic or fulfilling lives of his politically exiled mistress Antonia and his adolescent son Terry.[3] John Cooke in 1985, pursuing a general thesis suggested by his sub-title *Private Lives, Public Landscapes*, saw *The Conservationist* as Gordimer's clearest articulation of this opposition, in which the landscape of Mehring's farm becomes alive with all the irresistable public obligations Mehring's ordinary or private life suppresses. Cooke sees an 'excessive' (i.e. authorially heavyhanded) thematic contrast between Mehring's attempt to possess his farm and Gordimer's suggestions that the African farm labourers authentically or naturally possess it.[4] In 1986 Stephen Clingman, in a book with the same title as Cooke's, *The Novels of Nadine Gordimer*, but with the sub-title *History from the Inside*, presented the farm as a site of the return of a more specifically politically repressed. Like Cooke he sees a comprehensive contrast between Mehring's attempt to ground himself in the land and the lives of the Africans but, unlike Cooke, he sees nothing to blame and much to praise in what he takes to be Gordimer's deeply historical gesture of self-alignment with the blacks on the farm against the white owner.[5]

It is clearly right, I think, to see *The Conservationist* as a book about a failed authenticity project on the part of its white protagonist, Mehring. This view is in various ways shared by all three critics I have mentioned and indeed by nearly all criticism of the book I have encountered.[6] But how should we understand Mehring's failure to achieve satisfaction on his farm? How absolute a failure is it, and failure in contrast to what sorts of success? What modes of authenticity are offered as alternatives to Mehring's, and are they immune from the ironic attention the novel pays to Mehring's? To employ a set of terms I have elaborated elsewhere, does Gordimer in this novel present a clear enabling contrast between right and wrong ways of being in South Africa, or does *The Conservationist* seek out the areas of destabilizing threat to certainty of judgement I call the political uncanny?[7]

To seek such areas of uncertainty, and uncertainty at the expense of enabling beliefs or commitments, is a kind of literary courage which may sometimes work against clarity of political message, though in general, as Gordimer explores such areas in the minds of South African whites (and perhaps in her own mind) she is also, and not incidentally, underlining the outrageous nature of the apartheid system. But in *The Conservationist*, with its clear moments of uncanny political allegory (preeminently the return of the black corpse), Gordimer is also entering two more dicey areas of political uncanniness. The first appears as the book contrasts the life of the Africans on the farm to Mehring's life. The second emerges as the book explores Mehring's status as an exemplary capitalist.

The critical or theoretical issue to be raised here – one not without political overtones and consequences – is whether Gordimer in a contrast between white and black is contrasting inauthentic modes of being or occupation with authentic ones, as if there were an absolute or categorical distinction to be made, or whether her novel instead elaborates a contrast between less and more successful or authentic modes of occupation, so that the distinction becomes one of degree, and the novel charts areas or axes of similarity at the same time that it points to difference. Given Albie Sachs's suggestions about the political role of art as people prepare themselves for freedom, these axes of similarity may be taken politically to point to possibilities for negotiation or accommodation. Wade calls Mehring a 'super-pragmatist' in his book, as if that were a diagnosis of Mehring's problem;[8] I am inclined to see the book itself as an exercise in pragmatist critique and to feel that Gordimer's own critical intelligence in the novel is often hard to separate from the self-critical intelligence of Mehring. In general, then, I want to suggest that the failure of Mehring's authenticity project can be overgeneralized, and has been by the three critics I have cited.

Let me briefly sketch a two-stage argument about the blacks to whom Mehring is contrasted. First, they are part of a spectrum of such contrasts which displays Mehring's estrangement from his family and friends: Mehring the isolate *vs* the three-generation Afrikaner clan from a neighbouring farm (who stop by to borrow his bakkie), Mehring the isolate *vs* the four-generation Indian family running a shop (who sell him Christmas presents for the farm-workers and try to borrow his influence through his alienated son), Mehring the isolate *vs* the extended quasi-familial, quasi-tribal group of Africans under Jacobus's headship (who live on the farm to which Mehring holds legal title, borrowing the tractor for private trips). It blurs a comprehensive white–black contrast to see the Afrikaners as more like the farm Africans than they are like Mehring. All these groups of people treat Mehring in the same general way: manipulatively, with distance, and with some contempt.

Mehring is, moreover, though with greater intensity, in a similar relation of engagement and estrangement to his son and to his mistress. Mehring is useful to Terry and Antonia. His money and position, of which they are contemptuous, help them evade laws they wish to evade, and Mehring subsidizes the sites of their 'authenticating' experiences in pensioning Kurt and Emmy in Namibia (where his son vacations in preference to Mehring's farm) and in helping Antonia leave South Africa for a life as a political exile after her encounter with the police.

Obviously the novel does not elide, indeed it emphasizes, the huge social differences between the experiences of the farm blacks, the Indians, the Afrikaner farmers, and romantically left-liberal whites like Antonia and Terry. But the novel also presses on us the idea that all of them understand Mehring as someone specifically to be made use of while expressing distance from his values, ideas or desires. The things Mehring represents – technology, money, access, expertise – are things they all sometimes need. They take or seek what they need from Mehring relatively impersonally, evidently recognizing him as a representative of a depersonalizing system, though Antonia is the only character who might use these terms. In this sense the structure of differences which isolates Mehring suggests similarities among others, and while these parallels help promote the impression that Mehring stands apart precisely as a representative of capitalist control, these similarities also become focused as *uses* (in a specifically utilitarian sense) of Mehring, even though such a designation reverses the social and economic hierarchies Mehring lives in. Mehring becomes as much a factor of exchange as he is an agent, while the others act as agents even as they struggle with the politico-economic system they inhabit. The novel's treatment of authenticity, then, is more complex, more of a spectrum of different positions with competing claims to authenticity, than it is a stark white/black contrast.

Now for the second part of the argument about the novel's contrasts between black and white. *The Conservationist* explores the spiritual life of the farm blacks partly through a series of juxtaposed quotations from the Rev. Henry Callaway's *The Religious System of the Amazulu*, which has been interestingly discussed in an article by Judie Newman.[9] It is argued by Newman, and accepted by Clingman and Cooke, that these passages constitute, as it were, metaphysical or mythic support for black claims to authenticity on the land, to genuine conservation, which contrasts to Mehring's superficial or spurious conservation:

> The quotations [from Callaway] are the organizing points for a subtext which slowly comes into the foreground . . . The subtext, buried like the black man, rises to the surface of the novel and repossesses it, obliterating the 'paper' possession of Mehring and his story.[10]

These passages bear further discussion, however, both in their context in *The Conservationist* and in their context in *The Religious System of the Amazulu*, which, I will argue, Gordimer has read extensively and used in a more comprehensive way than Newman suggests.[11] Let me start with a general example from late in *The Conservationist*. Callaway, like Mehring a white with white cultural assumptions, exploring and attempting to possess part of Africa, discusses the creation with his Zulu informants, and discovers the absence of a transcendental myth of origins, a divine logos to authenticate or certify man's possession of the world. In short, he finds that the Zulu are a bit like Mehring.

> *'And who was Unsondo?'* – *'He was he who came out first at the breaking off of all things (ekudabukeni kwezinto zonke).* – *'Explain what you mean by ekudabukeni.'* – *'When this earth and all things broke off from Uthlanga.'* – *'What is Uthlanga?'* – *'He who begat Unsondo.'* – *'Where is he now?'* – *'O, he exists no longer. As my grandfather no longer exists, he too no longer exists: he died. When he died, there arose*

others, who were called by other names. Uthlanga begat Unsondo:
Unsondo begat the ancestors; the ancestors begat the great grandfathers;
the great grandfathers begat the grandfathers; and the grandfathers
begat our fathers; and our fathers begat us.' – 'Are there any who are
called Uthlanga now?' – 'Yes.' – 'Are you married?' – 'Yes.' – 'And
have children?' – 'Yebo. U mina e ngi uthlanga.' (Yes. It is I myself
who am an uthlanga.) (Conservationist, p. 247; Religious System, pp.
15–16)

Christians use a creation myth to establish such metaphysical abso-
lutes as the eternal authority of God and man's right to the fruits of
earth; the Zulu express by their creation myth the contingent transfer of communal authority from generation to generation. This particular passage from Zulu myth, then, illustrates a kind of African
pragmatism which is akin to, rather than philosophically opposed
to, Mehring's agnostic pragmatism. There is also, of course, a pathos
involving Mehring's failure to transmit inheritance to his son, and
the absence of his own parents in his consciousness, but Gordimer
here uses this quotation to show that Zulu religion does not offer any
myth of origin and possession beyond the locally historical claim to
have been on the land for many generations. And this allows us to
see similarities between the lives and traditions of the blacks and
Mehring's attempt to ground himself on his farm.

The episode in Callaway from which Gordimer takes three epigraphs is an extended narrative about a Zulu who has a nameless
'disease', and whose discomforts, inadequacies, and vision closely
resemble both Mehring's and those of Phineas's wife, the woman on
the farm who wants to become a witch-doctor and who has been
possessed by a spirit. The passages Gordimer quotes from Callaway
are in themselves very ambiguous.

once at night he was told to awake and go down to the river and he would
find an antelope caught in a Euphorbia tree; and to go and take it. (The
Conservationist, p. 83; Religious System, p. 194)

'So,' said he, 'I awoke. When I had set out, my brother, Umankamane,
followed me. He threw a stone and struck an aloe. I was frightened, and
ran back to him and chided him, saying, why did you frighten me when
I was about to lay hold on my antelope?' (The Conservationist, p. 92;
Religious System, p. 194)

That was the end of it, and he was not again told by anything to go and fetch the antelope. They went home, there being nothing there. (The Conservationist, p. 113; Religious System, p. 194)

These are all quotations from the story of James, who lives by himself ('the disease has separated me from you', he says to Callaway's informant), and who announces 'I have a disease with which I am not acquainted.' This disease 'reached the upper part of the body, and stopped in my shoulders, and caused a sensation of oppression, and there was a great weight here on my shoulders; it was as if I was carrying a heavy weight' (*Religious System*, pp. 186–7). Phineas's wife, once her dreams begin, 'held her shoulders like someone whose back has been burned by hot water and winced if anything touched it' (*The Conservationist*, pp. 164-5). Mehring finds that having the Africans talk about him in their language 'slightly taughtens the muscles in the thickness between his shoulder-blades, a fibrosis, as he feels them behind him, leaves him behind him' (*The Conservationist*, p. 75). James says

'There is not a single place in the whole country which I do not know; I go over it all by night in my sleep; there is not a single place the exact situation of which I do not know.

'I see also elephants and hyenas, and lions, and leopards, and snakes, and full rivers. All these things come near to me to kill me.' (*Religious System*, p. 188)

Phineas's wife describes 'how in her sleep there were also elephants and hyenas and lions and full rivers, all coming near to kill her, how they followed her, how there was not a single place in the whole country that she did not know because she went over it all, farther than Johannesburg and Durban, all by night, in her sleep' (*The Conservationist*, p. 166). Asked about his spiritual state, James replies,

'I do not think that I am still a man who can enter into a new position [i.e. become a Christian again], which I do not in the least understand. I do not know what I am. Attend, for I am a man who loves my children dearly. But now I do not care whether they are alive or not. The great thing is this disease alone.' (*Religious System*, p. 189)

And he adds:

> 'now I no longer love any one. My heart no longer loves men. It is
> as though I could stay where it is perfectly still – where there is
> not the least sound.' (*Religious System*, pp. 190–1)

James's description of his disease here closely resembles Mehring's
anti-social devotion to his farm, and his increasing tendency *on* the
farm to seek solitude. He

> always . . . ends up . . . down over the third pasture at the reeds.
> Peaceful, of course. They don't come down here any more, for
> some reason or other; not even the piccanins. (*The Conservationist*,
> p. 75)

Mehring has begun to seek the one place in the farm where the
Africans themselves will not go: the third pasture 'haunted' by the
dead man.

James's disease is possession by the ancestors, the *amatongo*, 'which
precedes the power to divine' (*Religious System*, p. 195); Jacobus tells
Mehring and Terry, 'the wife of Phineas she's want to be witch
doctor' (*The Conservationist*, p. 144), and her test will be to find the
hidden goat which is sacrificed and eaten at the dance, thus exhibit-
ing the power to divine which possession is supposed to precede.
Mehring, of course, like both Phineas's wife and James, is isolated
from others, hears voices, and is recurrently drawn to the hidden
dead man. He has no sex at all in the year or so of the book, unless
his molestation of the Portuguese girl on the airplane takes place
during that period; of Phineas's wife 'it was even said that the
woman would not sleep with her husband any more' (*The Conservationist*, p. 168).

Given this context in *The Religious System of the Amazulu*, we can
make more sense of the excerpts about the antelope caught in the
euphorbia tree by the river, quoted above. James has a chance to
confront and lay hold of the animal which will authenticate his
power, as finding the hidden goat authenticates the power of
Phineas's wife, but this confrontation may also release him from the
possession of the *amatongo*. Because of his brother, who throws a
rock which frightens him, James does not do this, and remains in the
possession of the spirits. The location of the antelope by the river

connects it to the dead black man on Mehring's farm; the interruption by James's brother may also conceivably connect the event to the crisis at the end of *The Conservationist*, where Mehring, full of vengeful thoughts towards Antonia and profound disturbance because of the return of the black corpse, is about to have sex for the first time in a long while, when he sees the legs of a white policeman and fears he's fallen into a trap. He is, in a sense, interrupted by his white 'brother'.

In any case, there is an extended parallel between the situation of Phineas's wife and Mehring, and both situations are elucidated by the episode in *The Religious System of the Amazulu* from which Gordimer takes her epigraphs. And there are other parallels. Mehring studies the flora of the farm, learning their Latin names; Phineas's wife 'knew about plants' (*The Conservationist*, p. 164). Alina, the housemaid, says of Phineas's wife,

> she feels the amatongo on her shoulders. It's the disease that means you're going to get the power. (*The Conservationist*, p. 169)

This accords with (and probably derives from) Callaway's account of James's disease as 'the disease which precedes the power to divine', but in James's case, as perhaps in Mehring's, this disease has as yet neither empowered nor destroyed him:

> The diviners tell James that he too is beginning, and will soon be a doctor. But they say he must not be treated with black medicines to lay the Itongo, for he will die, he must be just left alone. His friends therefore do not know what to do, since it is said, he will die. (*Religious System*, p. 196)

This parallel between Mehring and Phineas's wife in itself casts doubt on the claim that the epigraphs from *The Religious System of the Amazulu* produce an African subtext that authenticates African possession of the farm and denies Mehring's possession of it; the parallel suggests, rather, that African culture may have a diagnosis of what troubles Mehring. But more importantly, this hidden context for Mehring's obsession suggests an unexpected context for his final crisis in the mine-dumps. There, of course, he is encountering his equivalent of 'hyenas and lions and raging rivers coming to kill him' in the flood which has brought back the dead man; he is also experiencing with overpowering intensity the voices of his own *amatongo*, the departed ones who speak in his head: Antonia, Terry, but also those toward whom he feels guilty:

> *Trouble* – you said: the prominent industrialist associated with the economic advancement of the country at the highest level who helped his leftist mistress to flee abroad. He tried to interfere with me (that's the phrase that's used) when as a young prospective immigrant girl I sat beside him in an aircraft. He propositioned me in a coffee bar, trying to persuade me to sit in the dark with him at a cowboy film. If I had had my father's money I would have known better what to do with it than to pick up a prostitute and take her behind the trees.[12]

For the first time Mehring lets accusation flow over him without trying to provide a self-serving answer.

I suggest that we are exploring a system of diagnostic similarities as much as a system of differences here: black society as Gordimer treats it is more at home with and better at dealing with the uncanny than Mehring's white world, but it does not possess *certainties* which whites lack. The rituals of disenchantment or dispossession which take place on the farm may show that the Africans have better ways of dealing with feelings like Mehring's; on the other hand, their rituals in some ways resemble the process Mehring undergoes in the book. The resemblances in turn point to the openness of the book's ending. We as readers cannot be certain that Mehring's crisis in the mine-dumps is terminally disabling. It might even be cathartic, his equivalent of the ceremony of confrontation and sacrifice by which Phineas's wife casts out the *amatongo* and achieves power. But whether or not it is cathartic, we can see in the African culture surrounding Mehring not merely a stronger claim than his to proper possession of his land, but also a set of therapeutic practices applicable to his situation. Exploration of this latter side of the novel seems appropriate to me in light of the kinds of writing and reading for a new South Africa endorsed by Albie Sachs.

Let me turn now to the other side of the authenticity-contrast on which critics of *The Conservationist* have focused. Mehring is exceptional in Gordimer's work in that he is endowed with most of Gordimer's own intelligence and some of her sympathy, yet represents the segment of South African society she elsewhere treats with consistent contempt: the white English-speaking economic elite. Mehring is a representative of international capital. Through casually introduced or dropped facts we gather in the course of the novel that he is a quite major international industrialist, one whose deals and decisions shape the landscape in larger ways than the planting of expensive Spanish chestnuts in pits dug by his farm workers. He is a member of so many directorates that he turns new directorships down, sufficiently rich and sufficiently interlocked. He deals with persons he thinks of impersonally as 'the Metalgesellschaft Germans' or 'the Japanese' who channel international consumption of South African pig-iron. Mehring is also, as owner of a hobby farm, a representative of possessive individualism, the extension of self through possessions. One tends to think of these two – international capital and possessive individualism – as complementary, and to think of the successful capitalist as the possessive individualist writ very large, ceaselessly pursuing an ever-enlarging legal self: exemplified by Tamburlaines of modernity like Carnegie, Oppenheimer, Trump, etc.

Mehring's 'fall' – I have asked already what precisely it consists of – could thus be seen as a moral parable about the failure of possessive individualism and thus of capitalist development in South Africa: you can't live on the surplus value of others, Tamburlaine will die, raving and without Zenocrate, Jacobus's extended family will reassume Mehring's farm. Thus the novel may hint at a quasi-Marxist predictive integration of capitalist bad dreams, the failure of colonialism, and the black spectre haunting white South Africa in the service of historical prophecy. As both Cooke and Clingman point out, the prophecy is prefigured by the book's near-quotation of slogans about African resurgence in South Africa.

I do not think the novel encourages confidence about predictive history. I see it in fact as persistently deconstructive of such claims. By this I do not mean that the book sets itself against black liberation struggles or that its attention to them is anything other than the deep though inexplicit preoccupation charted especially well by Clingman. But I do think that Mehring is less *dismissed* by the novel than previous critical accounts of his failures claim. Mehring believes that people will mostly do what seems to work, and his irony dwells on the rationalizations with which people cloak their expediencies. His analysis is not easy to dismiss.

In some ways this is to argue that *The Conservationist* goes against the grain of Gordimer's other novels. She has, from the start, withheld sympathy markedly from the economic elite of English-speaking business people whose industrial arrangements have had such a profound effect on South Africa. Not only has she not made sympathetic characters of such people, she has treated them with a kind of dismissive contempt, as shallow, unimportant, even negligible factors on a political scene dominated by the struggle between Afrikaners and Africans with the liberal or radical whites who have often been her protagonists in an anguished middle. These whites are often refugees from the industrial capitalist elite, but they have nothing but scorn for it.

In *The Conservationist* as read by Cooke, Wade and Clingman, what Gordimer has done is, ultimately, to justify scorn and negligence by offering an in-depth case study of such a person, exposing his impotence, self-laceration, and failure. All of these critics, however (Clingman most clearly), note that part of the novel's strength lies in its countermovement to what they consider its controlling tendency – they agree with Antonia that Mehring is 'no ordinary pig-iron dealer'. How do we know this? In the novel his inner life remains hidden from those close to him, and what he says to them makes Mehring seem cruder and more committed to clichés of the rich than he seems to readers of the novel who know what he is thinking. Gordimer may conceivably be paying her respects – guarded and qualified, obviously – to an entire class of people rather than devoting herself to an exception. That she scorns the normal social life of this economic elite is clear; that she may be trying to do a complex kind of justice to the world-view of industrial capitalism and possessive individualism is less obvious, but perhaps only because the world of literary criticism and commentary on South African literature (and most literature) is separated by a gulf of mutual ignorance from the world of corporate capitalism.[13]

Let me illustrate by a passage in which Mehring is walking on the farm with his son Terry, who has spent his vacation in Namibia (then officially 'South West Africa'). Mehring comments to himself on Terry's insistence on the liberatory name:

Why Namibia? The great thing was once Spain. You are not the first. It's always been like that. Yes, it's all been thought, what you're thinking, a thousand times before. They went to fight in Greece, club-footed poet and the well-meaning romantic muddlers or freaks. They went off to Spain and lost the good cause and as a result today, despite the great loss to the country because a gipsy and her professor wouldn't dream of going there any more than they'd consider enjoying themselves in what she calls the Colonels' Greece (– But of course if you ever should have to get off your farm, the next thing'll be a villa in Malaga, eh. Isn't that the latest for rich South Africans –), yes the people are all better off today than they ever were. They have work and they eat. They wear shoes. A uranium deposit on that scale can raise the gross national product to a point where development – viability – becomes a reality, not a dream that depends on 'justice', wherever you're expecting to find that. (p. 147)

This is a complex communication which takes place entirely in Mehring's mind. He addresses it partly to his 16-year old son Terry, padding behind him on ostentatiously bare feet, partly to his former mistress Antonia, but partly also to the left-liberal community of readers, commentators, critics, taste-formers which is the main international audience for Gordimer's fiction – to us. The whole passage suggests Mehring's resigned apathy about political action and historical processes. Clingman notes, rightly, of Mehring's claim that black workers want 'shoes on their feet', that 'this is one of the most traditional (and cynical) excuses within the ideological armoury of imperialism'.[14]

Mehring's thumbnail sketch of the history of romantic involvement in revolutions (Byron in Greece, Auden or Orwell in Spain), targets literary romanticism generally, and Mehring seems to imagine himself specifically defending industrialism against romantics who find it distasteful, rather than defending colonialism. Franco's fascists are not colonialists; socialists build factories, and take pride in development. Mining uranium for the nuclear industry (and possibly for ultimate military use) is, of course, socially questionable ground on which to take such a stand; Mehring would do better to stick to his pig-iron, with its evident general utility. But Mehring seems to be ruminating an economic argument of W. W. Rostow's which was prominent in American discussions of the Third World in the late sixties and seventies: the notion that a nation needs rapid industrialization with attendant social inequalities and cultural dislocation to reach a 'take-off point' at which the economy generates so much wealth that some of these inequalities can be addressed (if not systematically rectified).

Trying to give Mehring's rumination an adequate response thus involves a tangle of historical, economic, and political judgements: his self-defence here is not self-evidently wrong and is even

associated with a then-fashionable economic theory. As read by
critics of Gordimer who want to see her as liberationist, however,
such thoughts are awkward and need to be dismissed. This is particularly the case when Mehring argues not, or at any rate not explicitly, for the maintenance of authoritarian government, but rather for
the social utility of large-scale industrial capitalism. Mehring concentrates on what capitalism does rather than on the forms of oppression with which it may be (and in South Africa obviously has
been) complicit.

This is what Mehring is thinking. But what is he saying? He is
acutely, sadly aware that his son is at the farm for only the last
morning of a vacation spent in Namibia; he recognizes in his son's
anti-government feelings a growing-away from him as father and a
potential moving away from South Africa as a country. They talk
about Khan Canyon, where uranium is now being mined.

> – You can't see anything? –
> – Nothing. You aren't even allowed on the approach road,
> where it turns off from the Swakopmund road. –
> – A tremendously valuable installation. Probably the biggest
> single find in the world. Millions sunk in it. . . . Swakopmund
> must have gone ahead? –
> If that's what interests you, the tone implies: – There's a whole
> new part of the town. I don't know how many houses, for the
> whites who work on the mine. – (p. 140)

Mehring then, disastrously, or perhaps with intentional uncompromising perversity (in the manner of fathers in covert argument
with sons) invites Terry to admire the new trilingual 'No Thorough-
fare/Geen Toegang/Akunandlela Lapha' sign on the farm road,
which he has put up. So Mehring's lecture to Terry on the utility of
industrial development never takes place, and Mehring instead associates himself in his son's eyes with exclusion and race separation
by pointing to the sign. Mehring is both an inept parent and an inept
apologist for capitalism, as far as Terry is concerned, but readers of
the novel know both that he cares more for his son than he shows
and that he has thought more clearly about social systems than he
demonstrates.

Mehring's retreat to his farm is an attempt to compensate for the
moral limitations of capitalism as a system and, though his farm is a
possession, his 'conservationist' relation to it does not fit conventional notions of possessive individualism as an ideology. He is not

even a small-scale Tamburlaine. While he represents a system which thrives on domination, he himself dominates just about nobody in the course of the book. In sexual relations he may sound like a male dominator, remembering how 'he drew [Antonia's] tongue into his mouth as he would suck the flame of a match up into his cigar' (p. 73), but while this records his complacent objectification of part of her body, it turns out mainly to mark the uncanny entrance of her consciousness, her ironically biting tongue, into his head, where it will reprove him and argue with him for the rest of the novel – a novel in which, as already pointed out, Mehring is celibate, despite thinking a great deal about sex. Though he blusters in mental dialogue with his wife, his mistress Antonia, his son Terry, all of them, like his neighbours and workers, in fact seem to get what they want from him. And though as 'owner' and 'farmer' he stands in a dominance relation to the blacks on his farm, he does not cast his relations to them in the mode of dominance and submission: rather he meditates on the limits of his communication with them and fantasizes about having more communication than he has. The available literary representation of the industrialist as domineering bully (traditional in the English novel since Dickens at least) who lives by self-imposition both on things and people is far from what Gordimer does with Mehring. His one consistent satisfaction comes from the belief that he and all others are enmeshed in a capitalist order he, unlike others, understands as an insider and has no illusions about. All this makes Mehring's pathos painfully clear, of course, and at times not much more attractive than the character of the bully presented in other fiction. But Mehring also seriously represents a disillusioned realism which accepts capitalism as a dominant presence. This is an idea Gordimer entertains, though not happily.

The Conservationist, then, concentrates on a mid-life crisis which does not alter very much. Mehring remains the owner of the farm. He continues to work at his job – Jacobus, getting permission from Mehring to 'make everything nice' for the reburial, notes that Mehring is 'leaving that day for one of the countries white people go to, the whole world is theirs' (*The Conservationist*, p. 266), thus persisting in his participation in the global flow of raw materials, finished goods, and money.

It is not Mehring's pragmatism that fails – pragmatism tells people to seek meaning in the communities in which meaning lives. What fails is his attempt to create meaning out of his farm without immersing himself in the community which constitutes his farm (the Africans on it), and the family he hoped to build or recover on the farm (Antonia and Terry). This points to a general failure of a kind of pragmatism which accepts with resignation the way things are as a boundary of imagination. The novel, in ways I have argued, alerts us to networks of similarity across race-barriers which Mehring accepts as boundaries, and in so doing suggests that if Mehring – and the dominant South African class he partly represents – had not reached a dead-end through the imposition of such boundaries, he might have understood his own situation on the farm better and so might have found there materials for reconstruction rather than for despair and isolation.

Good novels have in them the uncanny materials that let them continue to mean in different ways under new conditions of reception. South Africa, as Sachs's paper argues, has entered a process of change that justifies new ways of writing and new tendencies in reading. South Africa's future will very probably involve some form of capitalism, including private property and thus scope for possessive individualism, transformed (we may hope) in imaginative ways.[15] I have tried to show that *The Conservationist* speaks to this transformation even as it spoke to the apparent historical impasse which preceded it, and that it does so not by simply authenticating black claims and denying white ones, but by mapping subtle and largely unseen axes of similarity which coexist with the imposed differences of apartheid.

Notes

1. Albie Sachs, 'Preparing ourselves for freedom', paper prepared for an ANC in-house seminar on culture, 1989, quoted from Ingrid de Kok and Karen Press (eds), *Spring is Rebellious: Arguments about cultural freedom by Albie Sachs and respondents* (Cape Town: Buchu books, 1990), p. 20. Sachs does not refer to the question whether the Communist Sholokhov in fact composed *And Quiet Flows the Don* or whether, as has been suggested, he adapted it from the manuscript of a deceased White Russian, which would make it a less perfect example of what Sachs intends.

2. 'A Conversation with Nadine Gordimer', *Salmagundi* 62, Winter 1984, p. 16.

3. Michael Wade, *Nadine Gordimer* (London: Evans Brothers, 1978), pp. 190–227. See especially pp. 201–3.

4. John Cooke, *The Novels of Nadine Gordimer: Private Lives/Public Landscapes* (Baton Rouge: Louisiana State University Press, 1985), pp.

148–64. See especially pp. 150–1 and p. 163. For the claim that Gordimer identifies excessively with the Africans at the book's end, see pp. 212–13.

5. Stephen R. Clingman, *The Novels of Nadine Gordimer: History from the Inside* (Johannesburg: Ravan, 1986), pp. 135–69.

6. Compare, e.g. Andre Viola, 'The Irony of Tenses in Nadine Gordimer's *The Conservationist*', *Ariel: A Review of International English Literature*, Vol. 19, no. 4 (October 1988), p. 53: 'the appeased tone of the concluding lines unambiguously contrasts with the quasi-childless and rootless Mehring in their [sic] serene implication of a future that promises the Africans posterity and legitimate possession of the land'.

7. See Lars Engle, 'The Political Uncanny: The Novels of Nadine Gordimer', *The Yale Journal of Criticism*, Vol. 2, no. 2, Fall 1989, pp. 101–25.

8. *Novels*, p. 190.

9. 'Gordimer's *The Conservationist*: "That Book of Unknown Signs,"' *Critique: Studies in Modern Fiction*, Vol. XXII, no. 3 (1981), pp. 31–44.

10. Newman, p. 32.

11. In the following series of citations of passages in which Gordimer quotes Callaway, I cite page numbers from both works parenthetically, abbreviating Callaway's title as *Religious System* and retaining Gordimer's italics. See Nadine Gordimer, *The Conservationist* (Harmondsworth: Penguin, 1974) and the Reverend H. Callaway, *The Religious System of the Amazulu*, facsimile (Cape Town: Struik, 1970).

12. *The Conservationist*, p. 264. This section of the book is always taken with deadly seriousness (some early critics actually thought Mehring died in it), but this particular passage verges on comedy, partly because its affinities to a possible source in the 'Circe' episode of *Ulysses*: 'He surprised me in the rere of the premises, your honour, when the missus was out shopping one morning with a request for a safety pin. He held me and I was discoloured in four places as a result. And he interfered twict with my clothing' (New York: Random House, 1961), p. 461. Compare further accusations from other women on pp. 466–7. It will be remembered that Leopold Bloom emerges from Nighttown 'in complete possession of his faculties, never more so, in fact disgustingly sober', p. 614. An investigation of Gordimer's debts to Joyce in *The Conservationist* and *Ulysses* would be worth undertaking.

13. It is a distinctive mark of the subliterary, in fact, of the work of Wilbur Smith or Judith Krantz, to make these corporate figures into heroic centres of novelistic attention.

14. *Novels*, p. 142.

15. Altered policies in the South African liberation movements, the emergence of a negotiation process between the government and those movements, and the extraordinary changes in Eastern Europe and the Soviet Union all suggest this. Gordimer's own sense that something like a capitalist order will survive a change of power is suggested by passages in her two most recent novels: see *A Sport of Nature* (New York: Knopf, 1987), p. 340, and *My Son's Story* (New York: Farrar, Straus, Giroux, 1990), pp. 211–14.

7

The Interregnum of Ownership in *July's People*
ROSEMARIE BODENHEIMER

When Nadine Gordimer takes the Smales family to the South African bush in flight from a revolution they support, she deliberately invokes for the first time in her career the *Heart of Darkness* pattern of colonialist fiction. Marooned in an alien culture, the identities of the white liberals disintegrate, their morality and their language rendered impotent before the returned gaze of the black servant and the political paradoxes of black revolution. Gordimer's rewriting of this story accomplishes a number of important political reversals, beginning with the fact that the whites appear as dependent refugees rather than as imperialist adventurers; throughout the novel the old white fictions that control colonialist representations – fictions of adventure, ethnography, rural development, miscegenation – are elicited, diminished and dismissed.[1]

Perhaps the most central refocusing of the imperial quest story is the one signalled by the arrival of an entire white suburban middle-class family in the bush, complete with toilet paper, malaria pills, sporting equipment, and a toy electric race-car set. This is a story about the middle class and its possessions, its testing-ground a culture of poverty that immediately gives up its sensational secret: 'They had nothing.'[2] Set during an imaginary period when the political possession of South Africa is in question, its plot turns on the transfer of two power-objects, a car and a gun. Every painful phase of the disintegration of white consciousness is built around the struggle for an object; the heart of darkness is nothing more or less than the profound disorientation that is left when things are taken away. The special concreteness of Gordimer's narrative is a function of its political vision: as I understand it, *July's People* is largely a materialist fable in which political consciousness and identity are predicated less on race and power than on the fundamental economic facts of ownership and dispossession.

The text is devoted to the naming of objects; variants of the words 'possession' and 'belongs' virtually litter its pages. The story of revolutionary transformation begins in the language of fairy-tale, which tells how the 'yellow bakkie that was bought for fun turned out to be the vehicle' of escape, how the black servant July 'turned out to be the chosen one in whose hands their lives were to be held; frog prince, saviour, July' (p. 9). The fairy-tale diction is supplemented by the sounding of an ironically political keynote: 'In various and different circumstances certain objects and individuals are going to turn out to be vital . . . the identity of the vital individuals and objects is hidden by their humble or frivolous role in an habitual set of circumstances' (p. 6). What begins in the Smales's minds as a story of salvation evolves into a narrative of threat, as persons and objects are defamiliarized; not only are they experienced outside the grid of habitual circumstances, but they are resituated in a limbo of ownership. Struggling unsuccessfully to maintain the rights of possession, the Smales couple manifest the 'morbid symptoms' of a dying consumer culture in which identity is created by ownership and relationships are mediated by objects.[3]

The Interregnum of the novel is, then, a differently marked experience from the political necessities described in the essay 'Living in the Interregnum' (1982), written in the year after the publication of *July's People*.[4] Both novella and essay describe a contemporary state of ongoing revolution, a situation in which the liberal white must find her own way to a future which may or may not include a home for the white African; both represent Western capitalism as an impossible present for the black majority, and Gordimer ends 'Living in the Interregnum' with a plea for the possibility of 'an alternative left, a democracy without economic or military terror' (*EG*, p. 284). But while the essay is offered to its originally American audience as a series of general challenges – to the white South African, to the white African writer, to the Western left – *July's People* investigates the profound resistance to change offered by the psyche shaped to the specifications of Western consumer capitalism. A hint of that resistance appears fleetingly in the text of the essay, when Gordimer speaks of the difficult Interregnum between 'two identities, one known and discarded, the other unknown and undetermined'. If the white African is to fashion the possibility of a new home in South Africa, 'this depends also on our finding our way there out of the perceptual clutter of curled photographs of master and servant relationships, the 78 *rpms* of history repeating the conditioning of the past' (*EG*, 269–70). *July's People* records the stubborn persistence of the perceptual clutter, as well as its necessary imbrication with the machines (the camera, the phonograph, the car, the gun, the radio) that record and reify the old order. What appears in the essay as a series of separate topics – the need for new white identity, the need for a new economics – is deeply joined in the study of the Smales couple and their children, as if to suggest the virtual impossibility as well as the necessity of such alternations in the mental equipment of an adult white South African. Perhaps Gordimer glosses the nature of the difference when she remarks in 'Living in the Interregnum' that 'nothing I say here will be as true as my fiction' (*EG*, p. 264).

A 'curled photograph of master and servant relationships' appears early in *July's People* in an episode that forms a kind of parable within Gordimer's larger fable. Maureen Smales, thrust out of her suburban context into July's village, comes upon an odd object, a miner's BOSS BOY badge, stuck on the doorway of a hut where the village farm tools are kept. Signifying someone's now unpossessed past of dislocated labour, the badge recalls Maureen's own past, her childhood as daughter of the shift boss in a mining compound. She remembers her relationship with the family's black servant Lydia, a relationship she had imagined as intimate friendship and girlish collusion against the authority of parents. A photographer had taken a picture of Maureen and Lydia holding hands and crossing the street, Lydia carrying Maureen's school-case on her head; it appears later in another context, a *Life* coffee-table book of photographs documenting apartheid. Confronted with this book, Maureen asks the question she could not have asked as a child: 'Why had Lydia carried her case?' Yet although the image of the carried case is the sign that gives away the relation between the affectionately companionable bodies, it tells a truth Maureen still cannot name: 'Did the book, placing the pair in its context, give the reason she and Lydia, in their affection and ignorance, didn't know?' (p. 33)

Maureen's failure to read the photograph without nostalgia is a measure of the levels of resistance in her essentially honest consciousness. She understands that something is amiss, but she is unable to understand that Lydia would have known exactly what it was. The case belongs to the white child; it contains the books and gym suit that prepare her for a life of mental work and physical leisure to which the black woman has no access. Yet the woman who will never use it takes care of the object as object, takes the burden of its weight. It is the precise image of what is wrong with the Smales's apprehension of their relationship with July: while they imagine themselves defying the spirit of apartheid and 'treating him as a man', he is perfectly conscious that he is only employed to service and guard the things – as well as the children – that are the signs and conditions of their bourgeois life.

Gordimer's most brilliant achievement in *July's People* is to make the reader exquisitely aware of the meanings, histories and uses of objects as they enter new sets of circumstances. The yellow bakkie is, of course, the most prominent example. Bam Smales, who imagines his marriage 'back there' as an alliance against threats to liberalism that include 'the wine-tasting temptation of possessions' (p. 105), has sheepishly and defiantly treated himself to the bright yellow sporting van to celebrate his fortieth birthday; Maureen sees the action as an assertion of identity, 'a glimpse of the self that does not survive coupling' (p. 6). 'The vehicle', as it is insistently called, is formally introduced in the language of the consumer catalogue, its target-buyers designated as poor whites and coloureds or affluent whites who can afford a second car. Its first transformation from a superfluous leisure object into a 'vehicle' of salvation is quickly ironized when the gaudy colour threatens to give away the white presence in the bush. Once it is hidden in the village, Maureen sees the bakkie as 'a ship docked in a far country' which would 'rust and be stripped to hulk, unless it made the journey back, soon' (p. 14). It exists for her, as for its manufacturers, only in the context of its bourgeois origins, to which it promises to redeliver them.

In fact, however, the van becomes a 'vehicle' for the dissolution of the social contract under which whites own and blacks take care. The agonizing redefinition of July's relationship with his former employers flows from a single action: his appropriation of the bakkie. Under cover of his continuing role as servant to the Smales's needs, July manages to put the bakkie in a realm of ambiguous ownership: if he tells others it is his, it will be accepted as his. Thus he reassures the Smales couple that his driving will not give away their hiding place, but his implicit claim goes deeper, undermining the assumptions about property that keep the suburban couple afloat. As they manoeuvre to keep charge of the keys, to pretend that July is 'borrowing' the car, he denies the liberal pretence, offering Maureen his clear understanding that she has never known him as anything but a paid caretaker of her 'things'. His physical possession of the keys is all it takes to put the family in July's former position: they have no freedom of motion that is not in his hands.

The gun goes through similar transformations, but it works even more intimately as an index of Bam Smales's sense of identity. It too begins its bourgeois life as a leisuretime toy owned by a liberal white who would not on principle keep a revolver in the house to protect his family; the careful categorization of objects is part of the liberal mythology. In Bam's mind the rifle is transformed by the flight into a survival-necessity of the last resort, the moral equivalent of the revolver in the drawer. Bam keeps it in the thatched roof of the hut, hidden, he imagines, from the villagers, all of whom know exactly where it is. As his given name suggests, the gun and its promise of violent technological superiority is essential to Bam's sense of existence; the stubborn fantasy that he controls and conceals this identity comes through as a kind of comedy. When he goes through the village with his gun, preparing to kill wart-hogs, the narrative calls attention to the outdated image of the benevolent white hunter that he cherishes: 'He walked among them harmlessly; look, he and his gun were theirs' (p. 75).

Through Bam's consciousness Gordimer rehearses the repertoire of liberal white male imperial roles, and discovers their haplessness. Bam begins his life in the bush by imagining himself as a Third World development agency, bringing his technology and his expertise to the aid of the village. He helps mend the shared farming tools 'scarcely to be called equipment' (p. 24), and rigs up a water-tank to catch the rains, using July in his old role as an assistant around the house. As all-knowing older man he teaches the young black Daniel to use the gun, oblivious of its political implications. And when he kills his first warm-blooded animal, his epiphany is a much-diminished replay of the old imperial adventure story: the white man secretly thrills to discover himself as a killer – but leaves the blacks to do the dirty work of skinning and quartering (pp. 77–8).

It is not up to Bam, however, to determine the meaning of the gun under new political circumstances. That is done for him by the chief of July's tribe, who clarifies its status as a political object. The chief knows little of urban revolution and sees it as a threat to his tribe; Bam is to become a counter-revolutionary military trainer, helping the tribe defend itself against the black revolutionaries. It is the kind of dilemma Gordimer discusses in 'Living in the Interregnum', when she speaks of the need for whites to encounter within themselves the contradictions within the black movement. Bam is paralyzed by it; the old political languages fail to touch the actuality of the contradiction. But when Daniel solves the problem by taking the gun off to join the revolution, Bam is undone: he lies face-down on the bed in despair. While Maureen is able to grasp that Daniel 'only took what he had a right to' (p. 153), Bam's sense of manhood is destroyed with his last piece of power and property.

As the two power-objects are tentatively shifted into a black economy, the narrative engages the reader in a many-faceted confrontation with the questions 'What is stealing?' and 'What is garbage?' With stunning verbal economy, Gordimer records the village's appropriation and integration of the garbage generated by consumer culture. The pig-pen is constructed from 'a fusion of organic and inorganic barriers – thorny aloes, battered hub-caps salvaged from wrecked cars, crumbling tin, mud bricks' (p. 28); July brings milk in paraffin tins, milk in Golden Syrup tins (pp. 9–10); every old piece of string is hoarded and used; an old man makes rope from the plastic netting of discarded orange bags. In an upscale version of this improvisation, Bam keeps his bundles of cash in 'a moulded plastic-foam box that had once held a Japanese hi-fi system' (p. 7).

Maureen is accustomed to thinking of July as a repository for garbage: his room is furnished with cast-offs from the white family furnishings. In the village she finds little forgotten objects from her house that 'she privately recognized as belonging to her' and concludes that 'honesty is how much you know about anybody, that's all' (p. 36); in the heat of battle she later accuses July of theft. Yet she herself has guiltlessly looted a riot-torn Johannesburg drugstore for the many packets of malaria pills she brought into the bush. And the old ropemaker accuses her children of stealing one of the orange bags they define as garbage. What, then, is the difference between July's use of her discarded things and his appropriation of little objects that lie unused around the house? Between her looting and his taking? Between what July does with the bakkie and a friend borrowing the car? For the whites, the mere fact of ownership takes precedence over use-value. They fight for the right to define ownership even over unused objects, while the village runs on an economy of shared recycling in which property is defined by the person who can use it. Maureen never makes the connection between her looting and July's taking, but she does come to a theoretical understanding of Daniel's use-right to a gun which never belonged to her. In all these ways the novel blurs the clear lines of property which mark out the fundamental divisions of the bourgeois world.

The ethic of private property remains ineradicably etched in the white consciousness. When rage overcomes Maureen's guilty liberal concealments during her searing dialogues with July, she brings up from her depths not only accusations of theft but projections of the awful truths she is learning about herself. Attempting to have the last word, to possess at least the power of guilty knowledge, Maureen tells July to let Bam help him fix the bakkie, saying 'what nobody else should hear. – You don't have to be afraid. He won't steal it from you. –' (p. 101). Her taunt throws back July's earlier complaint that she has never trusted him with her things; her only power is to accuse him of the same paranoia of ownership that she has discovered in herself and Bam. In their final, all-destroying dialogue she accuses July of profiting by the war, of stealing the bakkie so he can 'drive around like a gangster, imagining yourself a *big man*, important,' until he runs out of petrol and the car rots in the bush, 'another wreck like all the others' (p. 153). The 'truth' she tells him here is presumably what lies deepest in her consciousness, the bourgeois fear that 'they' will take 'our' things and wreck them like children. The fight to retain possession continues into the post-revolutionary situation: the transfer of ownership is conceded, but the new owners are declared incompetent as users.

The fear that Maureen drags out of her repressions in the last pages of the novella has already been easily articulated by her son Victor at its beginning. Victor wants to show off his car-set to the village children, but he wants his mother to prevent them from touching and breaking his 'things'. The Smales children carry the theme of possession in scene after scene, first as unabashed representatives of the code in which they are reared, later moving beyond their parents into free intercourse with the village economy of poverty. As Stephen Clingman suggests, the children become transformed consciousnesses who make a future conceivable (Clingman, p. 197). But they function in other ways as well; in particular, Gordimer constructs the relationship between parents and children to show how it is mediated by things, and by the ideology of ownership. Back in the old life, 'Nothing made them so happy as buying things; they had no interest in feeding rabbits' (p. 6). When Victor kicks stubbornly at the tin bath, his mother reprimands not his moodiness but his destruction of others' property: 'Don't. D'you hear me? That's July's' (p. 14). When Bam goes hunting he can persuade his son to stay behind only by promising him the skin of the animal; 'his kind did not strike their children' (p. 76), but they do bribe them, in the familiar middle-class way of treats and deprivations. When Maureen wants to get the black baby, or the litter of cats, out of the overcrowded hut she tells the children to return baby or cat to its mother or owner; possession is the underpinning of discipline. Gina's friend Nyiko says, 'Nobody's got a cat', and the adults translate this into 'everybody has cats, just as cats have fleas', but by now at least the children understand that possession does not apply to the case (p. 87). Once the cats 'belong' nowhere, they do not signify except as vermin or garbage, and Maureen gets rid of them by drowning them emotionlessly in a bucket of water.

The children begin as mirrors of the adult values, unrepressed by liberal guilt. As their parents spar for the psychological upper hand in quarters that have become too close for sympathy, the children are 'locked in an endless game of tormenting one another' for possession of sleeping space on the carseats that form their beds (p. 42). A moment of intense race hatred between the Smales couple and July, emerging from their polite manipulations to regain control of the car-keys, is interrupted when the children burst in to accuse the villagers of stealing the water in the newly set-up tank, and the parents are allowed to relieve the tension by preaching to the children about common ownership of rainwater (pp. 62–3). But because they are unhampered by the adults' complicated defences, the children are quick to integrate themselves into the local economy. As July is discovered to have gone off with the bakkie, they are playing with homemade wire carts made by the black children and exhanged for Victor's racing-cars, now broken up and kept 'as objects in themselves by those who had so few that useless possession itself was the treasure' (p. 39). By the end of the novel they are scrounging and scavenging with gusto, abandoning the objects that their parents are no longer able to supply and control. Like the master–servant relation, the parent–child relation through objects becomes obsolete.

By the end of the novel Maureen has understood the meaning of dependency as a material rather than a personal condition. Formerly she had attributed July's irritability to the 'inevitable, distorting nature of dependency – his dependency on them' (p. 60), but her experience teaches her that dependency means having no access to things, having to ask for an aspirin, or the use of the phone (p. 155). In this way, as in all the others, *July's People* insists on the rooting of consciousness and relationship in the concreteness of possession. But Gordimer is also interested in the question of self-creation and self-possession, which she plays out most fully in the story of Maureen's consciousness. Always steps ahead of Bam in under-standing the changing meanings of old formulae, Maureen is en-gaged from the first in a struggle to ground herself in some adequate consciousness, to 'find a foothold' from which to speak. Her own situation as a dependent woman and wife, her sexuality defined by her place in the 'master bedroom *en suite*,' gives her the intermediary position that allows her to see more than the white man, and ends in a wish to flee the contradictions around which her identity is built.

This identity is rooted in the memories of objects. As the novel opens, Maureen comes out of the delirium of the three-day flight and finds equilibrium in a vision of her childhood room and an enumeration of the knick-knacks displayed in her collection. The objects are the small, damaged debris of empire or signs of feminin-ity: 'the miniature brass coffee-pot and tray, the four bone elephants, one with a broken trunk, the khaki pottery bulldog with the Union Jack painted on his back'; the lavender-bag, the girl's dressing table, the cut-glass scent bottle with a dented silver stopper (p. 3). Assem-bled, they somehow assemble the self; as James Clifford suggests in his critique of Western ethnography and art, identity is established through ritualizations of the desire to own: 'In the West . . . collecting has long been a strategy for the deployment of a possessive self, culture, and authenticity.'[5] It is here, rather than in the master bed-room of her marriage 'where her returning consciousness properly belonged' (p. 4) that Maureen orients herself, because in the master bedroom she herself 'belongs' as a possession, a sex-object, a wife. What does not belong to the self is an absence; thus Maureen sees the hut as 'empty' even though it contains a number of the village objects.

The movement of Maureen's consciousness in the narrative might be read as a kind of emptying-out of her collection of roles and attitudes, in preparation for the unknown identity ahead. But the difference between Maureen's theoretical meditations and her prac-tice complicates such a reading, and leaves ambiguities in Gordimer's representation of the possibilities for change. On the one hand, Maureen articulates the novel's abstract arguments about identity and possession; on the other she struggles fiercely to hold on to the power conferred by secret knowledge, as when she does not inform Bam about the return of July and the bakkie, keeping 'her knowledge of the vehicle as a possession to which she was curiously entitled' (p. 52). In a critical early scene Maureen finds herself unable to read a novel, and recognizes that her identity is threatened by the reality of village poverty as it had never been by 'the false awareness of being within another time, place and life that was the pleasure of reading'. Now 'She *was* in another time, place, consciousness; it pressed in upon her and filled her as someone's breath fills a balloon's shape. She was already not what she was' (p. 29). From this recognition she flees to the narrative of her past, to a memory and recapitulation of the Lydia story. Later, Maureen understands the inadequacy of the 'humane creed' in its assumption of the university of love, marriage, sex, or death; she sees that July's experience of love, marriage, and infidelity is determined by the material conditions under which he lives, just as the bourgeois experience is shaped by the possession of master bedrooms and access to clandestine hotel rooms (pp. 64–5). Yet this meditation is the prelude to the chapter in which she attempts to blackmail July with her knowledge of his 'city woman'; her urgent need for the possession of that power wins her only a bitter rhetorical victory. By the end of the story 'she was not in possession of any part of her life', finding no foothold in the present from which to recognize herself as a sequence or history conferring identity (p. 139). Having no place as wife, mother, mistress or friend, she has the feeling of not being there as life proceeds around her. But in the final dialogue between Maureen and July, each revels in the splendid destructiveness of truth-telling as they finally spit out in their different languages their essential contempt for each other. It seems clear that Maureen cannot think her way to a new consciousness; she is required to hear herself say the things that undermine every point of theoretical understanding.

Are those self-revelations purgative? Or are they the deeply-held 'morbid symptoms' that make change impossible? Similar questions might be asked of the moment in 'Living in the Interregnum' in which Gordimer responds to the South African writer's political challenge: should white writers write about blacks? 'I challenge my challenger to deny', she writes, 'that there are things we know about each other that are never spoken, but are there to be written – and received with the amazement and consternation, on both sides, of having been found out' (*EG*, p. 279). The dialogues in *July's People* – between mistress and servant, between husband and wife – are all about 'being found out'; as in the free zone of the novel, the Interregnum of ownership allows for the never-spoken to be said. Whether such writing and saying clears the way for a future or simply tells an alienating truth is subsumed for Gordimer in the special status of writing, which bears some resemblance to the hoarded possession of individual knowledge that she dramatizes in her heroine.

While the dispossession of the Smales couple forms the main plot of *July's People*, Gordimer sketches the black servant's identity problems in brief episodes of counterpoint.[6] In his own way July too must disinvest himself of his interests in apartheid capitalism. The possessive 'his white people' indicates a certain pride of status which the Smaleses confer on him in the eyes of his village, and he is at first prepared to save this 'possession' from revolution. He too associates his employers' identities with their things: when his wife criticizes Maureen's appearance, he claims that she looked different at home, with her cupboardfuls of clothes and elegant glasses for wine (p. 22). As he acquires the power of possession, July learns to invert the master–servant relation; his refusal to allow Maureen to gather food with the village women is an act of power, an reverse application of apartheid. It is also, however, an indication of the divided identity structure created by the homelands policy: July has created himself as someone who keeps the urban and rural parts of his life separate. As the Smales's servant he is called July; as the 'chief's subject' Mwawate; neither defines his 'real' name.

In the three dialogues with his wife that punctuate the narrative, July moves tentatively toward an integration of his two lives. Martha begins to question him, and deduces the possibility of the town woman. In the final dialogue July imagines Martha in Johannesburg with him, and mentions for the first time the United Building Society account that represented his literal investment in the white economy, while Martha imagines him using his capitalist skills to set up as shopkeeper in the bush. Despite these truncated experiments in imagining a future, July's story remains stuck in the imaginative limbo between identifications. He no longer carries his passbook, but he doesn't destroy it; 'he needed someone – he didn't know who – to tell him' that his legitimacy is no longer guaranteed by the Smales signature (p. 137). When 'his people' become redefined as his family and tribe, he is still confounded by the conflict between his chief and the urban revolutionaries, still willing to play in the ground between. Though by the end of the story Maureen herself, possessing nothing, has become an encumbrance that July is more than happy to throw away, the loss of his position as urban servant and dependent migrant worker leaves the question of his post-revolutionary identity as open as that of the whites.

Two large objects appear in the village at the end of the novel: the travelling red *gumba-gumba* and the helicopter. Displacing the car, the radio, and the gun, the new machines cannot be interpreted by the white refugees. The travelling phonograph, a machine ingeniously constructed from discards, comes up labouriously from the river carried on the head of its black entrepreneur; the unmarked helicopter springs from the clouds like an act of sexual violence, 'its landing gear like spread legs, battling the air with whirling scythes' (p. 158). But the occasion for either arrival is obscure. July refuses to tell the Smales couple what is being celebrated by the music, though a broken-off sentence suggests that it may be Daniel's decision to go off to the revolution. The possible political relationship between the celebration and the arrival of the helicopter is beyond the whites' speculative powers; it is only clear that someone else owns and controls the meaning of machines.

Maureen's run for the helicopter is an almost unreadable act. On the one hand, as Clingman points out, it is her first act of instinctive personal integration; she runs 'with all the suppressed trust of a lifetime' (p. 160) away from the worn-out roles of the past toward an unknown revolutionary destiny (Clingman, p. 203). On the other, it is a flight toward the only source of power that has manifested itself in the bush, a desperate run for 'civilization' in its undisguised aggressive and technological form. In the final paragraph the language of fairy-tale returns, slyly suggesting that 'the real fantasies of the bush' create mirages of civilized order and safety that power Maureen's deluded flight (p. 160); coupled with the present-tense suspension of Maureen running, this language also signals an overt return to fictionality, to the circular completion of the fable. But the invisible helicopter remains as a final sign of the ambiguous status of power-objects in the transitional world. At the endpoint of a story recording the breakdown of liberal bourgeois consciousness, it hovers in the bush as an elusive fantasy, signifying either a necessary point of departure or a dead-end.

Notes

1. See Susan Greenstein, 'Miranda's Story: Nadine Gordimer and the Literature of Empire', *Novel* 18 (Spring 1985): 227–42, for the argument that *Burger's Daughter* and *July's People* are the first of Gordimer's novels to avoid the literary colonizing of black African experience. She argues that the interpolation of 'the white woman's adventure' story makes this possible; in her discussion of *July's People*, she emphasizes the rewriting of the white story that July imposes on Maureen, and points to the irrelevance of the miscegenation fantasy.
2. Nadine Gordimer, *July's People* (New York: Penguin, 1982), p. 29. Subsequent page references will appear in the text.
3. The epigraph for *July's People* is a quotation from Gramsci's *Prison Notebooks*, from which Gordimer also derived the title of her essay 'Living in the Interregnum': 'The old is dying and the new cannot be born; in this interregnum there arises a great diversity of morbid symptoms.'
4. 'Living in the Interregnum', given as the William James Lecture, New York University Institute of the Humanities, 14 October 1982. Reprinted in *The Essential Gesture*, ed. Stephen Clingman (New York: Knopf, 1988), pp. 261–84. Further references to the essay will be designated *EG* in the text.

     Clingman, connecting essay and novel, reads *July's People* as the work in which Gordimer enacts the essay's commitment to the revolutionary future of South Africa. He rightly complicates this view by reformulating the novel's activity as 'seeing the present through the eyes of the future'; in his most penetrating and suggestive sentence, 'The deepest project of the novel is in this sense *semiotic* – decoding the signs and codes of the present in the light of their actual reality – and it is this reality that the projection into the future clarifies' (p. 202). Clingman's actual decoding emphasizes the breakdown of master–servant and male–female roles in the revolutionary situation. See *The Novels of Nadine Gordimer: History from the Inside* (London: Allen and Unwin, 1986), pp. 193–204.
5. James Clifford, *The Predicament of Culture* (Cambridge, Mass. and London: Harvard University Press, 1988), p. 218.
6. The sketchiness of the sections devoted to July and Martha is interestingly characterized by Susan Greenstein's argument that Gordimer only 'signals the presence of a shadow story'; that, insisting on its inaccessibility to whites, she 'neither ignores July's story nor presumes to tell it'. There is, however, somewhat more content in the sketches than Greenstein records. (Greenstein, pp. 241, 239)

8
The Politics of Place in *Burger's Daughter*
DAPHNE READ

I am the place in which something has occurred.
Claude Lévi-Strauss (epigraph, Burger's Daughter)

The old is dying and the new cannot be born; in this interregnum there arises a great diversity of morbid symptoms.
Antonio Gramsci, Prison Notebooks (epigraph, July's People)

One of the central tensions in *Burger's Daughter* lies in the question of 'place', in shifting definitions of 'place', in the boundaries between 'place' (whose place? what place?) and 'no place' (displacement; utopia; the margins that subvert 'place'). The opening epigraph suggests the novel's preoccupation with subjectivity,[1] with the construction of Rosa Burger as an individual, a fictional character in the novelistic discourse of liberal humanism. The subject is both 'I' and 'eye'. Yet at the same time the Western concept of the ego as centre of the universe is destabilized by the concept of 'place'. The 'I' (Afrikaner, middle-class, female, Communist) is positioned in relation to the 'place' of black Africans, a space 'where definitions fail' (p. 149), 'where categories and functions lose their ordination and logic' (p. 150).

In the opening scene of the novel, Rosa is both 'in place, outside the prison' and 'the place': 'outside the prison the internal landscape of my mysterious body turns me inside out, so that in that public place on that public occasion . . . I am within that monthly crisis of destruction, the purging, tearing, draining of my own structure. I am my womb, and a year ago I wasn't aware – physically – I had one' (pp. 15–16). The discussion of menstruation in conjunction with the arrest of her mother highlights Rosa's entry into adulthood, both as a woman and a political being. Yet perhaps more significantly, in terms of the novel's politics of place, the feminine experience of being turned inside out in the pain of first menstruation becomes an appropriate figure for the cognitive dissonance and restructuring that must occur, not only for Rosa, daughter of Afrikaner Communists, but for whites committed, like Gordimer, to building a South Africa with black majority rule and a place for themselves. This particular figuring of the white female body suggests the organic destruction of the white order in South Africa and its sterility, rather than fertility.[2] As the epigraph to *July's People* suggests, 'the old is dying and the new cannot be born', a lament that recurs metaphorically throughout *Burger's Daughter*.

Juxtaposed against the exploration of the construction of Rosa Burger as a white female subjective 'place' is the assertion of the place of black Africans. In the townships, home and dispossession are bound together in the tension of 'place': 'Fats' place, Marisa said. I said. Orde Greer said. Blacks don't talk about "my house" or "home" and whites have adopted the term from them. A "place", somewhere to belong, but also something that establishes one's lot and sets aside much to which one doesn't belong' (p. 149). For Rosa, searching for her own place in South Africa, 'This commonplace of any black township became to me what it is: a "place"; a position whose contradictions those who impose them don't see, and from which will come a resolution they haven't provided for' (pp. 150–1); in this place the new will be born in the 1976 uprising of the schoolchildren. In the cartography of the dispossessed, Rosa is brought face to face with the limits and contradictions of who she is. At Fats' place the proponents of Black Consciousness establish that she doesn't belong. And later, at a critical moment in the novel, the township is the site of her defection from her own familial and political coordinates: 'I was caught on the counter-system of communications that doesn't appear on the road-maps and provides access to "places" that don't appear on any plan of city environs. . . . I gained a cambered dirt road without signposts as one of those donkey-carts that survive on the routes between these places that don't exist was approaching along a track from the opposite side' (p. 207). For a moment the image of the cart in convulsion is, for Rosa, the symbol of universal suffering and the spectacle of apartheid, but it quickly resolves into a 'mad frieze against the sunset' of a drunken black peasant beating his donkey, terrorizing his wife, child, and beast into submission (p. 209). Paralyzed by guilt and fear that she will turn into 'one of those whites who can care more for animals than people'

(p. 210), she leaves South Africa: 'After the donkey I couldn't stop myself. I don't know how to live in Lionel's country' (p. 210).

For Rosa Burger, following in her father's path is not easy; she rebels against the commonsense ideology of her home – the ideology of the Communist Party – by finding her own way of understanding the world, through her own metaphors: 'I don't know what metaphors to use to describe the process by which I'm making my own metaphors for suffering' (p. 196). Later, when she returns to South Africa, she explains:

> I don't know the ideology:
> It's about suffering.
> How to end suffering.
> And it ends in suffering. Yes, it's strange to live in a country where there are still heroes. Like anyone else, I do what I can. I am teaching them to walk again, at Baragwanath Hospital. They put one foot before the other. (p. 332)

One set of axes of meaning in *Burger's Daughter*, then, is composed of the competing processes of ideology – the ideologies of South Africa, particularly those of the Communist Party, the Black Consciousness movement, and enlightened liberals – and metaphor – the personal and the literary process. In the shift from ideology to metaphor, from father to daughter, from political struggle to healing, the novel enacts a return to the terrain of liberal humanism.

Burger's Daughter juxtaposes two narratives: the idealized history of the father–hero, Lionel Burger, 'citizen of Africa', and the private story of the daughter, Rosa Burger, citizen of the people, citizen of the future. In Lionel Burger, Gordimer has created a figure who embodies not only the political praxis of the Communist community, but also the organic healing humanism of medicine. The political struggle in South Africa is, in part, translated into a model of disease. Lionel Burger, as a white Afrikaner, a member of the generation of the ruling race that constructed apartheid, attempts to cure the disease his people have caused. By the time he dies, however, the struggle has gone beyond the efforts of whites to 'cure' the situation and has been taken over by the blacks – Soweto marks the turning-point in *Burger's Daughter*. The struggle passes into the hands of the children and is reframed in terms of political conflict, no longer in terms of the suffering that comes from illness. Rosa, daughter of apartheid (born in the year and the month that the National Party which institutionalized apartheid came to power [p. 94]), is positioned on the margins of the struggle. Whereas Lionel was a leader and a healer (a Christ-like figure), Rosa provides palliative services, rehabilitating the wounded rather than curing the disease.

The novel explores the fusion of the political and private lives through Rosa's attempts to separate the two by trying to 'defect' from her father and all that he represents. However, though the novel is infused with history, it also partially refuses the determinations of history in a politics of 'place'. When Rosa returns to South Africa, she takes her place 'like anyone else' (p. 332), not like a hero, and inhabits her name in ways unforeseen by her father: she recognizes her own history. Rosa, named in part for Rosa Luxemburg (p. 72), assumes her place in a South Africa shaken by Soweto as one of the children for the future:

> Their children and children's children; that was the Future, father, in hands not foreseen.
>
> You knew it couldn't be: *a change in the objective conditions of the struggle sensed sooner than the leaders did*. Lenin knew; the way it happened after the 1905 revolution: *as is always the case, practice marched ahead of theory*. The old phrases crack and meaning shakes out wet and new. . . . The real Rosa believed the real revolutionary initiative was to come from the people; you named me for that? This time it's coming from the children of the people, teaching the fathers. . . . (p. 348).

Though she rejects the imperatives of her father's history, Rosa accepts the imperatives of her own historical location in a powerful image of rebirth: 'The old phrases crack and meaning shakes out wet and new.' She is Rosa Burger, not simply 'Burger's daughter'. Ironically, though her discourse is Marxist, Rosa's positioning of herself is compatible with liberalism. Again, using the process of metaphor, she takes her place 'like anyone else'.

What Rosa refuses is the inevitability of her 'destiny', an inevitability – in the eyes of the state, liberals like Conrad, the Party faithful – determined by her 'place' as Lionel Burger's daughter (familial and political history combined). Instead she accepts responsibility for her place, her location, a responsibility marked by her recognition that 'Nothing can be avoided. . . . No one can defect'

(p. 332). Adrienne Rich has also written about accepting responsibility for her location as a white woman:[3]

> It was in the writings but also the actions and speeches and sermons of Black United States citizens that I began to experience the meaning of my whiteness as a point of location for which I needed to take responsibility. It was in reading poems by contemporary Cuban women that I began to experience the meaning of North America as a location which had also shaped my ways of seeing and my ideas of who and what was important, a location for which I was also responsible. (*NPL*, pp. 219–20)

'Begin with the material', writes Rich (NPL, p. 213), counterpointing Rosa's coming of age, her acceptance of the material conditions of her life:

> It isn't Bassie-Zwel-in-zima, I must get the stress right – who sent me back here. You won't believe that. Because I'm living like anyone else, and he was the one who said who was I to think we could be different from any other whites. Like anyone else; but the idea started with Brandt Vermeulen. You and my mother and the faithful never limited yourselves to being like anyone else.
>
> I had met a woman in her nightdress wandering in the street. She was like anyone else: Katya, Gaby, Donna; poor thing, a hamster turning her female treadmill. I remember every detail of that street, could walk it with my eyes shut. My sense of sorority was clear. Nothing can be avoided. Ronald Ferguson, 46, ex-miner, died on the park bench while I was busy minding my own business. No one can defect (p. 332).

The process of Rosa's coming of age is structured dialectically in the novel's three parts. Each is marked by a rejection of her 'place' as Burger's Daughter, an attempt to locate utopia ('I want to know somewhere else' [p. 185]), and an undermining of that attempt by a realization of the material meaning of 'place' for black Africans. In the first part of the novel, by far the longest, she is set loose from the political moorings of her life by the death of her father. Through her relationship with Conrad, the 'you' in her dialogue who becomes a surrogate brother, her childhood is defamiliarized, the foundations challenged by a petty liberal individualism. When her father is imprisoned for life, Rosa retreats to Conrad's cottage, which 'was let without official tenure at an address that no longer existed. . . . It was safe and cosy as a child's playhouse and sexually arousing as a lover's hideout. It was nowhere' (p. 21). It is one of several attempts to escape her father's heritage and the place 'predestined' for her. In this place which is 'nowhere', she is allowed to regress politically, nostalgically, in her desire to 'know somewhere else' – to know a private life. She rebels against suffering and sickness: 'I grumbled one day, some commonplace – I'm sick of this job. – . . . [M]y silence hammered sullen, hysterical, repetitive without words: sick, sick of the maimed, the endangered, the fugitive, the stoic; sick of courts, sick of prisons, sick of institutions scrubbed bare for the regulation endurance of dread and pain' (pp. 69–70). Although this tantrum passes, she examines the metaphor of illness more closely:

> Even animals have the instinct to turn from suffering. The sense to run away.
>
> Perhaps it was an illness not to be able to live one's life the way they did (if not the way you did, Conrad) with justice defined in terms of respect for property, innocence defended in their children's privileges, love in their procreation, and care only for each other. A sickness not to be able to ignore that condition of a healthy, ordinary life: other people's suffering (p. 73).

But even as the certainties of a politicized childhood are called into question by Conrad's Freudian interpretation of life, with its emphasis on sex and death, Rosa reaffirms the simultaneous materiality of politics and childhood. 'You didn't want to believe that at twelve years old what happened at Sharpeville was as immediate to me as what was happening in my own body' (p. 115), she comments in her mind and, later, parenthetically, she reflects, '(I know you dislike my habits of naming private events with public dates, but public events so often are decisive ones in my life)' (pp. 193–4).

The second movement in the dialectic takes Rosa to France, to her father's first wife and a surrogate mother, the 'you' in the dialogue. Fleeing South Africa after the donkey-scene, she is seeking another life: 'I wanted to know how to defect from him. The former Katya has managed to be able to write to me that he was a great man, and yet decide "there's a whole world" outside what he lived for, what life with him would have been' (p. 264). Although her relationship with Conrad enables Rosa to see her childhood through the eyes of a liberal individualist and to mourn her travestied private life, she is unable to remake her life differently as long as she remains in South Africa, 'Lionel's country'. Her relationship with Katya, however, enables her to experience a private life not dominated by politics, though still tenuously linked with the history of Lionel Burger. In France, she becomes an invented creature: 'It was a room made ready for someone imagined. A girl, a creature whose sense of existence would be in her nose buried in flowers, peach juice running down her chin, face tended at mirrors, mind dreamily diverted, body seeking pleasure. Rosa Burger entered, going forward into possession by that image' (pp. 229–30). The seductiveness of this image is inscribed in the lyricism of this part of the novel. The image by which Rosa is possessed satisfies a longing to be free of her historical context.

The difference between Rosa's 'existence' in France and her existence in South Africa is pinpointed in a discussion with her lover Bernard Chabalier:

They looked at painting. – In Africa one goes to see the people. In Europe, it's pictures. –

But she was seeing in Bonnard canvases . . . a confirmation of the experience running within her. The people she was living among, the way of apprehending, of being alive, at the river, were coexistent with the life fixed by the painter's vision. And how could that be? –

. . . These pictures are proof of something. It is the people I'm living among I'm seeing, not the pictures. –

– And do you know why, my darling? – [He points to two paintings.] In the fifty years between the two paintings, there was the growth of fascism, two wars – the Occupation – And for Bonnard it is as if nothing's happened. Nothing. Look at them. . . . He could have painted them the same summer, the same day. And that's how they are, those ones up there round the château – that's how they live. It's as if nothing has ever happened – to them, or anybody. Or is happening. Anywhere. . . . Look here – and there –– the woman's flesh and the leaves round her are so beautiful and they are equal manifestations. Because she hasn't any existence any more than the leaves have, outside this lovely forest where they are. No past, no future. . . . Your forest girl and the vase of mimosa – c'est un paradis inventé. – (pp. 286–7).

'She hasn't any existence . . . no past, no future': this is the critical subtext of Rosa's life in France as her identity shifts from one man's daughter to another man's mistress:

> There's nothing more private and personal than the life of a mistress, is there? Outwardly, no one even knows we are responsible to each other. Bernard Chabalier's mistress isn't Lionel Burger's daughter; she's certainly not accountable to the Future, she can go off and do good works in Cameroun or contemplate the unicorn in the tapestry forest. 'This is the creature that has never been' – he told me a line of poetry about that unicorn, translated from German. A mythical creature. *Un paradis inventé* (pp. 303–4).

The unicorn is the antithesis of the lion. What destroys the spell of the mythical for Rosa (and of the liberal separation of public and private) is her encounter with the black man whom she knew as her brother 'Baasie', but whose name is Zwelinzima, 'suffering land' (p. 318). The lion[4] and the unicorn: Lionel Burger, Africa, suffering land, versus a 'creature that has never been'. A poetic two-page passage (pp. 340–1), tellingly placed in the third part of the novel, offers an allegory of sorts, a recapitulation of the Bonnard paintings. The invented creature that Rosa might have been, had she followed through her plans to transplant her life into Bernard's orbit, sits gazing:

> There she sits, gazing, gazing.
>   An old and lovely world, gardens and gentle beauties among gentle beasts. Such harmony and sensual peace in the age of the thumbscrew and dungeon that there it comes with its spiral horn
> there she sits gazing
>   bedecked, coaxed, secured at last
> by a caress – O the pretty dear! the wonder!
> Nothing to startle, nothing left to fear, approaching –
>   There she sits, gazing, gazing. And if it's time for the museum to close, she can come back tomorrow and another day, any day, days.
>   Sits gazing, this creature that has never been (p. 341).

Located in the moment of Rosa's return to South Africa, this invented memory, a daydream, inscribes an impossible idealism that nonetheless sustains a utopian possibility.[5]

If we conceive of the dialectical movement of the novel in terms of thesis/antithesis/synthesis, or as condition-of-being (the given)/ negation/transcendence, then the second movement of *Burger's Daughter* may be regarded rather dismissively as an aberration, a 'defect' in Rosa's activity, as indeed the epigraph for Part Two suggests: 'To know and not to act is not to know' (p. 213). But what does Rosa 'know'? The lion/unicorn dualism inscribes the issues raised in the novel about the relationships between the political and the private, between the activist and the artist, the materialist and the idealist. In the final movement Rosa clearly opts for the 'lion': she returns to the father/land, entering into dialogue with her mentor, her dead father. But to dismiss the second movement – the 'unicorn' movement – as a critique of the 'unicorn' is to misread.

The first and second movements of the novel may be read as a double negation of the father and his heritage, but both also inscribe a utopian longing. If the first is the utopian longing for a kind of childhood 'innocence', a rejection of the father's authority and a longing for his death, the second realizes the longing for the mother. Where Rosa's mother had 'sacrificed' the daughter's vulnerability for the political cause, denying the personal and prostituting the romantic, Katya 're-parents' Rosa, offering the intimacy of mother–daughter bonding and honouring the possibility and pleasures of heterosexual romance. In spite of the internalized perspective of her father which rather uncompromisingly and harshly judges Katya as 'lesser' (pp. 263–4), Rosa moves forward into possession of the romantic image Katya has prepared for her and reenacts Katya's defection from Lionel, her relocation in a community where 'nobody expects you to be more than you are' (p. 250), and her love affair with a married man that promises a happiness she has never before known. Seduced by the image of sensuousness, pleasure, romance, she inhabits her body differently than in South Africa. And beginning with the body (whether with her first period or with her first apolitical love affair) is, as Rich has argued, a necessary step towards 'locating the grounds from which to speak with authority *as* women' (*NPL* 213).

Posing as an allegory of universalism and eternity, yet marked by its absence of suffering ('that condition of a healthy, ordinary life', as Rosa drily notes), the unicorn tapestry reflects critically on liberalism and its blindness to history and oppression. In addition it comments on the inadequacies of a liberal epistemology of vision. In an essay on the centrality of vision in classical philosophy, Evelyn Fox Keller and Christine Grontkowski focus on three aspects of vision that have led to its appeal as 'a model for knowledge' (p. 218). Following the work of Hans Jonas, they identify, first, the 'simultaneity of presence' in the act of seeing, or 'the distinctively spatial rather than temporal character of vision'; second, the 'dynamic neutrality' of vision, or 'the peculiar lack of engagement entailed by seeing, the absence of intercourse'; and third, its objectivity and perspective – 'its uniquely advantageous dependence on distance' (p. 219). Keller and Grontkowski conclude:

> [T]here is little doubt that vision, by virtue of its apparent atemporality, both invites and lends itself to an atemporal description of truth and reality. Similarly, there is little question that its equally apparent disengagement from action, experience, and dynamic interaction invites and lends itself to a model of truth which transcends the more body-bound, materially contingent senses. And, of course, the possibilities of perspective it grants us, and the gain the visual sense derives from distance further contribute to a model of truth based on distance between subject and object, knower and known (pp. 219–20).

The model of knowledge implicit in the unicorn tapestry comments retrospectively on Rosa's encounter with the tableau of the donkey-cart, the donkey and its black male abuser. Rosa flees South Africa when she is brought to the abyss of the ways of seeing of liberalism, when from the vantage point of distance the suffering of a donkey becomes a metaphor for universal suffering: 'I didn't see the whip. I saw agony. Agony that came from some terrible centre seized within the group of donkey, cart, driver and people behind him. They made a single object that contracted against itself in the desperation of a hideous final energy. Not seeing the whip, I saw the infliction of pain broken away from the will that creates it' (p. 208). Rosa's reaction is implicated in the 'disengagement from action, experience, and dynamic interaction' that is characteristic of vision:

> I rolled to a stop beyond what I saw. . . . And then I put my foot down and drove on wavering drunkenly about the road, pausing to gaze back while the beating still went on. . . . I could formulate everything they were, as the act I had witnessed; they would have their lives summed up for them officially at last by me, the white

woman – the final meaning of a day they had lived I had no knowledge of, a day of other appalling things, violence, disasters, urgencies, deprivations which suddenly would become, was nothing but what it had led up to: the man among them beating their donkey. I could have put a stop to it, the misery; at that point I witnessed. What more can one do? That sort of old man, those people, peasants existing the only way they know how, in the 'place' that isn't on the map, they would have been afraid of me. I could have put a stop to it, with them, at no risk to myself. No one would have taken up a stone. I was safe from the whip. I could have stood between them and suffering – the suffering of a donkey.

As soon as I planted myself in front of them it would have become again just that – the pain of a donkey.

I drove on. I don't know at what point to intercede makes sense, for me (p. 209).

Though Rosa is immobilized in the contradictions between what she 'sees' and what she 'knows', she recognizes the culpability of a white liberal epistemology of vision, where the objective stance of the Eye/ I sees abstract universality, and from the distance that creates perspective, blots out specificity and history – the conditions and causes of suffering.

Yet, while Rosa identifies and rejects her potential complicity with white liberals – 'I couldn't bear to see myself – her – Rosa Burger – as one of those whites who can care more for animals than people' (p. 210) – her flight to France is complicit with the chastity of the Lady and the Unicorn. Rosa's coming to know, or perhaps her resistance to knowing ('To know and not to act is not to know'), is framed by the donkey tableau 'in the "place" that isn't on the map' and the later imaginary reading of the unicorn tapestry. This visual framing of Rosa's epistemological journey from seeing-without-acting to a unity of sight/insight/acting illustrates the culpability of the liberal gaze: 'nothing can be avoided . . . no one can defect'.

Burger's Daughter deconstructs the liberal epistemology of vision, the notion that seeing is the source of knowing, of knowledge. Citing Mongane Serote in 'Living in the Interregnum', Gordimer has noted the necessity to question the authority of the white 'I am', the white Eye: 'Blacks must learn to talk; whites must learn to listen' (p. 267). Seeing privileges the individual who sees; listening forces engagement with the 'other', suggests the possibility of connection, dialogue, and mutual understanding. The clash between Rosa and Zwelinzima Vulindlela at the end of Part Two of *Burger's Daughter* jolts Rosa from her liberal reveries of another life into a recognition that 'no one can defect'. In her dialogue with her dead father in Part Three, she says, 'I cannot explain to anyone why that telephone call in the middle of the night made everything that was possible, impossible' (p. 328). The telephone call counterpoints the donkey-scene at the end of Part One, which sent Rosa fleeing to France, in a paroxysm of fear, alienation and white guilt. Though Rosa denies she is a liberal, the phone-call dredges up the language and responses of the liberals Rosa despises. Zwelinzima Vulindlela forces Rosa to 'see' in the dark: 'Put on the light, Rosa. I'm talking to you' (p. 319). He forces her to 'see' herself as capitalizing on her identity as Lionel Burger's daughter; she defends herself against his criticisms of her behaviour by defending her father. In response to her challenge to prove his political credentials and the implicit taunt that he too has fled the country, he says, 'I don't know who you are' (p. 322). He challenges her identity, her perceptions, her knowledge, her relationship to the struggle and to her past in which 'Baasie' exists, reified in unexamined assumptions of a shared childhood. In her later private self-criticism, Rosa reflects: 'Repelled by him. Hating him so much! Wanting to be *loved*! – how I disfigured myself. How filthy and ugly, in the bathroom mirror. Debauched. To make defence of you the occasion for trotting out the holier-than-thou accusation – the final craven defence of the kind of people for whom there is going to be no future. If we'd still been children, I might have been throwing stones at him in a tantrum' (p. 329). This analysis echoes in telling ways her analysis of her decision to leave South Africa: 'the suffering – while I saw it was the sum of suffering to me. I didn't do anything. I let him beat the donkey. The man was a black. So a kind of vanity counted for more than feeling; I couldn't bear to see myself – her – Rosa Burger – as one of those whites who can care more for animals than people' (p. 210). She is unable to 'read' Zwelinzima when she meets him, seeing only a version of herself reflected in him, but in her self-criticism after the phone call, Rosa makes the shift from the arrogant authority of seeing-and-knowing to the humility of listening and insight.

The focus on how others see her and on how she sees herself reveals another important angle of vision in *Burger's Daughter*. The female subject – Rosa – is constructed in terms of the gaze: the male gaze, both public and private, and the mirror. The subject is divided,

constituted from the outside by the public gaze and by state surveillance ('When they saw me outside the prison, what did they see?'
[p. 13]), and from the inside by a subject alienated from her self ('I
couldn't bear to see myself – her – Rosa Burger – as one of those
whites' [p. 210]; 'To be free is to become almost a stranger to oneself;
the nearest I'll ever get to seeing what they saw outside the prison'
[p. 81]). The divided self is marked as female: it is a woman who
asks, what did they see when they saw me? 'I shall never know. It's
all concocted. I saw – see – that profile in a hand-held mirror directed
towards another mirror' (p. 14).

The motif of woman-and-mirror is repeated throughout the novel;
marking stages in Rosa's growth to autonomy. In France the alienation of the subject under double surveillance – state and self – disappears in the fullness of the love affair: 'In the bar where she had sat
seeing others living in the mirror, there was no threshold between
her reflection and herself' (p. 272); and, 'It's possible to live within
the ambit of a person not a country. . . . There's the possibility with
Chabalier, my Chabalier' (p. 302). However, the confrontation with
Zwelinzima Vulindlela reorients her self-vision away from this male-
centred 'awareness of her own being' (p. 272). Finally, the narcissism
that Rosa has rejected, the distortion of self in the mirror, is reflected
in the unicorn tapestry: 'On an azure island of a thousand flowers
the Lady is holding a mirror in which the unicorn . . . sees a tiny
image of himself. But the oval of the mirror cuts off the image just at
the level at which the horn rises from his head' (p. 340).

Rosa's divided self, the self split by the public and private gaze, is
resolved in a double gesture. The first is the conclusion of the internal dialogues that have punctuated the novel; the two 'conversations' with her father in the last part of the novel (pp. 328–32, 348–52)
mark the resolution of their relationship for Rosa and her acceptance
of her self. Not surprisingly in a realist novel, she is 'centred' in her
'self' (in the discourse of liberal humanism). The internal dialogue,
the silent reading of self and society, is displaced into writing, a
more public form of communication; the letter Rosa sends at the end
of the novel is written to a 'real person', another woman. The centred
individual moves out of the self-absorption of her scrutiny of the
meaning of freedom into political action to expand the meaning of
freedom, to make it concrete for others beyond herself. In prison she
takes up sketching in an inversion of the observer–image theme
throughout the novel. Her still-lifes are 'clumsy' and 'naive' and
show problems with perspective and light (p. 355) but, like the

patients she helps in the hospital, Rosa puts one foot in front of the other.

The emphasis on the father–daughter relationship, structurally foregrounded in numerous ways throughout the novel and at the end, in particular, by the internal dialogues, obscures the second gesture marking the repositioning of Rosa as subject. Rosa moves out of her orbit around men into self-affirmation in conjunction with other women. She reclaims the Otherness of femininity; that is, though socially positioned as Other in relation to men, she moves beyond that definition. This shift from an immobilizing awareness – and occasional fear – of the defining gaze of male interlocutors (the state, surveillance, journalists, father, 'brothers', lovers), to autonomous self-defining activity, is not, however, a deliberate feminist strategy rooted in gender-consciousness. It is, rather, one of the multiple deconstructive processes that occur in the novel in response to the pressures of the social and political conditions of South Africa. That is, by pushing at the limits of what she perceives as her fixed identity, Rosa repositions herself in a way that is compatible with, but not informed by, feminism.

Rosa's defection to Katya, to an exploration of private life, enables her to return, not just to her father/land, but also and just as importantly, to Marisa Kgosana, the wife of a black leader incarcerated on Robben Island. Rosa's relationship to Marisa before she defects is somewhat enigmatic, if not romanticized. Rosa meets Marisa by chance on the first anniversary of her father's death and the two women embrace:

> To touch in women's token embrace against the live, night cheek of Marisa, seeing huge for a second the lake-flash of her eye, the lilac-pink of her inner lip against translucent-edged teeth, to enter for a moment the invisible magnetic field of the body of a beautiful creature and receive on oneself its imprint – breath misting and quickly fading on a glass pane – this was to immerse in another mode of perception. As near as a woman can get to the transformation of the world a man seeks in the beauty of a woman. Marisa is black; near, then, as well, to the white way of using blackness as a way of perceiving a sensual redemption, as romantics do, or of perceiving fears, as racialists do. In my father's house, the one was seen as the obverse of the other, two sides of false consciousness – that much I can add to anyone's notes. But even in that house blackness was a sensuous–redemptive means

of perception. Through blackness is revealed the way to the future (pp. 134–5).

'Blackness was a sensuous–redemptive means of perception': Rosa must deconstruct this tenet of her childhood teachings into its component parts before she can reconstruct its meaning for herself. Though Marisa offers an immediate resolution of her dilemma to Rosa, Rosa backs off, runs away, in order to explore the meanings of 'sensuous', 'redemptive' and 'perception'. When Rosa meets Marisa after her father's death, she experiences a longing that is later differentiated into the child's for the mother and the lover's for complete union: 'I felt a dangerous surge of feeling, a precipitation towards Marisa. . . . A longing to attach myself to an acolyte destiny; to let someone else use me, lend me passionate purpose, propelled by meaning other than my own' (p. 155). Marisa embodies the charisma of sexuality, motherliness and revolutionary energy. Although Rosa is attracted by the sensuality and the community, she is unable to commit herself to the proposition: 'The vanity of being loved by and belonging with them offered itself. But I know it can't be taken for nothing. Offered freely – yet it has its price, that I would have to settle upon for myself' (p. 169). She is on her way to say goodbye to Marisa when she encounters the donkey; the farewell is never made. Instead she explores 'the vanity of being loved and of belonging' in France, where there is no obligation and where she comes freely to accept her connection with others, through the separate experiences of surrogate mothering, sisterhood and romantic love. Then she is able to return to South Africa and to a political sensuous–redemptive relationship with Marisa. Rosa's return to the black woman leader is understated, signalled, fittingly, by the state's intention to implicate Rosa in a major prosecution of 'Kgosana's wife' (p. 354). But concealed in this return is an important question: to what extent does Marisa, in her blackness, represent a romantic or exotic Other for Rosa?[6] Has Marisa simply replaced Bernard? The explicit link between the male gaze at the female beloved and the white female gaze at the sensuous black woman marks a disturbing alignment in the power of the gaze: white and male.

Rosa's positioning of herself is compatible to a certain extent with both liberalism and feminism. However, while the dominant political discourse in *Burger's Daughter* is that of revolutionary struggle (the discourses of the Communist Party, the African National Congress and the Black Consciousness Movement), the novel lacks a feminist discourse for analyzing the relationship between the political and the personal for women. But in the attention to detail that is one of the defining characteristics of realist fiction, the categories that are the foundation of the private sphere for the white bourgeoisie and of the social construction of female subjects – the nuclear family, heterosexual romance and marriage, the authority of the father – are deconstructed, destabilized. And these categories are destabilized by the place of black Africans, by the existence of a place beyond white Johannesburg, the place-not-mapped (by the white authorities) of black Africans. Where radical feminists would start with a critique of the categories of the personal for women, and move from the private to the public, *Burger's Daughter* begins with the public and an already-politicized private life. In the process of investigating the fusion of the political and the personal that is the condition of everyday life for the Burger family, the private is further deconstructed, as is absolutely necessary in a rigorous analysis of the conditions of white power – those that sustain it and those that undermine it.

Yet ultimately the novel's investigation is tentative. The privilege of whiteness, as Gordimer describes in 'Living in the Interregnum', enables a distance from the struggle against apartheid. She notes the undermining of the authority of the white I/eye. She identifies the fear for whites of 'being without structures', which reinforces the privileged distance from the struggle: 'however hated and shameful the collective life of apartheid and its structures has been to us, there is, now, the unadmitted fear of being without structures. The interregnum is not only between two social orders but also between two identities, one known and discarded, the other unknown and undetermined' (pp. 269–70). And finally, Gordimer admits that for her 'struggle is still something that has a place': 'Between black and white attitudes to struggle there stands the overheard remark of a young black woman: "I break the law because I am alive." We whites have still to thrust the spade under the roots of our lives; for most of us, including myself, struggle is still something that has a place. But for blacks it is everywhere or nowhere' (p. 271). *Burger's Daughter* explores the interregnum between two identities; Rosa moves into the unmapped place opened by the Soweto schoolchildren. The novel ends, as it begins, with a metaphor of the interregnum. In Rosa's letter to Katya, 'there was a reference to a watermark of light that came into the cell at sundown every evening, reflected from some west-facing surface outside; something Lionel Burger once mentioned. But the line had been deleted by the prison censor. Madame Bagnelli was never able to make it out' (p. 361). In 'Living in the Interregnum', Gordimer comments: "The sun that never set over one or other of the nineteenth-century colonial empires of the world is going down finally in South Africa' (p. 262). The watermark of light at sunset, like menstruation, 'that monthly crisis of destruction', signals that 'the old is dying'.[7]

Notes

1. Other discussions of Rosa Burger as a female political subject present differing critical (and ideological/political) perspectives regarding the significance of the intersection of race, gender and politics. See, for example, Boyers, Clingman, Liscio, Meese, Newman, Radhakrishnan, Visel, and Yelin.

2. Meese makes a similar point (p. 76). The connection between the female body and the sterility of white South African society is made quite explicit later in the novel when Rosa visits Brandt Vermeulen, an Afrikaner, and encounters a plastic female torso with 'anatomical novelties' (p. 189). The plastic representation of the headless female body with the transverse vulva is a grotesque caricature of female sexuality – reductive and non-reproductive. In contrast, in *A Sport of Nature* Hillela represents a fertile white female sexuality married to black male revolutionary power. Her sexuality becomes the route to politicization.

3. The reference to Adrienne Rich is not arbitrary. Rich credits *Burger's Daughter* as the source of her phrase 'an end to suffering' in 'Sources' in *Your Native Land, Your Life*, and in her essay 'Notes toward a Politics of Location' (1984), she traces a path similar to Rosa Burger's in coming to terms with her identity as a white woman. Echoing the epigraph to *Burger's Daughter*, she writes: 'I need to understand how a place on the map is also a place in history within which as a woman, a Jew, a lesbian, a feminist I am created and trying to create' (p. 212). Since Gordimer's reservations about Western feminism clearly refer to radical feminism, it is fascinating to note the shift in thinking of such a powerful radical feminist writer as Rich and the convergence in their concerns. It is also quite ironic that in the process Rich effectively implicates Gordimer in a feminist literary history.

4. The lion and Africa are linked in Gordimer's story 'A Lion on the Freeway'.

5. See Newman and Meese for interpretations of the unicorn tapestries based on the work of Erlande-Brandenburg.

6. Greenstein argues that Rosa's lapse into romanticizing Marisa is rectified in her reaction to the women's meeting convened by Flora Donaldson and that her affiliation with Marisa in prison at the end of

the novel is a relationship of 'genuine sorority' (p. 237). 'In *Burger's Daughter* and *July's People*', Greenstein argues, 'the white woman's adventure in Africa, which breaks the mold of the classic adventure tale, frees Gordimer to purge her fiction of the remnants of the age of imperialism' (p. 231). I am not sure that *Burger's Daughter* is completely purged of 'the quest of white for black' characteristic of the literature of empire (p. 227).

7.   As Lionel Burger is loosely modelled on Bram Fischer, Fischer's concluding comments in his statement from the dock (*The Sun Will Rise*, ed. Mary Benson, pp. 35–50), are of interest in relation to the metaphor of sunset. Just as Gordimer might have referred to menstruation as a metaphor for life rather than destruction, she might also have chosen sunrise over sunset. Fischer concluded his statement from the dock by quoting from a speech by President Kruger, 'one of the great Afrikaner leaders,' in 1881. The translation of the quote is: 'With confidence we lay our case before the whole world. Whether we win or die, freedom will rise in Africa, like the sun from the morning clouds' (p. 50).

Works Cited

Benson, Mary (ed.), *The Sun Will Rise: Statements from the Dock by Southern African Political Prisoners*, rev. edn (London: International Defence and Aid Fund for Southern Africa, 1981).

Boyers, Robert, 'Public and Private: On *Burger's Daughter*', *Salmagundi* 62 (1984): pp. 62–92.

Clingman, Stephen, *The Novels of Nadine Gordimer: History from the Inside*, (Raven: Johannesburg, 1986).

Erlande-Brandenburg, Alain, *La Dame à la Licorne* (Paris: Editions de la Réunion des Musées Nationaux, 1978).

Gordimer, Nadine, *Burger's Daughter* (1979: Harmondsworth: Penguin, 1980).

_____ , *July's People* (1981; Harmondsworth: Penguin, 1982).

_____ , 'A Lion on the Freeway', *A Soldier's Embrace* (Harmondsworth: Penguin, 1982), pp. 24–7.

_____ , 'Living in the Interregnum', *The Essential Gesture: Writing, Politics and Places*, ed. Stephen Clingman (1988; Harmondsworth: Penguin, 1989), pp. 261–84.

_____ , *A Sport of Nature* (1987; Harmondsworth: Penguin, 1988).

Greenstein, Susan M., 'Miranda's Story: Nadine Gordimer and the Literature of Empire'. *Novel: A Forum on Fiction* 18 (1985): pp. 227–42.

Jonas, Hans, 'The Nobility of Sight', *Philosophy and Phenomenological Research* 14 (1954): p. 513.

Keller, Evelyn Fox and Christine R. Grontkowski, 'The Mind's Eye', *Discovering Reality: Feminist Perspectives on Epistemology, Metaphysics, Methodology, and Philosophy of Science*, ed. Sandra Harding and Merrill B. Hintikka (Dordrecht, Holland: D. Reidel, 1983), pp. 207–24.

Liscio, Lorraine, '*Burger's Daughter*: Lighting a Torch in the Heart of Darkness', *Modern Fiction Studies* 33 (1987): pp. 245–61.

Meese, Elizabeth A., 'The Political Is the Personal: The Construction of a "Revolutionary Subject" in Nadine Gordimer's *Burger's Daughter*', *(Ex) Tensions: Re-Figuring Feminist Criticism* (Urbana: University of Illinois Press, 1990), pp. 50–77.

Newman, Judie, *Nadine Gordimer* (London: Routledge, 1988).

Radhakrishnan, R., 'Negotiating Subject Positions in an Uneven World', in *Feminism and Institutions: Dialogues on Feminist Theory*, ed. Linda Kauffman (Oxford: Blackwell, 1989), pp. 276–90.

Rich, Adrienne, 'Notes toward a Politics of Location', *Blood, Bread, and Poetry: Selected Prose 1979–1985* (New York: Norton, 1986), pp. 210–31.

_____, *Your Native Land, Your Life* (New York: Norton, 1986).

Visel, Robin, 'Othering the Self: Nadine Gordimer's Colonial Heroines', *ARIEL: A Review of International English Literature* 19.4 (1988): pp. 33–42.

Yelin, Louise, 'Exiled In and Exiled From: The Politics and Poetics of *Burger's Daughter*', in *Women's Writing in Exile*, ed. Mary Lynn Broe and Angela Ingram (Chapel Hill: University of North Carolina Press, 1989), pp. 396–411.

9

Making Metaphors/ Moving On: *Burger's Daughter* and *A Sport of Nature*

SUSAN WINNETT

I

Soon after its publication in June 1979, *Burger's Daughter* was banned by the South African Director of Publications. After a month of international protest that received considerable attention in both South African and foreign newspapers, the Director of Publications appealed against his own committee's ban and commissioned both a special board of literary experts to review the book and an expert on state security to issue a separate report on the threat the novel represented to the safety of the State. The literary experts overturned the decision of the censorship committee, charging it with 'bias, prejudice, and literary incompetence' (WHBD, p. 1); the expert on state security decided the novel represented no threat to the State. After *Burger's Daughter* was unbanned, Gordimer persisted in documenting the affair in a publication entitled 'What Happened to *Burger's Daughter'*. By refusing to accept the government's 'rehabilitation' of her novel, Gordimer insisted upon its controversiality; just because the State was forced to reverse its ban does not mean that the novel is any less subversive than it was originally perceived to be. And indeed, it was in order repeatedly to provoke the mutual interrogation of narrative and political authority thematized in the novel that Gordimer documented her experiences with the censors.

Gordimer has written that *Burger's Daughter* is about the 'human conflict between the desire to live a personal, private life, and the rival claim of social responsibility to one's fellow men' (WHBD, p. 17). Her fiction is the site of a related conflict between writing psychological novels about middle-class white South Africans like herself and dedicating her writing to a political struggle that is – to put it mildly – not concerned with such luxuries as the psychologies of middle-class white people. Both the historical moment recorded in *Burger's Daughter* – the rise of the Black Consciousness movement – and its polyvocal narrative call into question the authority of any narrative faithfully to chronicle this conflict, partly because to assume narrative authority means – whether intentionally or not – to silence other voices, and partly because the whole story will always also be the story of a reception a text can anticipate but not guarantee. It is relatively easy for Gordimer to orchestrate the novel's many voices – Rosa's, the impartial third person narrator, the narrative of surveillance – in such a way that the novel testifies eloquently to the impossibility of the kind of totalizing knowledge that allows the apartheid state to declare with such obscene certainty what is black, what is white, what is coloured, and what to do with these distinctions. She has far less control over the voices that will respond to the novel, since her nuanced provocation forces the monolith apartheid to return her attacks by wielding its authority to determine in what ways and to whom a novel is a political event. Gordimer's refusal to appeal the original decision to ban the novel is emblematic of this bind: she would make her appeal only to the authority of common law, because she wanted her text to engage directly the same forces of oppression it names. When the state chooses to subject *Burger's Daughter* to a different tribunal, the story of what happened to the novel *Burger's Daughter* enters into a complicated dialogue with the story of what happens to the character whose name and situation it takes for its title. To ask the question 'What will happen to *Burger's Daughter*?' is to raise an issue Gordimer takes up in her penultimate novel, *A Sport of Nature*: what will happen to the novel when the realization of its political imperative – or even tomorrow's step toward this realization – might render a South African novel about a Burger's daughter an anachronism, a contradiction in terms, even reactionary self-indulgence?

'Imagine, a schoolgirl: she must have somebody inside' (p. 9). The novel begins with a description of a group of people outside a prison, their arms filled with parcels of clothes for last night's harvest of detainees. The schoolgirl Rosa Burger does indeed have someone inside: her mother, a Communist opponent of apartheid. Several pages after the third-person narrative voice presents this scenario and introduces us to the Rosa Burger known to her classmates and their parents, Rosa takes over the narrative, describing what was happening to her that day. Describing what no outsider could have seen:

> But real awareness is all focussed in the lower part of my pelvis, in the leaden, dragging, writhing pain there. . . . [O]utside the prison the internal landscape of my mysterious body turns me inside out, so that in the public place on that public occasion . . . I am within that monthly crisis of destruction, the purging, tearing, draining of my own structure. (*BD*, p. 16)

'Imagine, a schoolgirl. She must have somebody inside.' Rosa already knows about revolution, 'the crisis of destruction, the purging, tearing, draining of [a] structure', but this consciousness is not what the partisans see when they look at her, nor is it the kind of experience her parents' generation of revolutionaries consider politically relevant. For the world that will publish her mother's arrest, try and imprison her father, ban her, as well as read and ban *Burger's Daughter*, Rosa's experience is indeed 'inside out'. And yet the novel insists upon the authority of Rosa's insides and on the private process through which she formulates what she calls 'the metaphors for suffering' that will govern her public attempts to bring suffering to an end. But like *Burger's Daughter* itself, Rosa Burger is also in search of the audience that will test her authority to tell the story of that somebody inside: inside her body, inside South Africa, inside history, and at the end, inside the prison and thereby, back inside both her family plot and that of revolution.

Halfway through the novel, Rosa has an experience that deprives her of the authority to tell the kinds of stories and formulate the metaphors with which we attempt to assimilate the suffering we hope never to know to something we do know that we remember as suffering. Rosa, who has watched her mother die of MS, seen her brother drown, and witnessed her father's trial, conviction, and death through medical neglect 2 1/2 years into a life sentence, sees a poor, ragged black man beating his donkey:

> I didn't see the whip. I saw agony. . . . Not seeing the whip, I saw the infliction of pain broken away from the will that creates it; broken loose, a force existing of itself, ravishment without the ravisher, torture without the torturer, rampage, pure cruelty gone

beyond control of the humans who have spent thousands of years devising it. (*BD*, p. 208)

All of a sudden even the political narratives and the metaphors that had made sense for her of the suffering – her own, and that of those whose cause was her entire inheritance – lose their authority because she, Rosa, the white woman, could have put a stop to the donkey's misery by handing a black man over to the police, a man about whose story she knew nothing.

> I could formulate everything they were, as the act I had witnessed; they would have their lives summed up for them officially at last by me, the white woman – the final meaning of a day they had lived I had no knowledge of, a day of other appalling things, violence, disasters, urgencies, deprivations which suddenly would become, was nothing but what it had led up to: the man among them beating the donkey. (*BD*, p. 209).

Rosa knows that telling this story calls into question her authority to tell all stories. Her education has given her a litany of general explanations for the awful spectacle, but none of them give her a clue as to what she should do: 'they would have been afraid of me. I could have put a stop to it, with them, at no risk to myself . . . I was safe from the whip. I could have stood between them and suffering – the suffering of the donkey.' There is no place for her in the story she has entered *in medias res*. She decides to leave South Africa. 'Earth, guts – I don't know what metaphors to use to describe the process by which I'm making my own metaphors for suffering' (*BD*, p. 196).

Gordimer has repeatedly described the 'interregnum' of contemporary South Africa in Gramsci's formulation: 'The old is dying and the new cannot be born.' In a television interview with Susan Sontag, she responded to Sontag's doubts that an artistically successful novel can take politics – indeed, any contemporary problem – as its subject by explaining that she has had no choice and has never felt a conflict between what Sontag was calling 'aesthetic' or 'modernist' criteria and the issues we expect to encounter in her fiction: 'I don't choose apartheid as a subject. I write about what I know and feel and see. [Apartheid] is in the air I breathe, in the bus, in the cinema, at the library. It seeks me, I don't seek it.' The writer who sees art as a world elsewhere, a retreat from a modernity of political struggle, will want to protect her perfect prose from the messy language of debate and dissent, the misspelled manifesti of the Soweto Students Representative Union that Gordimer reprints in *Burger's Daughter*, as well as from those excruciating situations that challenge the boundaries we draw between right and wrong, art and life. Yet these are precisely the situations that Rosa Burger – and her creator – need in order to discover the 'metaphors for suffering' that help determine what to make of their lives and privilege.

Both Gordimer's notion of the 'interregnum' and Rosa's preoccupation with the process of making metaphors anticipate change, without knowing when or how this change will come. *Burger's Daughter* is about the stories we can tell while we're waiting (and working toward) a new beginning. In this sense, the novel can only rehearse possibilities, prepare individuals for the end of the interregnum. Will the Marxism of Rosa's father, Lionel Burger, create a state which has abolished the economic oppression that makes poor black men beat their donkeys? Or will whites, even Marxist martyrs to the cause like Lionel Burger, be expelled so that poor black men won't be subject to the racial oppression that makes them beat their donkeys? Or do men of all colours, rich and poor, beat whatever creatures are weak enough to be their donkeys? Something is going to happen, but, as Gordimer says of the present, 'You don't know what to build a sense of continuity on.' She continues, 'I have to rack my brains to think of something I'd like to see preserved in South Africa.'

With this, I think we have to see Gordimer's recognition that the institution of the white novelist may well fall victim to her own cry for revolution. On the other hand, it is only in the fictions of a community of South African visionaries, black and white, that she can build the sense of continuity that is necessary in order to imagine and register political and social change. But she also recognizes that this sense of continuity, because it is a fiction, must remain subject to revision, reimagination, or far more violent upheavals. We see this, in fact, in Rosa Burger's career. It is taken for granted that she will continue her parents' work. Indeed, the torch was handed to her so early in life that everyone assumes that the plot of radical dissent will dictate her as it seemed to dictate everything her parents did. But when Rosa's father dies in prison, Rosa 'defects'. The story of her defection, from the movement, from Lionel Burger, from South Africa, and ultimately from defection itself, culminates with a reunion in London with a militant black separatist whom Rosa knew as

Baasie when Lionel adopted him as a boy. Baasie lived with the Burgers and was closer to Rosa than her own brother until he disappeared from her life. After the party, Baasie phones her late at night and subjects her, her life, and her politics to a brutal verbal assault. In the light of his tirade, Rosa must ask herself anew: what can she, a white, middle-class, South African woman do, and for whom is she doing it? Is she now in the place of the donkey, being tongue-lashed by a victim of what she saw then as 'other appalling things, violence, disasters, urgencies, deprivations' that her father's programs, the righteousness of well-intentioned whites thought would keep the blacks from turning on them? Rosa writes, 'In one night we succeeded in maneuvering ourself into the position their history books back home have had ready for us – him bitter; me guilty' (*BD*, p. 330). All the Burgers' attempts at living different plots and telling different stories before the next chapter can be written in the history books are overridden by the text of apartheid. Rosa gets off the phone and vomits. As in the scene outside the prison, the political subject is a body in revolt.

Rosa takes her body back to South Africa, where she resumes work as a physical therapist. Like her father, she works in a hospital for blacks, putting children's bodies back together. Unlike her father, she serves, rather than leads, a movement whose 'ideology' is in the making, rather than preformulated and imposed from without:

> No one can defect. I don't know the ideology. It's about suffering. How to end suffering.
> And it ends in suffering. Yes, it's arrange to live in a country where there are still heroes. Like everyone else, I do what I can. I am teaching them to walk again. . . . They put one foot before the other. (*BD*, p. 332)

If Rosa is 'teaching' the children 'to walk again', they are determining the direction of the movement:

> The old phrases crack and meaning shakes out wet and new. They seem to know what is to be done. They don't go to school any more and they are being 'constantly reeducated by their political activity.' The parents . . . have been radicalized – as the faithful would say – by their children. . . . The real Rosa [Luxemburg] believed the real revolutionary initiative was to come from the people. . . . This time it's coming from the children of the people,

teaching the fathers – the ANC, BPC, PAC, all of them, all acronyms hastening to claim, to catch up, *the theory chasing events.* (pp. 348–9, emphasis mine)

During the midnight telephone call, Baasie tells her that his name is not the Afrikans, Baasie, but Zwelinzima, which means 'suffering land'. This too, is a metaphor for the suffering, but it's not of Rosa's making; she can hardly pronounce it; it is not the name of her Baasie, her childhood. She cannot be the author of all the metaphors for suffering; she is not part of the same process that gave Zwelinzima his name, nor is her history the same as the process that made Lionel Burger dedicate his life to the same battle she has begun again to wage. Gordimer's epigraph to *Burger's Daughter* is Lévi-Strauss's statement, 'I am a place where something has happened.' What Rosa and the reader of the novel recognize is that even within a culture where one thing – apartheid – is happening with such prominence and violence, its occasion in each individual is different, an intersection of plots both self-generated and inflicted from without. She may share the goals of the 1976 children's uprising, but she has not had their experience: 'They can't spell and they can't formulate their elation and anguish. But they know why they're dying.' She can help them 'put one foot before the other', but she can't tell them where to go. Nor can she tell their story. *Burger's Daughter* is profoundly aware of the limits of which stories it is entitled to tell.

II

Through the process of 'defection' which the novel chronicles, Rosa generates and takes possession of her own metaphors for suffering so that the jail sentence she is serving at the end of the novel is truly her own and not simply an extension of her father's or mother's. Yet in a world of 'acronyms hastening to claim, to catch up, the theory chasing events' (*BD*, p. 348), the activity of metaphor-making identifies Rosa with the racial and class privilege that assumes that the individual can indeed take possession of her actions, that one's *own* metaphors are worth making: 'Earth, guts – I don't know what metaphors to use to describe the process by which I'm making my own metaphors for suffering' (p. 196). Rosa needs *metaphors to describe the process of making metaphors.* For a character so caught up in a political process into which she was born, this act of taking stock

by making metaphors to describe the process of coming to consciousness – which in Rosa's case means appropriating the spectacle
of pain for herself – is crucial, and Gordimer uses this process of
metaphor-making to chart the development in the novel of a personal commitment. Rosa's metaphors enable us to recognize her
voice in the chorus of inmates that ends the novel. They distinguish
the particular individual within a collective process of revolution
which, however – and this is the point I want to stress – is as
essentially non-metaphoric as it must be impersonal. Rosa's bourgeois origins and limitations are manifested in her need for metaphors to describe both process and pain; the Soweto students, in
whose movement (in both senses of the word) Rosa gets caught up
in upon her return, seem not to need the metaphors for metaphor-
making that characterize the white South African's negotiation between self and society: 'They can't spell and they can't formulate
their elation and anguish. But they know why they're dying.' Rosa
takes her place within their plot, their movement, and while she
never stops making metaphors for suffering for herself, the final
chapters of the novel suggest that they have become entirely irrelevant to the process to which she has rededicated herself, or that
they are relevant only to the extent that they enable her to function
within a plot of someone else's making. As *Burger's Daughter* resolves Rosa Burger's quest for her place in the struggle against
apartheid, it raises the question of whether or not the struggle can be
hers at all.

Gordimer published *Burger's Daughter* at the end of the seventies,
a period in which a large number of South African blacks rejected
the African National Congress's conviction that whites can opt out
of class and race privilege and identify with black liberation. At the
end of the decade in which the Black Consciousness movement
refused any affiliation with whites whatsoever, Desmond Tutu wrote:

Whites unfortunately have the habit of taking over and usurping
the leadership and taking the crucial decisions – largely, I suppose, because of the head start they had in education and experience . . . of this kind. The point is that however much they want to
identify with blacks it is an existential fact . . . that they have really
not been victims of this baneful oppression and exploitation. . . . It
is a divide that can't be crossed and that must give blacks a
primacy in determining the course and goal of the struggle. Whites
must be willing to follow. (*EG*, p. 267)

The South African poet, Mongane Wally Serote, has said the same
thing in a way that delineates the specific challenge to the white
South African writer dedicated to the abolition of apartheid: 'Blacks
must learn to talk; whites must learn to listen' (*EG*, p. 267). Metaphors for suffering no longer confer upon their makers the authority
to narrate the plot of change; only an experience of pain that the very
fact of whiteness would seem to deny to whites can, in Tutu's words
'determine what will be the priorities and strategies of the struggle'.
Now the role of follower and listener cannot come easily to a writer
of novels, who is by nature and practice a maker and articulator of
plots. And yet, the first step in the white author's compliance with
the imperatives of the 'order struggling to be born' with which she
identifies would be to follow the dictates of those she acknowledges
as her future leaders.

III

Much as Rosa Burger finds that her work for the revolution requires
that she surrender the authority for scripting its plot that was her
father's way of participating in the struggle she rejoins, Gordimer
too writes with the awareness that the accomplishment of the vision
informing her novels might well result in her own exile or disenfranchisement. As Zwelinzima's (Baasie's) rage suggests, *Burger's Daughter* runs the risk of being banned again by those inheritors of the
unspecifiable future to which Gordimer has committed herself. Indeed, Rosa herself has been banished to the margins of Gordimer's
1987 novel, *A Sport of Nature*, where she has a walk-on role so
minimal that it can only be calling attention to the relative insigni-
ficance of her plot among the many vying for the authority to forge
a new South Africa:

> A girl younger than Hillela was brought to the house by Joe; but
> a schoolgirl with the composure of someone much older. On her
> the drab of school uniform was not a shared identity but a con-
> vention worn like a raincoat thrown over the shoulders. She turned
> the attention of a clear smile when spoken to yet, as an adult gets
> out of the way polite acknowledgement of the presence of chil-
> dren, firmly returned the concentration of her grey eyes to Joe,
> who read through documents those eyes were following from
> familiarity with the contents. . . . The girl drank fruit juice and ate

steadily without a break in the span of the room's preoccupation, while Pauline hovered with small services in the graceful alertness of a cocktail party hostess.

– D'you know who that was? – Pauline came into the bedroom where Carole and Hillela had holed up.

– Daddy said. Rose somebody. I see she goes to Eastridge High. Horrible school. –

Pauline's vivid expression waited for its import to be comprehended.

– That's Rosa Burger. Both her parents are in prison. – (*SN*, pp. 23–4)

Gordimer herself has already made something new happen to Burger's daughter.

The novel in which Rosa reappears as the 'schoolgirl . . . [who has] somebody inside' of the first pages of *Burger's Daughter* and then disappears again almost entirely eschews the exploration of individual subjectivity in order to pursue a double project: *A Sport of Nature* both tells the particular story of a white South African woman and realizes the process in which South Africa blacks author and star in their own revolution. If *Burger's Daughter* is about positioning and repositioning – making metaphors about the process of making metaphors, *A Sport of Nature* is about change as it becomes revolution-in-progress and its incompatibility with the metaphor-making that gives the white liberal subject the luxury of figuring out ever anew who she is and where she stands. Hillela, the novel's protagonist, is uncannily able to outgrow metaphors; she is, as the novel puts it, someone who can 'move on'. Hillela – her last name is as irrelevant as Rosa Burger's was decisive – has none of the compelling family, social, and political allegiances that bind a character like Rosa to plots that predate her. In the words of one of the aunts with whom Hillela spends her youth, '[s]he's amoral. I mean, in the sense of the morality of this country. – ' (*SN*, p. 44). This amorality enables Hillela to venture through the world without the preconceptions that paralyze the South African bourgeoisie on both the right and the left. Hillela is Gordimer's child of the South African 'interregnum', '[t]he white . . . [who] does not know his place "in history" at this time' (*EG*, p. 276). She honors neither conventional taboos nor sentimental ties for their own sake. What she carries with her of the past is that which speaks to the demands of the current situation.

A Sport of Nature is a picaresque charting the exploits of a woman with an enormous heterosexual appetite and the talent to satisfy it, and many – in fact, most – of the situations Hillela so deftly navigates are erotic, or begin as erotic situations. Expelled from boarding school for dating a coloured boy, expelled from the home of her activist aunt and uncle for sleeping with her cousin, Hillela leaves South Africa because her lover is apparently in political trouble. When he disappears, she becomes one of the regulars in an exile community, where she sleeps with a revolutionary leader, the Belgian ambassador, and a melancholy German economic adviser – among others. This promiscuous curriculum vitae culminates in her falling in love with, marrying, and having a child with Whaila Kgomane, an ANC leader-in-exile whose political confidante she gradually becomes. When he is assassinated by South African government agents, Hillela dedicates her life to his cause, working (and having affairs) in England, in Eastern Europe, and finally in the United States. She becomes a prominent spokeswoman for African aid agencies, and seems about to marry a New York yuppie and settle into a brownstone existence when, on a trip to Africa, she begins sleeping with Reuel, a general who had led an army coup in his country, returned it to civilian rule under his presidency, escaped the counterinsurgents of the former colonial power, and is in the process of plotting what will be his successful return to power. Hillela becomes Reuel's closest political confidante and his deftest operative, someone 'who could keep abreast of him, moving on' (*SN*, p. 269). As a member of Reuel's revolution, Hillela unites the personal and the political: she can transform the pain of Whaila's death into a crusade 'to get rid of it' (*SN*, p. 268).

Even, however, as Hillela's passions become increasingly – the narrative even ponders, exclusively – political, Gordimer insists upon keeping track of her erotic plot. Reuel's meditation on his revolution and her sexuality is characteristic of the novel's persistent dual focus:

> The language of their intimacy was as much the terse anguish when supply lines of ammunition broke down . . . as it was love-talk. Her sexuality, evident to every man watching her pass as he sat in the bush oiling his gun, or stood at attention for review before the General, was part of the General's command. For him it seemed to grow, to be revealed with the success of his push towards the real capital. Her small, generous, urging, inventive

body was the deserts of success; some bodies are made only for consolation, their sweetness touched with decay. But he had known from the first time he made love with her that that was only an experience of her possibilities – without realizing exactly what these would turn out to be. (*SN*, p. 283)

Hillela's body as the experience of revolution? As the analogue for a new kind of novel that is writing toward the 'experience of possibilities – without realizing exactly what these would turn out to be'? The narrative continues:

Everyone has some cache of trust, while everything else – family love, love of fellow man – takes on suspect interpretations. In her, it seemed to be sexuality. However devious she might have to be (he realized he did not know why she should have wanted to be chosen by him) and however she had to accept deviousness in others, in himself – she drew upon the surety of her sexuality as the bread of her being. (*SN*, p. 283)

The novel registers human bodies minutely: breasts, penises, hands, facial lines, toes, and hair perform the function in this novel that the African landscape performs in so much of Gordimer's early work. Rosa Burger's metaphors for suffering originate in 'earth and guts'; the story of Hillela registers the metonyms of the human body as they register each other, touch, pass in and out of each other, age. Whereas understanding and knowledge are the goals of the narrative voices of *Burger's Daughter*, the narration of *A Sport of Nature* seems content to represent what it knows and claim ignorance of what it doesn't. What we see of Hillela's political and personal development is unabashedly linked to the succession of men with whom she sleeps. Yet the ignorance of her motivations and movements that the narrative repeatedly claims forces us to wonder whether the story that has been put together for us is a story of her life that the novel's protagonist would recognize.

Nor, in the final analysis, is it important why Hillela has done what she has done or whether any particular event is told the way it happened. What is important in *A Sport of Nature* is that South Africa gets liberated. Its protagonist does not end up in jail, contemplating a spot of reflected western light on the prison wall that her father must also have seen. In the final scene of *A Sport of Nature*, Hillela is attending the ceremony proclaiming the 'new African state that used to be South Africa' (*SN*, p. 337). She is there, a white woman, at the side of her black husband, who is the Chairman of the Organization of African Unity. The 'Western-style military drums' are 'beaten out by the tremendous blows of African drums' (*SN*, p. 330). It is important to note that the process that led to the liberation of her native land has nothing to do with anything Hillela herself has done – or has been shown to do in the novel. Her husband's government has helped the South African black leaders, and she has helped her husband, but the novel refuses us the specifics of the process. It shows us, in place of the private dream of the 'rainbow family' she envisaged creating with her first husband Whaila, a panoply of splendid colours, of flags, banners, and costumes that share a celebration one day and represent conflicting interests the next. In the aftermath of Whaila's assassination, Hillela realized the deception of any individual attempt to invent 'a category that doesn't exist', a family of children who are, as she put it, 'our colour'. The 'rainbow family', the fantasy of a white Jewish South African princess with a knack for survival, is a political reality of starving and dying bodies that cannot be wished away by a white woman and a black man who love each other:

> The real rainbow family stinks. The dried liquid of dysentery streaks the legs of the babies and old men and the women smell of their monthly blood. They smell of lack of water. They smell of lack of food. They smell of bodies blown up by the expanding gases of their corpses' innards, lying in the bush in the sun. (*SN*, p. 251)

If this is a 'metaphor for the suffering', it has an entirely different valence than those metaphors Rosa Burger was formulating for herself, 'because this metaphor has neither to do with Hillela's need to figure out who she is nor with what we would call a private life – of that we see precious little in the novel. It is, instead, a useful representation of a past that 'is not a haunting, but was a preparation, put to use' (*SN*, p. 341).

A Sport of Nature is preoccupied with bodies because apartheid is preoccupied with bodies. Hillela muses that the political exiles on Tamarind Beach 'have no home – not out of clumsiness, a tendency to break what is precious – but because they are brave and believe in the other kinds of love, justice, fellow man – and inside each other, making love, that's the only place we can make, here, that's not just a place to stay'. The reason for their homelessness, and thus for the need of the desperate carnal consolation she describes, is that their *other* home has decided, on the basis of bodies, whom it will harbour and how. Lying next to Whaila, Rosa

> examines his body minutely and without shame, and he wakes to see her at it, and smiles without telling her why: she is the first not to pretend the different colours and textures of their being is not an awesome fascination. How can it be otherwise? The laws that have determined the course of life for them are made of skin and hair, the relative thickness and thinness of lips and the relative height of the nose. That is all; that is everything. . . . The stinking fetish made of contrasting bits of skin and hair, the scalping of millions of lives, dangles on the cross in place of Christ. It has mattered more than anything else in the world. (*SN*, p. 178)

The personal begins with the body and is political. And the political is the only personal that matters to Nadine Gordimer until every South African is a person in the same way. Hillela is sufficiently the bourgeois subject to support a narrative about her life. But this narrative is in the service both of a new non-bourgeois subject and a yet unrealized form of the novel that will chronicle it. Unlike *Burger's Daughter*'s eponymous heroine, whose name ties her to the claims of her roles as daughter, citizen, Afrikaner, woman, Marxist, Hillela is a 'sport of nature' which, the epigraph informs us, is '[a] plant, animal, etc. which exhibits abnormal variation or a departure from the parent stock or type . . . a spontaneous mutation, a new variety produced in this way'. *A Sport of Nature* represents an attempt at a new novelistic undertaking that calls into question the importance of the personal life and the metaphor-making of the individual. The novel is too much the institution of the personal story and Gordimer is too much the child of the Interregnum for her altogether to abandon its traditional foci. But by wrenching our attention away from her protagonist's emotional life and forcing us to watch the body that is its vehicle, she both shows us the facts of colour and skin that make political action necessary and frees her narrative from the metaphor-making that impedes this action. At the end of *A Sport of Nature*, as the flag of Whaila's country 'writhes one last time and flares wide in the wind, is smoothed taut by the fist of the wind', the narrative muses: 'It . . . may be true that a life is always moving – without being aware of this or what the moment may be and by a compass not available to others – towards a moment' (*SN*, p. 341). Elsewhere Gordimer has written: 'The black knows he will be at home, at last, in the future. The white who has declared himself or herself for that future, who belongs to that white segment that was never at home in white supremacy, does not know whether he will find his home at last' (*EG*, p. 270). This white person is in the position of those political exiles whom Hillela described as at home only in their own fleeting pleasure, 'making love, that's the only place we can make, here, that's not just a place to stay'. For Gordimer, this small and temporary place of pleasure and its narrative is what's legitimately left to the personal story for whites who are discovering what it means to live in a body that is defined as coloured.

Works Cited

Gordimer, Nadine, *Burger's Daughter* (Harmondsworth: Penguin, 1979) (abbreviated in text as *BD*).

Gordimer, Nadine, *What Happened to 'Burger's Daughter'* (Emmarentia, SA; Taurus, 1980). (*WHBD*)

Gordimer, Nadine, *A Sport of Nature* (New York: Knopf, 1987). (*SN*).

Gordimer, Nadine, *The Essential Gesture: Writing, Politics, and Places* (New York: Knopf, 1988). (*EG*)

10

A Sport of Nature: Identity and Repression of the Jewish Subject

MICHAEL WADE

Any exploration of the Jewish theme in Nadine Gordimer's writing, especially her novels, is an exploration of the absent, the unwritten, the repressed.

The significance of this statement may be better understood if we try to imagine the works of a Bellow, a Roth or a Malamud with the same lack of attention to Jewishness as Gordimer paid – up to the publication of *A Sport of Nature*.[1] Gordimer's creative and political milieus, so far as these were white, were Jewish in much the same way as the world of progressive politics or literary culture in the main urban centres of the eastern seaboard of the United States possessed elements of a Jewish character from the 1930s through the end of the 1960s – in other words, Jewishness functioning as a mysterious but ineluctable cultural component of individual identity and expressed as an aspect of the nominally Jewish writer's particular, unique quest for identity in a heterogeneous society.

Gordimer was born in 1923, and the first seventeen years of her life saw the South African Jewish community grow rapidly both in numbers and in proportion to the rest of the white population. This increase was almost entirely the result of developments in Eastern and Central Europe, which led to accelerated emigration of Jews living in the Soviet Union and the former Austro-Hungarian empire. The highest proportionate level, 4.5 per cent, was measured in the 1936 census. In 1938 the South African government closed the country to Jewish immigration from Europe. When Gordimer was born the vast majority of the 70 000–80 000 Jews living in South Africa – probably more than 80 per cent of them – were either themselves immigrants from Lithuania or the children of such immigrants. Nadine Gordimer's father came to South Africa from Lithuania. Her mother was a rarity on the South African scene; she was an English Jewess. As she grew up in the South African Jewish community, Nadine Gordimer was subject to assimilationist pressures emanating mainly from her socially ambitious mother. During this period the Jewish community was moving rapidly up the social scale, though the fundamental direction of its self-identification in the racially-divided South African community was inwards.

Apart from a few short stories, mostly emphasizing painful or embarrassing (to the writer) aspects of Jewishness or analogous immigrant experience, only minor characters in Gordimer's novels since her first, *The Lying Days*, up to *A Sport of Nature* have been designatedly Jewish – except Antonia Mancebo in *The Conservationist*, and she is an empty space in the central character Mehring's perception of the landscape. The most remarkable thing about Antonia is her absence. The reasons for this unusually powerful mechanism of concealment in a body of work whose telos is to reveal, may be sought in the circumstances of time and place in which it was produced, in the personal history of the producer of the work, and in the interactions between these two categories.

John Cooke[2] in his 1985 study which uses more biographical material than had hitherto been fashionable or possible, sketches a scenario of repressed conflict in Gordimer's parents' home as she grew up. Her ambitious Anglo-Jewish mother wished to integrate into suburban middle-class Gentile English-speaking society in the Witwatersrand mining town of Springs; this ambition must have been to an extent frustrated by the fact that Gordimer's father, the immigrant Jew from Lithuania, certainly spoke Yiddish as his mother-tongue, English with an accent, and no doubt possessed a different view of the English-speaking (and seeming?) suburban ideal from that held by his wife. In her first collection of short stories to appear in the United States, *The Soft Voice of the Serpent*,[3] published in 1952, Gordimer included no fewer than four stories presenting Jewish identity or experience as highly problematic. In the following year she published her first novel, the *bildungsroman*, *The Lying Days*. In it she resolves the emotional conflicts associated with Jewishness in the earlier stories by making one of her major characters, Joel Aaron, who is Jewish and a Zionist and notable for his integrity and intelligence, leave to live in Israel at the end of the book. The emotional intensity associated with Jewish identity then dies down for a long time in her work, and disappears from the novels as distinct from the short fiction.

I want to focus on the relationship between this 'resolution' and one of the most anguished and complexly structured of the Jewish stories in *The Soft Voice of the Serpent*, called, unambiguously, 'The Defeated'. The story, like *The Lying Days*, is set in a small mining town on the Witwatersrand, and much of it takes place in an area described in the opening passage of *The Lying Days* – the cluster of mine-compound stores run on a concession basis, mostly by Jewish immigrants from Eastern Europe, for the patronage of black goldminers. Its timespan covers the period of mass Jewish immigration prompted by the Russian Pale of Settlement laws of 1883 to the later stage where the Jewish community had stabilized in numbers and the first generation born in South Africa was energetically pursuing the rewards of upward mobility.[4]

In the opening sequence of *The Lying Days* Gordimer presents the stores as a taboo area, forbidden to Helen Shaw by her parents and in addition charged with hints of precocious sexuality. In 'The Defeated' the story opens with an identical delineation of the topography; the young girl, like Helen Shaw in the opening passage of *The Lying Days*, defies her mother's ban because 'I felt that life was going on down there at the Concession stores'. There one day she meets a child in her class at school, a pretty girl called Miriam Saiyetovitz, whose parents run one of the stores, and who apparently takes her unsuitable surroundings for granted.

The narrator and Miriam become friends and the friendship persists through high school and university, where both study to become teachers. War breaks out; the narrator enlists and trains as a nurse, serving in North Africa; she hears that Miriam has meanwhile married a doctor. Back in her home town, on an impulse she goes to visit the Saiyetovitz parents at their Concession store.

When his wife had gone into the back of the shop to refill my teacup, old Saiyetovitz went silent. . . .
. . .
And then he told me that they had seen Miriam's little boy only three times since he was born. Miriam they saw hardly at all; her husband never. Once or twice a year she came out from Johannesburg to visit them. . . . She had not invited her parents to her home at any time; they had been there only once, on the occasion of the birth of their grandson.[5]

The narrator's response to the Saiyetovitzes' abandonment and defeat is, in the context of the story, unexpected and even gratuitous. 'I stood there in Miriam's guilt before the Saiyetovitzes, and they were silent, in the accusation of the humble.'

How do we account for the narrator's unexpected guilt, and the equally surprising suggestion that she is the target of the 'accusation of the humble'? The puzzlingly close identification by the narrator of herself with Miriam is, I think, meant to suggest just that: Miriam is a version of the narrator, they are doubles, the difference between them is Gordimer's necessary artistic mask for relating this experience. Miriam's punishment of her parents for their otherness is severe and complete, and conceals Gordimer's own desire to avenge her sense of displacement on her parents for their otherness. Gordimer is highly specific in her identification of the source of this otherness. Here is her description of Miriam's mother:

> Ugly, with the blunt ugliness of a toad; the ugliness of seeming not entirely at home in any element – as if the earth were the wrong place, too heavy and magnetic for a creature already so blunt. . . . And yet her ugliness was without repellence. . . . She was only ugly. She had the short, stunted yet heavy bones of generations of oppression in the Ghettos of Europe; breasts, stomach, hips crowded sadly, no height, wide strong shoulders and a round back.[6]

The frustrated, helpless fury scarcely concealed as the energizing force of this description is also present but handled very differently in the presentation of Joel Aaron's mother in *The Lying Days*.

> Her body in a cheap silk dress that had the remains of an elaboration of black cotton lace and fagoted trimming round the neck was the incredibly small-hipped, thickened body of Jewish women from certain parts of Europe, the swollen doll's body from which it seems impossible that tall sons and daughters can, and do, come. The floral pattern of the apron she wore was rubbed away over the bulge of her breasts and her stomach. . . .[7]

The crucial difference between Miriam and Joel is that one rejects her parents and her background while the other not only accepts his but does so effortlessly and naturally. In these two characters, so widely divided in their answers to the question of identity, Gordimer was testing possible resolutions to her own acute uncertainty in this respect. Joel and Miriam have identical starting points: both are children of lower middle-class, 'simple' Jewish immigrants from Eastern Europe who have failed to pick up the fabled gold from the pavements of Africa. In each text the writer inscribes in close detail the relationship of the character to his (and her) parents and their objective surroundings. In both, the character at grips with the question of Jewishness is closely shadowed by a double – the narrator in 'The Defeated' and Helen Shaw, the heroine, in *The Lying Days*. Both Helen and the narrator of 'The Defeated' are spokespersons for the author. Significantly, despite the differences of their responses to their parents and childhood environment, both Miriam Saiyetovitz and Joel Aaron leave home on reaching maturity, and in each case the departure amounts to a complete rupture.

We might argue that for Gordimer there were two possibilities, each involving leaving behind, for ever, at least the blatantly immigrant component of her parental background. The received version, based on interviews she has given since her mother's death, is that her socially-aspiring mother was the powerful member of the family constellation, and her father, in every outward respect the alien other, an ineffectual person. In the story 'The Defeated', Miriam's father articulates the experience of defeat.

... John Saiyetovitz was a gentle man, with an almost hangdog gentleness, but when he was trading with the natives, strange blasts of power seemed to blow up in his soul. Africans are the slowest buyers in the world. . . . They must go carefully; they nervously scent pitfalls on every side. And confronted with a selection of different kinds of the one thing they want, they are as confused as a child before a plate of pastries; fingering, hesitating, this or that . . . ?
. . . .
And then Mr Saiyetovitz swooping away in a gesture of rage and denial; don't care, sick-to-death. And the boy anxious, edging forward to feel the cloth again, and the whole business starting up all over again; more blankets, different colors, down from the shelf and hooked from the ceiling. . . . Mr Saiyetovitz throwing them down, moving in jerks of rage now, and then roughly bullying the boy into a decision. Shouting at him, bundling his purchase into his arms, snatching the money, gesturing him cowed out of the store.

. . .
   With me, he was shy. . . . He always called me 'little girl' and he
   liked to talk to me in the way that he thought children like to be
   talked to, but I found it very difficult to make a show of reply,
   because his English was so broken and fragmentary.[8]

By locating Mr Saiyetovitz's frustration on the level of his dealing
with blacks, and by stressing his economic failure (the narrator says
he does not have the 'peasant cunning' that helped many owners of
such stores to become wealthy) and his lack of an appropriate language, Gordimer suggests an identity, certainly never to be realized
consciously by the parties involved, between the immigrant generation and the newly-urbanized, disoriented blacks, torn by sheer
economic need from their poverty-stricken rural lives to work on
contract in the gold-mines. The anger of the one and the confusion of
the other are really shared possessions, reactions to very similar
senses of inadequacy in relation to their surroundings.

   This is an early equation in Gordimer's work of the immigrant
and the black experience and it occurs in a context of exculpation, in
which she is trying to explain and accommodate the incompetent
immigrant father's weaknesses. The otherness of being black and the
otherness of the immigrant Jew seem to have much in common both
for the young author and her young narrator. Much of Gordimer's
writing life has been spent in attempts to understand and integrate
the black experience into her psyche, to overcome its otherness as
part of an enterprise aimed at achieving a specifically South African
wholeness of identity. But for most of her career the primary otherness
of the Jewish immigrant, of her father and his family, was too threatening to be dealt with, except through repression and denial.

   Her most powerful and specific treatment of the inadequacy of
the immigrant father (again, in relation to a sensitive adolescent
daughter) is a story called 'Harry's Presence', which appeared in the
collection *Friday's Footprint*,[9] at the end of the same period in her
writing, and in which she defuses the whole question of Jewishness
through an astonishing act of denial. The father is a Greek rather
than a Jew. The text contains plenty of internal evidence for its
strongly autobiographical provenance; the hapless immigrant father
plays the card game klaberjas with his Greek friends, and while
klaberjas (Gordimer spells it 'Klabberyas') is widely known in different parts of Europe, in South Africa it was the quintessentially

Jewish immigrant game. The shape of the family dissected is identical to Gordimer's own: domineering native English-speaking mother, two daughters, both at convent schools, unsatisfactory (in this instance in terms of status rather than money: he is a garage-owner, scarcely a genteel occupation in English-speaking South Africa) immigrant father. The narrator, the younger daughter, who is at the onset of sexual maturity, having 'just turned fourteen', speculates: 'Perhaps it is the fact that my father is a Greek that has prevented our family from having a real circle of friends among the other people of the town. People simply accept the fact that Greeks stick together . . .'. For Greek read Jew.

In Gordimer's own childhood, the outward identity of Jewishness, of otherness, of the quality of not belonging, must have been associated strongly with her father. Because of the Oedipal pull in a family situation full of unresolved conflicts this opened two opposing possibilities to her: over-identification with the father *as other*, or rejection of him, imitative of her mother's attitude. This mirrors the strain of equal but opposite authorial impulses – the need to inscribe the experience, and the need to escape it. In this story the need to escape the situation in which the father is actually released by the mother from his sexual status as husband and made available by her to her adolescent daughters reflects the intolerable nature and degree of that strain. The uneasy balance of frustration is destroyed by the entrance of Harry, who is a 21-year-old good-for-nothing second cousin on the mother's side. Harry takes over the odd jobs around the house, the practical discussions with the mother about 'how the garage ought to be run', the ritual nightly search for the intruder (unmentionably, in this inscription, black), while the narrator's father is exiled to the porch to read his newspaper. Sometimes his younger daughter joins him there; but when Harry comes into the bedroom she shares with her older sister and 'lie[s] across the bottom of my bed . . . while Edith sat on her bed and did her homework', she has to 'hide away my doll Vera, who was expecting a baby and who was married to a very rich, middle-aged man who adored her'. There is no resolution to the entanglement of Oedipal passion and immigrant otherness in 'Harry's Presence'; it ends in an undignified bathroom scuffle as the father tries to restore his paternal possession of his older daughter and reprimands her for performing her morning toilet dressed in her slip, in the shared bathroom, as she prepares for her school-leaving examination.

'Harry's Presence' is Gordimer's only treatment of the Jewish/immigrant theme that does not involve or even mention the existence of blacks. Its discourse is neurotic, promising only endless repetition of the same trapped behaviour on the part of all the members of the family described.

A major area of difficulty, then, is that of her relationship with her father; and she was compelled to make him both the sign for Jewishness in her life and the object of her rejection. Both these ways of relating to the father-figure inevitably involve the subject in feelings of guilt, and the connection between rejection and guilt strikes the narrator of 'The Defeated' through the final statement by Miriam Saiyetovitz's father – 'It doesn't come out like you think,' followed by the revelation that his daughter has ruptured her ties with her parents. In 'Harry's Presence' it is clear that the identity of otherness is the exclusive attribute of the father. At the same time, the closeness of the narrative persona to the authorial presence allows more intimate and potentially shattering possibilities to surface. The narrator-daughter's relationship with her father is charged with Oedipal potential, to the point where she utters a specific denial which carries powerfully sexual overtones and is directed in different ways at both Harry and her father (though the real object of the remark is the omnipotent, manipulative figure of her mother): 'There's no danger that he [her father] would want to handle my thoughts'. The use of 'thoughts' to substitute for the fulfilment of the physical image initiated by the word 'handle' alerts the reader to what is being denied.

The problem in its specifically Jewish manifestation then disappears from the surface texts of Gordimer's novels. *A World of Strangers* (1958), with its ambience of leftwing and bohemian whites contains an occasional reference, an old man at a party who speaks with a strong East European accent and who looks comic by contrast with his beautiful, blonde wife; *Occasion for Loving* (1963) has Boaz Davis, about whom the only Jewish thing is his name; the question of Jewish identity is unimportant, and he, as a character, has virtually no dimensions. Again, the ambience here is middle-class, white, left-wing, intellectual and bohemian, politically aware and involved; the absence of the Jewish dimension as an element in the discourse could be seen as a falsification, though I would prefer to regard it as an escape from a ghost haunting the author. In *The Late Bourgeois World* (1966) we encounter a similar gap as the world of the previous two novels comes to an end.

Then in a story written in all probability between *The Late Bourgeois World* and *A Guest of Honour* (1971), called 'A Third Presence',[10] the monster surfaces again and we find ourselves in what looks like the world of Miriam Saiyetovitz, suitably updated. Rose and Naomi Rasovsky are the 'daughters of poor Rasovsky the tailor': in the first line of the story the trope of the inadequate immigrant (Jewish) father is slapped at the reader like a carp on a fish-shop counter. Naomi is pretty and marries her businessman who transports her to the suburbs (a version of Miriam Saiyetovitz's fate, though Naomi retains close ties with her family, which includes an ugly, nearly blind widowed mother – note the parallel with Mrs Saiyetovitz's impaired vision) who eventually comes to live with her, and a mentally-retarded brother. But she does have three children and they follow conventional paths.

Rose, on the other hand, 'who cruelly bore her name along with the sad Jewish ugliness of her face, was clever and must get a job to help support the family'.[11] She is seen by her mother as 'the other one, a good girl, the image of her father, with her thick glasses and sad, heavy nose'.[12] She has 'the face of some old Talmudic scholar from Eastern Europe'. She works as a secretary in Johannesburg, sending part of her salary each month to the day-care centre where her brother is taken care of, and returns dutifully each month to the small Reef town to visit her sister and her family. Rose's intelligence and her sensitivity to other people's needs, presented in the story as a necessary accretion to her character resulting from her lack of physical attraction, lead her into a relationship with a Hungarian refugee professor who makes it in the big time when a book Rose helps him translate is noticed by an Oxford don; with an Afrikaner radical intellectual who brings her into contact with the world of radical anti-apartheid politics and even evinces jealousy of her former lover, long since gone to England to take up a chair in a new university. When her Afrikaner lover leaves South Africa permanently, she becomes the companion of a British correspondent and her photograph appears with his on the social pages of the newspapers.

The narrative perspective in the story is authorial and authoritative, though occasionally Gordimer allows Rose's inner voice to pronounce judgement on the self-satisfied world of her sister and brother-in-law and their children. The message is that the physical ugliness which is the outward mark of Rose's Jewishness is the key to her growth, her becoming mature and separate, while her sister's beauty leads only to narcissism and emotional stasis:

Like many sexually-unawakened women, Naomi was a born tease. Rose gave surcease and even joy to Ferovec but no man ever glanced twice at her as she went about her work in her quiet clothes, making the best of herself.[13]

By subtle variation of the narrative viewpoint Gordimer keeps the matter of Jewish identity in the forefront of her discourse. Rose, of course, never says anything direct about it, though her consciousness of it is associated with the pain of ugliness. But Gordimer links this, as if of necessity, with the pain of growth, and goes on to show that maturity has substantial compensations. Rose is intellectually, physically and emotionally fulfilled and even materially rather well-off, buying herself a new car when her sister is stuck in the no-longer-so-fashionable suburb, in the house built for her on her marriage. Do these compensations amount to an acceptance of the experience of Jewishness, with the barriers to entry in the larger world that it raises? Is the Jewish component in Rose's consciousness of herself responsible for her growth and fulfilment? Is the Jewish focus (in the story's terms, anyway) on the primacy of family life the reason for Naomi's failure to grow beyond narcissism to maturity?

The story's ending indicates that Gordimer had not yet broken through the wool-and-iron barriers of confusion and conflict aroused by the question of her Jewish identity. On Naomi's fortieth birthday Rose arrives to celebrate and her sister notices a change in her: '"Something's been done to your nose." . . . "I hated my nose more than anything," said Rose.'[14] Her nose is the key to the Jewishness, identified with ugliness in the story, of Rose's appearance, specifically linked as noted above with her father's looks. Does this point to yet another clash between the mature Gordimer and the shade of the father who failed her in her childhood struggle for separateness from her mother – and thus to a reiteration of her angry rejection of the imposed Jewish component of her identity?

'A Third Presence' may be read as a transition to the very much more comprehensive confrontation with the question of Jewish identity which permeates the text of *A Sport of Nature*. In the short story two possibilities issue from the fact of being Jewish, and one reading would suggest that a painful conflict over acceptance or rejection of the identity is morally superior to an unthinking acquiescence in it. This points forward to the three sisters of *A Sport of Nature*, whose lives are conditioned by their responses to the question of Jewishness.

I have noted elsewhere the existence of a hidden Jewish text in *A Sport of Nature*.[15] The overt pattern of Jewish identity in the text involves Hillela's heritage from the three sisters responsible for her existence and upbringing. Her mother, who bolts with her Portuguese nightclub-dancer lover when Hillela is little more than an infant, may be seen in this kind of crude schematization as responsible for her daughter's later sensuality and keen idea of how to satisfy it; her Aunt Olga, poolside student of Hebrew and antique collector, gives her both warmth and an appreciation of the material side of life against which she must (and does) rebel in the course of growth to maturity; Aunt Olga cannot face the crucial choice between living in South Africa or going elsewhere and dies of cancer; and liberal Aunt Pauline, who sees her through adolescence, gives her a moral framework for political judgement and action, but balks when Hillela seduces Sasha, Aunt Pauline's son and her own first cousin.

Where are the Jewish men in this account? Hillela's own father, deserted husband, failed commercial traveller in Rhodesia, involved with and then married to a brassy blonde immigrant from England, in love with his daughter but entirely without the emotional resources to provide her with a stable home; Olga's husband, the intensely conventional businessman whose money hedges him from the human realities of South African life and who, in any event, is ruled by Olga without knowing it; Pauline's husband, Joe, the liberal lawyer, an ineffectual figure set against the power of his wife's personality, always counselling caution and acting within the ever-diminishing framework of the law; and their son Sasha, whose mother never allows him to escape to maturity and whose rebellion is correspondingly extreme though self-defeating, because it involves actions of which she could not disapprove – he becomes an ANC militant and spends years in jail before South Africa's eventual liberation – these are the Jewish men, the foolish men in patriarchal guise, the descendants of the Talmudic scholars of Eastern Europe, the various fictive inscriptions of the immigrant father a generation or two later. Thus they are written out of the significant action – a familiar scenario in Gordimer's work where this has concerned itself with Jewish identity and family structures, but its first transportation on an important scale to a novel.

And what of grandfather Hillel, for whom Hillela, the wild gene, the sport of nature, is named? The significance of naming in

Gordimer's work varies but is often quite intense, nowhere more so than in *A Sport of Nature*. The mysteries of the names Reuel and Jethro – and of Hillel – have been elucidated elsewhere;[16] but where is the man himself, bearer of the greatest name in the Jewish moral tradition, whose famous aphorism: 'If I am not for myself, who is for me? But if I am for myself alone, what am I? And if not now, when?' constitutes both framework and ironic comment on Hillela's course through life. In the book's extended analytical statement about South Africa's political reality, a letter written to Hillela by her cousin Sasha while he is being held incommunicado before his trial on charges of conspiring to overthrow the state and furthering the aims of the African National Congress, the name of great-grandfather Hillel does occur, right at the end.

> There has been madness since the beginning, in the whites. Our great-grandfather Hillel was in it from the moment he came up from the steerage deck in Cape Town harbour with his cardboard suitcase, landing anywhere to get away from the Little Father's quotas and the cossacks' pogroms. It's in the blood you and I share. Since the beginning. Whites couldn't have done what they've done, otherwise.[17]

The passage suggests that Sasha, Oedipally wounded by his mother, trapped (and trapping her) into suffering for the kind of rebellion of which she must approve, has no notion at all of the historical resonance of his cousin's name, no idea at all of Jewish experience having its own historical and ethical framework.

One way of reading this passage would be: Hillel is Gordimer's father's generation; he bore a name of the greatest moral significance, a tradition which produced that significance; why didn't he (metonymy for his whole generation of Jewish immigrants) transmit any of these matters to his spiritually needy offspring? John Saiyetovitz, the Greek father of 'Harry's Presence', the ugly Talmudic scholar in the photograph in Joel Aaron's house in *The Lying Days*, all surface here. The failed father in the Jewish family resonates from Gordimer's personal experience throughout her work.

A sign of the persistent depth and power of these feelings is the astonishing presence of mistakes in *A Sport of Nature*. A factual error in a Gordimer text is a matter of extreme rarity; her precision about such matters is legendary in the world of writers, obsessional.

Hillela was invited by her Aunt Olga to the special dinner connected with Passover (Olga liked to keep up these beautiful old Jewish traditions which the girl, named in honour of her Zionist great-grandfather, would certainly never be given any sense of in Pauline's house)......[18]

At Olga's Friday night *seder* there was in the background a radio report of hut-burnings and murders between chiefs who, Joe told in the other house, opposed the government and those who were bribed to support it. Arthur did not submit to Olga's objection that the temporal babble of the radio had no place in the timeless state of grace invoked at a Friday night ceremonial dinner.[19]

Each of these passages has its specific context in the political narrative, and the time-frame is South Africa in the late 1950s and early 1960s (the Treason Trial, the republic referendum, Sharpeville), and I do not wish to present them outside of it. But Gordimer's terminological glitch suggests its own hidden context. She makes frequent reference to Jewish ceremonies, always held in Olga and Arthur's household. Their domestic regime signifies the triumph of materialism over morality in one version of Jewish life in South Africa – for Gordimer. This perception is, for her, an emotional issue of some urgency, compelling lapses in her usual meticulousness. As most Western secular readers in English (South Africans included) know perfectly well, 'the special dinner connected with Passover' referred to in the first quotation above is universally called a *seder*. The ceremonial Friday night (sabbath eve) meal has the same sacramental framework (candles, blessings over wine and bread), and in a technical sense is also a *seder*, though the word is never used to describe it in ordinary discourse (except by Gordimer, in the second quotation above). Gordimer was poorly served by her editor here; but in no other text with Jewish content does she commit this kind of elementary blunder.

There is more. Her association (almost an equation) of Jewish orthodox religious practice with Zionism betrays a highly impressionistic and careless presentation of Jewish life in South Africa in the earlier period. The repeated insistence in the text that great-grandfather Hillel was a Zionist does not receive a historical context. What does 'Zionist' mean in the fictive present of Gordimer's narrative? What are its connotations within the author's radical world-view? What distance has been traversed since great-grandfather Hillel's 'Zionism' and the use of the term by Hillela to Reuel, Pauline to Hillela? Is its meaning presented as stable, unchanging in history? If we compare Gordimer's historiography of the Jewish experience in South Africa here with her dramatic and accurate historical account of the South African Left in *Burger's Daughter*, the former appears slapdash and impressionistic:

> My sister went on a holiday with you to Lourenco Marques when you were two, and it's not quite the way they've told you . . . if they've told you anything. She's quite unlike me in most ways, but I understand her. You see, she had been handed over from our father to Len, there were his mother and aunts watching her waist to see if she was going to be pregnant, as she should be, in the first year. They were an orthodox Jewish family – . . . There were the family dinners on Friday nights, the cake sales for Zionist funds, and especially the same old parties – weddings, barmitzvahs; those tribal Jews don't know what it is to enjoy themselves spontaneously. . . . That's what she kept going back for. To wash off the Calvinism and koshering of this place.[20]

The perspective is that of Pauline, Hillela's liberal aunt, and she is explaining to the liberal Hillela why her mother, Ruthie, abandoned her when she was two years old for a Portuguese nightclub-dancer in Lourenco Marques (now Maputo). This is Ruthie's own account, many years later in Luanda, in her brief reunion with Hillela, by now the consort of Reuel, soon to be president of his own country:

> Ruthie followed as if she had planned it all herself. Now she could put a hand out and place it over Hillela's, a parental blessing bestowed upon a bowed head. – Hillela, I'm so glad you've really lived. I knew you'd be well taken care of by my family but at the same time I felt ashamed that it would mean you'd grow up like them, and never know anything different. Every time I remembered you I thought that. It would come upon me suddenly in the most unlikely moments, moments when it seemed that the things I was doing, the things that were happening to me – they made it impossible that what I left behind in Johannesburg had ever existed, that I had ever been Olga and Pauline's sister and Grandpa Hillela's favourite granddaughter and married someone under a canopy. –[21]

The problem with these accounts is their ahistoricity – and that is emphasized by their congruence, despite the years of narrative time that pass between them. Jewish life in South Africa (whose historical significance for the individual is actually denied by Ruthie in the above passage!), left behind by Joel Aaron, Miriam Saiyetovitz, Rose Rasovsky, Ruthie and Hillela in their different ways, did not remain static – if it ever much resembled the icon in Pauline's description. Nor was it ever lacking in diversity of expression or identity. For the majority of East European immigrants of Gordimer's father's generation, arrival in South Africa was a welcome opportunity to shed the shackles of religious obscurantism, outworn custom, and superstition. For most, embracing this opportunity also meant developing new ways rather quickly of expressing Jewish identity. While the rate of assimilation was low, the speed and flexibility of adaptation was high. For Gordimer (daughter of an immigrant), on the other hand, the immigrant Jewish experience seems to be a timeless matrix imprisoning a part of the imagination. Unlike her great American contemporaries, she seems unable to make conscious use of either Jewish identity or her relative closeness to the immigrant experience to obtain for her, as insider, the luxury of an outsider's objectivity and critical perspective on her society.

In the end she forces the issue (of resolution to the problem of Jewish identity) through Hillela, a character with Nietzschean transcendental capacities; Hillela's 'rainbow family' (though only partly realized) is the sign of transcendence, working through a unification of all versions of the other – Jews, blacks – in Gordimer's perceptual universe. Both Hillela's husbands are black; of her lovers, the two most important are an ageing East European dissident and an upper-class East Coast American liberal disfigured by a facial birthmark – both precisely delineated as figures of otherness. Her adolescent seduction of her first cousin Sasha is both an outreach to his alienated, Oedipally-trapped soul and a transcendence of taboo. But the intractability of the problem of the meaning of Jewish identity remains and is emphasized by Gordimer's setting the resolution, the final act of the transcendence, in an indeterminate future state.

Resolution of the Jewish issue, through all the steps taken towards it in Gordimer's work, is always signified through a break in continuity. Every one of the main characters in the stories dealing with the question departs from the Jewish scene (except the adolescent narrator of 'Harry's Presence', who is trapped in time and place in a classically Oedipal stalemate, and is still too young to move away, and Sasha, in *A Sport of Nature*, who takes *his* Oedipal prison with him when he goes). In both 'The Defeated' and *The Lying Days* the commanding trope in the enactment of resolution of the conflict is the act of leaving and not coming back. Joel Aaron gets to live in Israel; Miriam Saiyetovitz cuts herself off from her parents and her childhood home. This is the structural *sine qua non* of Gordimer's efforts to respond to the emotional demand her Jewishness imposed on her. And in her most protracted and systematic attempt to enforce a resolution, *A Sport of Nature*, her failure to solve the puzzle of historical continuity in relation to the meaning of being Jewish in a particular place and time is made clearest through the repetition of precisely this structure: Hillela (like Ruthie before her, like Pauline eventually, like Joel Aaron and all the others, except the narrator of 'Harry's Presence' and Sasha) departs, escapes, leaves the scene, breaks the (inarticulable) continuity, never to return in a recognizable fictive present. Thus Gordimer incorporates the resolution to this problem, her own struggle with Jewish identity, into her prophetic statement about a wider, future resolution of the whole South African conflict.

What is the signification of 'Jewish' for Gordimer? For writers in plural societies – the 'new', frontier or open societies of the twentieth-century, Jewishness is nearly always a sign of outside. For Jewish writers participating in the secular culture of these societies, for at least the first sixty years of the century, the 'outside' signification of 'Jewish' endowed them with the space for critical manoeuvre. Their choice to participate in the secular realm constituted a proposition of rebellion or freedom from enclosure within an exclusive culture which interacted with the majority culture only pragmatically at best. They started as sceptics in relation to Jewish culture, and, *once outside*, found this a natural condition (of course, rejection by the mainstream played its part); hence the critical perspective and the prophetic and moralistic strain in much Jewish writing in the United States. But these very writers, though in the vanguard of secular rebellion against social and cultural forms imported from Eastern Europe, by and large did not alienate themselves from a deeper, more inclusive signification of Jewishness. They did not pretend not to be Jews. The Jewish experience of their childhood and adult lives permeated the texts they wrote, providing a perspective for criticism and prophecy.

The categories of inside and outside did not work in the same way in the South African plurality, where the power of whiteness was such an overwhelming sign. For Gordimer, given her unusual family experience, Jewishness was a trap; it was either a version of 'English'(-speaking), and therefore very much inside the cultural segment that regarded itself as dominant as she grew to maturity, or it was foreign without being liberating, without endowing her with that same room for manoeuvre. Jewish was 'outside', but at the same time, because it took on the power of the sign of the right colour, it was ineluctably 'inside', not-other. It also denied her easy access to what seemed (in a shallow sense) culturally desirable. In her early and middle novels she tried to create that space by writing Gentile, as it were, trying to use and later to adapt European liberal and radical stances to her situation as white South African writer of fiction, social critic and prophet.

Throughout her writing life we see much evidence that the failure to find a correct sign for Jewishness discomforted her. In most of Gordimer's work the Jewish character is depicted at his or her best as the one who departs the Jewish scene (especially the immigrant or immigrant-influenced version), leaving it for a greater stage or lesser, but leaving it. By writing *A Sport of Nature* in the transcendent style she chose, she tried again to give meaning to her personal muddle over Jewish identity and experience, this time by creating Hillela, whose name represents the deepest moral and prophetic tradition in Jewish history, and who, united with Reuel (=Jethro), the great (not-Jewish) guide and adviser of the beginnings of that history, is able to resolve the inherent contradictions of (the writer's?) white-South-African-radical-Jewish identity. But Hillela is perhaps the most striking example in all Gordimer's writing of 'the Jew that went away', and it is not clear that she succeeds in creating the new sign she seems to have sought.

Notes

1. Gordimer, Nadine, *A Sport of Nature* (London: Jonathan Cape, 1987).
2. Cooke, John: *The Novels of Nadine Gordimer: Private Lives/Public Landscapes* (Baton Rouge and London: Louisiana State University Press, 1985).
3. Gordimer, Nadine, *The Soft Voice of the Serpent* (New York: Simon and Schuster, 1952; London: Victor Gollancz, 1953; page references are to the New York edition).
4. See Dubb, 'Demographic Picture', in Arkin (ed.), *South African Jewry: A Contemporary Survey* (Cape Town: Oxford University Press, 1984),

pp. 37–8. Dubb argued in 1977 that Jewish social mobility had probably reached its upper limits, with Jews better educated and holding better-paid employment than other whites; but up to *A Sport of Nature* Gordimer's substantial Jewish characters, mainly in the short stories, were part of a community moving upwards and away from immigrant experience and status.

5. 'The Defeated', in *The Soft Voice of the Serpent*, p. 212.
6. Ibid., p. 206.
7. Gordimer, Nadine, *The Lying Days* (London: Victor Gollancz, 1953), p. 117.
8. 'The Defeated', pp. 202–3.
9. *Friday's Footprint* (London: Victor Gollancz, 1960), pp. 167–78.
10. 'A Third Presence', in *Livingstone's Companions* (London: Jonathan Cape, 1972; Harmondsworth: Penguin, 1975; page references are to the Penguin edition), pp. 43–53.
11. Gordimer, Nadine, *Livingstone's Companions*, p. 43.
12. Ibid., p. 48.
13. Ibid., p. 46.
14. Ibid., p. 52.
15. See my review of *A Sport of Nature* in *South African Review of Books*, Vol. 1, no. 1, Summer 1988, pp. 13–14.
16. Reuel and Jethro in the Old Testament are the same person, Moses' father-in-law who helped guide the Israelites through the desert during their exodus from Egypt to the promised land. Some commentators stress the advice given by Jethro to Moses early in the process of nation-building, to delegate authority by appointing judges and officers, thus bringing authority into closer contact with the people. Jethro/Reuel was head of the Kenite clan. (Glueck, Nelson: *Rivers in the Desert: A History of the Negev* [New York: The Norton Library, 1959, 1968], p. 134 and *passim*). Other traditions suggest Jethro's daughter Ziporah, Moses' wife, was black.
17. *A Sport of Nature*, p. 374.
18. Ibid., p. 35.
19. Ibid., p. 65.
20. Ibid., pp. 58–9.
21. Ibid., p. 343.

11

A *Sport of Nature* and the Boundaries of Fiction

STEPHEN CLINGMAN

In her essay 'Living in the Interregnum' (1983) Nadine Gordimer introduces her discussion with an apparently self-invalidating confession: 'nothing I say here will be as true as my fiction'.[1] The idea is to say the least paradoxical: not only was the essay originally given in the personal voice, as a speech, but it also contains probably Gordimer's most intensely individual account of the implications of living as a white and a white writer under apartheid – especially during the period of rising revolutionary tempo of the early 1980s in South Africa when the speech was given. The statement might be read as a conventional defence of the superior value and priority of fiction as against non-fiction, but at least partly because of the context, the tone and the subject matter of the speech, it does not seem to be offered in a conventional way. Instead, taken in context, it reads as a candid admission of the impossibility of reaching any adequate degree of depth in non-fictional writing; depth, that is, adequate to Gordimer's situation and priorities as a writer.

Yet 'Living in the Interregnum' is notable precisely for the degree of personal and social depth it does evoke; also, and perhaps not incidentally, for the way in which Gordimer mobilizes (in a more licensed way than hitherto) many of the stylistic and structural features of her fiction in a non-fictional essay. Because of these paradoxes, the statement begins to invite specific questions. What *are* the boundaries between Gordimer's fiction and non-fiction? How is the one transmuted into the other? At what level must we read the 'truth' of her fiction, and does this 'truth' mean that the fiction is in some sense more 'non-fictional' than the non-fiction? Also, does it then mean that we should go back to Gordimer's essays and read them in some 'fictional' way in order to establish their 'truth'? Not all of these questions can be answered at once; but the availability of Gordimer's non-fictional essays now seems to require that we return to ask some of them. I propose to do this in relation to Gordimer's ninth novel, *A Sport of Nature* (1987), which as a work of fiction covers and draws upon a good deal of 'non-fictional' ground.

There is another reason to do this with specific reference to *A Sport of Nature*. For it is a work which has set off heated debate among critics and reviewers, precisely over the boundaries of fiction in the novel. *A Sport of Nature* is the story of a young white girl, Hillela, abandoned by her mother, brought up by her aunts, who through a succession of events ends up marrying a black African National Congress (ANC) leader in exile in Ghana, only to see him gunned down brutally by South African agents in Lusaka. Much later she marries again, this time to an African general who becomes (for the second time) President of his country and (for the first time) head of the Organization of African Unity. It is by his side that Hillela returns as a honoured guest to witness the celebrations at the moment of liberation of South Africa. Through all of this Hillela appears to be motivated primarily by her sexuality, moving from one man to another until her destiny is achieved; but it is still a kind of secondary and supportive role that she plays, even at the moment of liberation.

Gordimer has suggested that her novel is in the picaresque tradition (and is at that a kind of *feminized* picaresque),[2] but it is easy to see why others have been perplexed. Is Hillela's progression towards the climactic moment of the novel's ending the product of wish-fulfilment, a fantasy imposed without justification on the recalcitrant material of South African reality? What about Hillela's sexuality: is it the sign of her personal liberation, or of her ultimate submission to patriarchal hierarchies? Even aesthetically – and then perhaps morally – there may be problems, for the fact is that throughout the novel Hillela is presented from the outside, and we have no real access to her inner feelings; some have found this to be a fatal flaw both for the novel's central character and for its wider vision. Thus, Lionel Abrahams, writing from South Africa, considers that *A Sport of Nature* is Gordimer's 'poorest novel' because she has surrendered her art to the pressures of political demands. As he sees it, Gordimer has taken an ideological short-cut to revolution – a route which is in 'drastic conflict' with the characteristic stylistic complexity of her fiction, apparent in other aspects of the work.[3] On the other hand, Linda Weinhouse, writing from America, and taking a deconstructionist and Lacanian view, sees only the victory of art over life. In her view, far from prophesying the revolution triumphant, *A*

Sport of Nature inscribes its perpetual postponement – not least because of the construction of Hillela, who functions as a sign of permanent absence and displacement.[4] Working through the relationship between life and art in the novel Diane Johnson sums up the frustration of many readers by remarking that the novel 'calls into question the generic assumptions of the book, the rules by which we must try to understand it'.[5]

Hillela as empty signifier, sexual paradox, or overdetermined cypher of triumphant revolution; *A Sport of Nature* as wish-fulfilling fantasy of future liberation, or as the deconstruction of that triumph: what are the rules for reading this novel? In my previous work I have tried to show that such conflicts about, and contradictions within, Gordimer's fiction are not new, but can be related to contradictions within her situation and historical position over time. Of these the deepest relates to what I have called Gordimer's 'split position' – the fact that her situation has been a divided one in so many ways, historically, socially, culturally and psychologically.[6] In approaching Gordimer's fiction, therefore, we need to keep multiple levels in view. There are invariably inner dialogues within her work – between different modes, forms, and kinds of vision – which make the deeper logic of her work appear. It is quite possible that frustrations with *A Sport of Nature* are the result of 'monological' expectations, aesthetic or otherwise, while readings which find an unproblematic single 'vision' in the book are bound to be mistaken in some way. This is not to say that Gordimer's novels are never resolved in a particular direction; in my previous work I have tried to show that they are; but their resolutions are always the product of an intense inner debate and self-testing. From this point of view, restoring a sense of the central dialogue between the fictional and non-fictional in *A Sport of Nature* may allow us to pick out the underlying logic of the novel, and yet again open up the 'inner history' which Gordimer's fiction writes.

Certain of the non-fictional aspects of *A Sport of Nature* are clear enough, working on a number of levels. The most explicit of these concerns what we may think of as the 'historical supplement' to the fiction – that is, the way in which it fills in the historical ground and background of its own operations. At this level we learn through the novel (in a far more exhaustive way than in any of Gordimer's previous works) of a whole chronology of South African developments, running from the 1950s right through to the 1980s. The pass-burning and Defiance Campaigns; the Alexandra bus boycott and the Sharpeville massacre; the All-in African Conference and the 1961 national stayaway; the exploits of Nelson Mandela underground, and the Rivonia and Fischer trials; the beginning of Umkhonto weSizwe operations in Zimbabwe in August 1967; the Black Consciousness era of the 1970s and the death of Ahmed Timol; the Tricameral Parliament of the 1980s and the Detainees Parents' Support Committee: all these (and many other developments besides) become a sustained element of the narrative. Towards the end of the novel there is one event which was 'prophetic' at the time *A Sport of Nature* was written, but which became reality just a few years after: the release of the major political prisoners, including the leaders of the ANC. Finally this dense chronology leads to the 'fictional' culmination of the liberation of South Africa at some point in the future, and given the events of 1989–90 we are entitled to wonder how far we are to read this as purely imaginary.

At another level this account means that Gordimer is in some sense bringing her own past 'writing-life' into her fiction, going over the ground that her previous novels have worked through, and one can see this not so much as a matter of intertextuality as a kind of non-fictional reference to previous fictional concerns. There are varying degrees of 'secondary revision' involved in this: Gordimer's second novel, *A World of Strangers*, was set in the 1950s, which *A Sport of Nature* engages with yet again. The figure of Donsi Masuku, Pan-Africanist Congress functionary, who comes to Hillela's aunt Pauline for help, as well as Pauline's response to him, may relate to the decisive moment of *The Late Bourgeois World*, in which Elisabeth must decide whether or not to aid Luke Fokase, who comes to her from the PAC underground. Lionel Burger (from *Burger's Daughter*) enters *A Sport of Nature* as a reference, Rosa Burger as a character. Hillela's mother Ruth's passionate affair in Lourenco Marques recalls Gordimer's second unfinished novel, which establishes a similar polarity of (in that case more-or-less willing) entrapment within a bourgeois marriage, and suppressed passion, partly in the setting of Lourenco Marques.[7] Roving the streets of Johannesburg, working underground for the ANC, Hillela's husband Whaila is the equivalent of 'something out there' – the title of Gordimer's novella of 1984.

At a third level the novel's reference appears to be directly to Gordimer's non-fictional writing itself but, more precisely considered, it is to the autobiographical and social experience which has been worked into the non-fictional essays as well as the novel. Thus, the dignified ANC leader who stays in Pauline and Joe's house clearly relates in some way to Chief Luthuli, who stayed in Gordimer's house at the time of the Treason Trial in the 1950s, and whom Gordimer wrote of in her biographical essay.[8] A figure very much like Nat Nakasa, the black South African writer whom Gordimer wrote about in 'One Man Living Through It', appears in the novel to intrigue and exasperate Bradley Burns. Certain resonances are passing and casual, though they give moments of readerly pleasure when recognized: the old man who fights for sweets on one of Hillela's trips to Africa contrasts with the children in Gordimer's essay on Botswana who carefully share the sweets she hands out to them ('Pula!', *EG*, p. 210); Gordimer's descriptions of the unnamed West African country that Hillela goes to with the French ambassador and his wife clearly derive from her own trip to Abidjan, which she wrote about in 'Merci Dieu, It Changes'; the elephants which gaze on after Hillela's car crash with the General recall that strange moment for Gordimer when she found herself among elephants in 'The Congo River', while the European hotel-keeper, whom Gordimer mentions in that same essay, and whom she has described elsewhere,[9] sounds distantly related to the sexually transgressive and rather charming owner of Archie's African Arts Atrium in Dar es Salaam in the novel.

In these instances of non-fictional reference times and places have been shifted around, but other echoes go to the heart of the work. Thus, the sign which Hillela reads on the dashboard of a taxi in Accra, 'IT CHANGES',[10] and which Gordimer read in similar circumstances on her own trip to Ghana, is surely one of the central themes of the book. The very fact that Hillela and Whaila are married in Ghana, and that their child is born there at the exact moment of Nkrumah's downfall, provides the poignant and central motif of the promise and postponement of Africa's revolutionary potential which Gordimer explores in 'Merci Dieu, It Changes'. Hillela's discoveries in Eastern Europe – particularly in conversation with Karel – adumbrate issues of radical and dissident solidarity in the ideological wastes of the 1980s: a major theme which Gordimer approaches in 'Living in the Interregnum'.

That same essay suggests further possibilities: when Hillela thinks about her previous life in South Africa (including her semi-incestuous relationship with her cousin Sasha, for which she was expelled from her aunt's house), she considers that it seems 'impossible that what was left behind, there, had ever existed' (p. 344). In 'Living in the Interregnum' Gordimer points out that a South Africa 'in which white middle-class values and mores contradict realities has long become . . . unreality, to me' (*EG*, p. 278), and talks of her determination – much like Hillela – to enter a different kind of future. Again, in the essay, at virtually the same instant that Gordimer maintains that nothing she has to say will be as true as her fiction, she also says to her audience, 'I have to offer you myself as my most closely observed specimen' (*EG*, p. 264). As *A Sport of Nature* opens, Gordimer remarks of Hillela that 'Nothing can be more exact than an image perceived by itself' (p. 14). The reiterated motifs of self-inspection and transformation across the essay and the novel are not exact equivalents, but they are nonetheless suggestive: in what sense, and at what level, might we think of the novel as autobiographical? For repetitions of this kind cannot be entirely arbitrary or accidental; they suggest that the relations between the fictional and the non-fictional, the autobiographical, the social and the 'imaginary', and between their different kinds of 'truths', might well be closely and complexly meshed.

This leads to the feeling that it is not at the surface level of reference or echo that the more significant relations between the non-fiction and the fictional are to be found – indeed, that one should distinguish between surface and depth relations in this regard. In fact the paradox is that it is when one approaches the deepest thematic and figurative drives of the novel that its most profound levels of 'non-fictional' reference emerge. Here we might consider Hillela, the figure at the core of this book. For Hillela is neither an overdetermined cypher of revolutionary wish-fulfilment nor an indeterminate signifier of pure absence; instead there are deeper issues at work through her constitution as a character, and she has a specific kind of presence which is far from insignificant: a *bodily* presence.

Throughout the novel Hillela is represented as an 'organic body': organic in the sense that mind and body are harmonious extensions of one another, and that her whole being is in tune with nature. (She is after all a 'sport of nature' – the exception to the customary rule, but also nature's ultimate flourish and unrestrained example, and perhaps the key to some kind of evolutionary principle.) Hillela has a 'bodily intelligence' – Sasha tells her, 'You are the most intelligent person in this house' (p. 98) – and there seems to be a philosophy of the body being worked out through her. For in Hillela's case consciousness comes from the body, and not the other way round.

Indeed, *in* her sexuality, in her animal-like self-fulfilling presence, Hillela's is an identity which seems both pre- and post-Cartesian in an unexpected but thrilling direction: like her mother she might say 'I'm all over my body' (p. 62). And precisely because this identity is based on a principle of the organic body, it is one which takes Hillela entirely beyond frameworks or limitations – in the same way that the body in its essence always moves just beyond the edge or grasp of thought. It is then primarily a bodily drive that takes her from one successive stage of her life to the next, from her aunts' houses in Johannesburg, to Tamarisk beach in Tanzania, to the Ambassador and his wife, to Whaila, America, Eastern Europe, and finally back to Africa and the moment of South African liberation.

That Gordimer is directly concerned with the idea of the 'organic body' is indicated (sometimes by contrast, sometimes by equation) through other characters and relationships in the novel. Sasha, Hillela's cousin but also symbolic 'brother', exists for the major part of the novel in contrast to her. His real name is Alexander, but like a character from a nineteenth-century Russian novel he bears his nick-name as his identity. More to the point, like many of the dissatisfied youthful male figures of pre-revolutionary Russian fiction, Sasha is the archetypal 'useless man' – a figure deeply aware of oppression and injustice, but also agonizingly of his own social impotence and irrelevance (this is compounded psychologically in the novel by his relationship with his mother). In contrast to Hillela's organic mobil-ity, but like the typical 'useless man', Sasha exists in a world of physically paralyzed 'mentality' – in which his consciousness of his own irony feeds off and circles on itself endlessly. Where Hillela is bodily and light, Sasha is heavy and grave: after the two have made love it is he who is woken by the flapping shutter of an open window of the house – vulnerable to the murmurings of the world outside him and internally to his subconscious – while Hillela sleeps on in bodily ease. Towards the end of the novel Sasha does become in-volved physically in political action – and it is a matter of huge release for him – but even when detained in prison he is subjected to 'sensory deprivation' (p. 369) – something which no one would ever think of saying about Hillela. In prison his letters to Hillela are never sent, or if sent are never received;[11] his 'solitary confinement' in that setting, although of course very real, is also a symbolic accentuation of his condition all along. It may be true that Sasha is the 'real hero' of the novel in that it is he who undergoes and works through various crises of doubt and conscience,[12] but it is also true that he cannot go where Hillela can go – not into the future with her bodily instinct.

In order to do this Hillela needs to escape the incestuous relationship with Sasha (as if they were two halves of one entity – body and mind – which can come together, but which cannot escape the closed circle of the self) and find other bodies, organic like her own, to match her and challenge her. Thus it is that Whaila, her first husband and only true love in the novel, is represented in unmitigatingly physical terms. Hillela first sees Whaila when he arises from the sea, 'pure hardness against the dissolving light', to announce a horribly physical fact – that a comrade has been killed by a car bomb (p. 164). Later it becomes apparent that part of Whaila's magnetism for Hillela is that even his innermost qualities are like material extensions of his physical being – his 'spirit resistant and brain bright as obsidian' (p. 236). When he himself is killed the novel presents a physical tribute which is filled with the same kind of spirit: 'the obsidian god from the waves, the comrade was buried in the gold, green and black flag he died for' (p. 251). And it is true that throughout their conjunction Hillela and Whaila's relationship has an unrepentant and deeply moving physicality to it, as she for example examines the minutiae of his black body with loving wonder and attention. In this light it is apparent that Hillela's bodily drive – which is fundamentally a sexualized drive – has a political analogue. It is Hillela's sexuality that will take her beyond the artificial boundaries and limits of customary morality, and certainly beyond the boundaries of apartheid into a new world. More deeply than anything else Hillela trusts only the authenticities of sexual love – there can be no cheating here, at this level of bodily truth, and sexuality is in a sense for her a true 'home' – but the opportunity that comes to her, partly through chance, partly through trauma, and partly through the logic and necessity of her nature, is to ethicize this bodily politics by transforming it in social terms. This she does through her continuing commitment to Whaila's body and the world that it stood for, after he has been killed.

Why should this 'organic body' be at the centre of Gordimer's preoccupations? If we think back to her previous novels we see that each of her characters has searched for and found this sort of unity with varying degrees of success. Within the framework of liberal humanism Toby Hood finds a limited organic unity in *A World of Strangers*, but the collapse of this framework in *Occasion for Loving* means a corresponding implosion for Jessie Stilwell, who ends entirely out off from action and trapped within a world of 'mentality'. Liz Van Den Sandt (in *The Late Bourgeois World*), Rosa Burger, and Maureen Smales (in *July's People*) are three female figures who find climactic moments of organic unity in crises of political decision. For Bray, in *A Guest of Honour*, it is cut off by death, while Mehring, in *The Conservationist*, who desires it most desperately, could not be further from it as a bastion of apartheid.

In *A Sport of Nature*, however, this organic unity is fully achieved, and present in Hillela from beginning to end: this *is* her identity, and some of the symbolic reasons why this should be so are apparent. For one thing, in so far as Hillela represents an evolutionary principle – as the genetic 'sport of nature' which holds the key to the future – this must be registered primarily in the body, and then, as a consequence, in terms of consciousness, for this is our basic measure of evolution: a new state of body and mind. But there are also more localized reasons. As Hillela herself intimates, where apartheid has divided according to the body, only the whole body can be a sign of reintegration: 'Skin and hair', the narrative points out, 'It has mattered more than anything else in the world' (p. 206). Also, at the level at which the organic body establishes its own imperative teleology of liberation, the white body – at last in Gordimer's fiction – realizes a form of necessity corresponding to that of blacks in South Africa. There is no understanding of the full enormity of apartheid like that which is impacted in the body. In this sense it is through her body that Hillela is identified with the black world – and nowhere more so than through her love for and marriage with Whaila, whose violent death she herself experiences as a bodily shock (losing the second child in her womb), and as whose living partner she comes to reclaim a liberated South Africa at the end of the novel.[13]

From this point of view there has been another major turn for Gordimer's vision in *A Sport of Nature*. In *The Conservationist* it was the improperly buried black body which returned at the end of the novel to claim the land; in *A Sport of Nature* at last the white figure is one with that body, returning in a sense to claim it with him and for him. (It is perhaps no accident that she is a female figure, for the earlier novel showed how the hierarchies of apartheid were inseparable from Mehring's definition of male sexual supremism.) Also in contrast to *The Conservationist*, Hillela is one with the repressed black world; the subjective analogue of this is the redeemed identity, the unrepressed unconscious whose reality can only be the organic body.

Indeed, Hillela is Gordimer's first central character not to be subject
to a 'return of the repressed', because she is identical with it, and this
reintegration allows other previous splits in Gordimer's fiction –
between nature and history, 'whiteness' and 'Africanness', for
example – to be resolved.[14] In that light the 'organic body' becomes
a sign of oneness with the African continent, which is the ultimate
scene of Hillela's ranging operations. Unlike Bray in *A Guest of
Honour*, Hillela is able to achieve an identification with Africa *and
live*, and all figurations of her 'animality' in the novel combine the
sense of her organic unity with a belonging in Africa. From all these
points of view Gordimer is following through and completing a
specific symbolic logic which she has generated in her fiction. But it
is a development which also registers an ontological claim: that in its
non-recognition of imposed limitations the organic body is fundamentally connected with a revolutionary drive.

It is at this level that the 'non-fictional' reference in the fiction
begins to emerge and, interestingly, in its range it appears to satisfy
autobiographical, psychoanalytic demands on Gordimer's own behalf, wider cultural issues in the novel, as well as the deeper realities
of the 1980s, when the novel was written. The autobiographical side
of things has begun to be explored by John Cooke and Michael
Wade, and certainly what they say is borne out in *A Sport of Nature*.[15]
Here the essential thing is that *as* 'organic body' Hillela displays and
may be intended to resolve a critical anxiety of identity for Gordimer.
Hillela grows up 'without parents', as it were – her mother unknown
to her from the age of two, her biological father in doubt. In her
various foster families her relations are close but not directly genetic:
she is 'like' a daughter or sister, but not the actual thing in the flesh.
In leaving behind her aunts Hillela also sheds the accretions of her
Jewish identity – something that Wade is correct to point out has
constituted an issue of subjective distancing for Gordimer. On the
other hand, there is not a total divorce: after Whaila has been killed,
Hillela declares, inside to herself, *'What am I without him? And if,
without him, I am nothing, what was I?'* (p. 250). In these words, their
intonation and syntax, we are sure to hear the echo and variation of
the renowned ethical paradox of Rabbi Hillel: 'If I am not for myself,
who will be? If I am for myself only, what am I? And if not now,
when?' Hillela at some level has the same impulse to mutuality and
the urgency of the present as Hillel, but hers is perhaps intended as
a further elaboration on that commitment – in that her being can
simply have no existence without another. In this there may be an

additional cultural echo, of the African proverb, later incorporated into a poem by Jeremy Cronin, that 'a person is a person because of other people'.[16] For Hillela 'other people' includes all others, irrespective of racial or ethnic divides. From this point of view – if we are thinking of her cultural identity – Hillela is well on her way to her final name in the book, 'Chiemeka', her African name, meaning 'God has done well' (though she still calls herself '*Hillela* Chiemeka').

Nonetheless, it remains significant that mothers are especially troubled and troubling figures in the novel – not least because, counting her lost mother and her aunts, Hillela in some sense has *three* of them. Where the mothers in the novel are real (Pauline in relation to Sasha, for example) they are claustral and cloying figures, themselves trapped in emotional circles of misunderstanding. For her part, Hillela's major satisfaction as a mother is 'not to have reproduced herself' (p. 228). Again, the way into the future seems to be through variation (not to reproduce the genetic types of apartheid), and there is some suggestion – especially in Hillela's metaphor of her larger African 'family' – that a non-nuclear African culture is not subject to the same kinds of Oedipal tensions as the European.[17] But still, there may be a deeper existential issue here for Gordimer: one remembers the words of one of her much earlier female characters, thinking of her child: 'You don't know how horrible it is to reproduce yourself like that.'[18] Also, for much of the novel Hillela appears to be searching for an absent father (one thinks of her relationship with Karel in Eastern Europe, not to mention the 'fatherly' nature of the General).

All of this may well have some origin in Gordimer's own complex family setting, particularly in relation to her own mother, who cut off Gordimer's highly physical life when she was about ten or eleven, and the memory of which constituted a kind of mental and bodily anguish for a long time after.[19] Gordimer has also spoken (with some degree of self-consciousness) of the ambiguity of her father who, himself an oppressed Lithuanian Jewish immigrant, nonetheless quickly absorbed and reproduced the habits of segregrationist South Africa.[20] Any full psychoanalytic reading of *A Sport of Nature* would require more time, evidence and gumption than is available here, but we can note these areas of complexity and repetition in the novel. The essential thing is that as organic body Hillela is virtually a *tabula rasa* as far as her identity goes; there is a symbolic condensation which may allow her to resolve issues of personal repression as far as Gordimer is concerned, establish wider cultural resonances, *and* at the same time represent a wholly unrepressed revolutionary potential politically considered, beyond all frameworks, limitations, known categories. It is an extraordinary kind of symbolic intersection and layering.

At this point it is worth stating the obvious: that we cannot interpret Hillela simply as a *realistic* character. Expectations of a certain kind of realism lead to the complaint that Hillela 'has no inside', no inner being to make her interesting. On the other hand purely symbolic readings can lead in two possible, but opposite directions: that Hillela represents an (overdetermined) impetus to revolution, or that she represents its perpetual postponement. In terms of sexual politics, are we to interpret Hillela's relations with men as a sign of her sexual and political dependency on them, or is her wide-ranging sexuality a vision of her inner liberation, her canny political intelligence of the body? The fact of the matter is that in this, as in Gordimer's other novels, we need to keep many levels of representation in mind at once. On a realistic plane Hillela may well represent a negotiation of the realities of power (including gender power in the Third World) in the 1980s, while symbolically there is the innate drive of the organic body to liberation, which might affect women and men, black and white, equally. In this we have to understand what we might think of as the *agenda* of Hillela's conception. Milan Kundera, considering his own forms of characterization in his fiction, remarks that 'to apprehend the self in my novels means to grasp the essence of its existential problem. To grasp its *existential code*.'[21] In that light, *A Sport of Nature*, for all its evident differences from Kundera's fiction, has something in common with it; in the best sense – just as a Kundera novel might – it reads as a fictionalized essay on the body. In Hillela, for her own complex reasons, Gordimer has taken the 'existential code' of the body and explored its politics, its destiny, its ambiguities, its versions, inversions and reversions, on realistic and symbolic planes, in both the personal and social spheres. In that sense the body – in this case Hillela's body – generates its own genre: the genre of this novel, which otherwise might appear inexplicable.

It is in the social sphere that Hillela's nature allows a political allegorization, breathtaking both in its scope and in the extent to which this has a larger kind of 'non-fictional' reference. Here it is Sasha who provides the clue. When he hears that Hillela has married Whaila he knows this is not some cheap attempt to overcome the barriers of apartheid through sex or transcendent interracial love, but instead, in one of his undelivered (though pre-prison) notes, he identifies the basic drive of the organic body as 'utopian', contrasting his mother with Hillela in this respect:

> Reformers are . . . totally rational, but the dynamic of real change is always utopian. . . . Instinct is utopian. Emotion is utopian. But reformers can't imagine any other way. They want to adapt what is. . . . Don't you see? It's all got to come down, mother. Without utopia – the idea of utopia – there's a failure of the imagination. (pp. 217–18)

In Sasha's understanding Hillela is no 'reformist', but the quest of her body for complete solutions has taken her in its logical direction. In Hillela's body Gordimer has imagined the utopian drive.

Suddenly, in this light, everything becomes clear, for in her utopian guise Hillela represents not only the 'organic body', but the 'resurrected body' as well. Surprising as it may seem, there are numerous figurations of resurrection in *A Sport of Nature*. Propounding to Hillela the need for a violent struggle in South Africa, Whaila tells her that she too has been born in 'sin' – the sins of her white people; but as she emerges bodily from the bath in which he is talking to her it is clear that she in some way has been 'saved', and the conversation is like a 'baptism' (pp. 242–3). After Whaila is killed the difference between Hillela's past and future life is marked by way of an inner death for her and a more sombre, more resolved resurrection: 'even if she had not been hit [by the bullet] the little beach girl was buried' (p. 252). In a book in which sexuality is central, Udi Stück – whose own flesh has literally been unable to 'resurrect' since the death of his wife in a car accident (for which he has felt overwhelming guilt) – explains to Hillela the difference between grief and tragedy. Grief belongs to death, but tragedy to the resurrections of struggle in the face of death (p. 251). Hillela, who never feels guilt (but who does feel loyalty), and who is able to survive a car accident with her General, and laugh about it, commits herself to that resurrection.

To be precise: at a symbolic level Hillela proceeds from parthenogenesis (unknown parents), to life as the organic body, through death (Whaila's, which she feels bodily as if it were her own) and resurrection (her resuscitated afterlife alone and with the General) to political Paradise – liberated South Africa. In many respects Hillela can be seen as a transcendent archetype: it is not just the fact that

Hillela is 33 years old (the age of Christ's death and resurrection) when she marries the General that makes one wonder whether Gordimer's early life at a convent school had a more significant effect on her fiction than we might have thought![22] This, however, is not the spiritual paradise – literally 'utopia' or 'no place' – in the usual sense, but a secular, politicized vision of wholeness, completeness, liberation.

It corresponds to fundamental realities of the 1980s, but also allows the novel to register a certain degree of doubt or division in relation to them. Primarily we might suggest that the organic body and its physical, utopian drive to political paradise at some figurative level relates to the rising climacteric of the 1980s in South Africa, which was characterized by a sustained bodily drive towards revolution. In the townships, in the streets, in the unions and mass organizations, in the innumerable 'bodies' and groups which proliferated (Sasha writes that South Africa has become a country of acronyms), there was a real sense of a physical drive towards power. Moreover, for some whites in Gordimer's position this meant a renewed form of participation in that drive. She herself was a founder member of the new writers' body in South Africa – the Congress of South African Writers (acronym, COSAW); and in at least one incident at the height of the State of Emergency she – together with other whites – was able to place her body between those of the police and the residents of Alexandra township.[23] In the same way that the organic body does not in itself recognize imposed limitations, this physical drive to power was in its most undiluted form, in Sasha's words 'to overthrow the State' (p. 365) – the entire framework of limitation which currently existed. It was in some sense a quest for utopia, and it led, by early 1990, to the release of Nelson Mandela and other political leaders, and a vision of the end of apartheid.

Yet if the organic body is not subject to conventional limitations, then it is also not primarily an ethical principle: in following the code of the body the novel begins to register more ambiguous realities. Towards the beginning of the work Sasha and Hillela are reading *The Brothers Karamazov* which, in the legend of the Grand Inquisitor, contains one of literature's most profound dialogues between pure, utopian virtue on the one hand and the realities of worldly politics on the other. In Dostoevsky's novel the figure of Christ is the ultimate 'organic' body: though he says not a word the luminosity of his presence speaks intimately and overwhelmingly of a higher truth to the Inquisitor. Yet the essence of the Inquisitor's response is that worldly authority – precisely because it has an ultimate 'good' in mind – must make do with worldly ethics and practices; that it must enter into contract with what the General in *A Sport of Nature* calls 'the currencies of power' (p. 356). And there is indeed a sustained dialogue running through *A Sport of Nature* on the question of power and its compromises – registered chiefly through the figure of the General, who gains rather virtuous ends for his country through compromised and mercenary means. The General is militaristic, macho, and dynastic; his view of power is characteristically material: 'you get there with guns and you stay there with money' (p. 310). Even his name, Reuel ('Rue', 'Rule', 'Royal'?) sounds like an ironic commentary. He jokingly refers to his regained Presidency as 'the Second Empire'; this is a form of bodily resurrection, but it is a Bonapartist reversion nonetheless. If one considers the revolution which began the novel – Nkrumah's in Ghana – and compares it with this, one sees a long and winding path only of ironic circularity.

And yet this is partly the point. The problem with Nkrumah's revolution, we might think, was precisely that it was utopian and idealist, but fell to the blandishments and realities of power nonetheless. Far better perhaps to have a regime that is conscious of power, and is still able to maintain some ethical momentum; this is surely the import of the fairy-tale-like mixed economy which Reuel is able to sustain in his country, in which major resources have been nationalized, but where agriculture has not, and small shopkeepers have been left alone, because the General has learned from 'the disasters elsewhere' (p. 383). At some level, it is clear, Gordimer has accepted irony and 'political mortality' – the historical nature, so to speak of the 'fallen' and not God-like body – and embedded it in the very structure of the novel. Indeed, the novel is riddled with irony: even the phrase which everyone uses of Hillela – 'trust her' – combines an acceptance of her essential integrity with an ironic perception of her personal ability to survive. Elsewhere we see that Hillela's child Nomo – named for Winnie Mandela – goes to Bedales and becomes a fashion model, while when liberation comes to South Africa it is Hillela's cousin Clive – who had by no means been alien to the structures of apartheid – who has been invited to serve on a Ministry of Agriculture Commission. (In his own opportunistic capacity Clive has provided, along with the help of Afrikaner and Indian capital, the liberation T-shirts which the joyous crowd is wearing.) In these ways the novel seems to hold together an acceptance of the commerce of power – Sasha, in prison in South Africa, accepts that the General, in his country, must also have prisoners – with an ironic vision of its ethics and its dangers. Indeed, there is a direct link between Hillela, in the State House in Reuel's country, and Sasha, who in prison is a 'guest of the State' in South Africa: the State – politics – is inextricably bound up with power, and all are infected by its reality.

All of this corresponds to specific patterns in the 1980s in a global dimension – a period of fantastic cynicism (one is talking now about the period primarily *before* 1989 – but perhaps after, as well) in which people had to find their ethical way, and keep political faith, through an almost bodily intuition, and in which the realities of power became profoundly apparent. (In this respect, if one compares *A Sport of Nature* with *A Guest of Honour* one sees the demise of a purer version of socialism in Africa, the world more generally, and in Gordimer's consciousness.) And this is surely the reason for the presence of Eastern Europe in the novel in the first place – for the politics of Eastern Europe posed exactly those questions of political realism, betrayal, and the possibility of a sustained deeper loyalty to a moral vision that Gordimer confronted in 'Living in the Interregnum'. Karel tells Hillela that her search for 'somewhere to go is right at the heart of this century' (p. 259). It is significant then that for all Hillela's 'realpolitik' of the body, whether in Africa, Eastern Europe or America, the one thing she never loses is her larger and sustaining sense of loyalty to her projected community. So at one level Gordimer appears to accept – and as the end of the novel indicates – even celebrate this political and ethical complexity.

Yet – and accentuating now the novel's ironic vision – there are at least two signs of division in the resolution of *A Sport of Nature* which we should note. Sasha – who has indeed learned to make his way from the entrapments of mental confusion to physical resistance – is finally left in Holland, an outsider when the moment of liberation comes. From there the legacy of his mental and ethical struggle seems almost like a reproach to the bodily opportunism of Hillela. But even Hillela, who is present for the climactic moment, is herself a visitor. This is partly a sign that she does not 'own' the revolution, that it must be surrendered to the people in whose name it has taken place; and this is why she must finally play a secondary and supportive role. But everything about the novel leaves open the question: who will participate in utopia? (The lives of both Hillela and Sasha indicate this will not simply be a matter of race.) Perhaps even more to the point: how, and in what specific forms, will the utopian movement, in its bodily or physical teleology, enter into contract with the currencies of power? The complexity of Gordimer's novel, combining both hope and irony, realism and symbolism in exploring the code of the body, suggests that after the climactic moment of liberation and release there will be some hard thinking to do; that all kinds of questions that have been suspended in the utopian drive will need asking and answering. In this respect *A Sport of Nature* may be South Africa's first genuine pre- and post-revolutionary novel; Gordimer has raised the configurations of her 'split position' to a higher historical level. In all these ways, ranging from its psychoanalytical and cultural dimensions to a deep 'inner history' of South Africa in the 1980s, this is the kind of non-fiction that Gordimer's fiction tells.

Notes

1. In Nadine Gordimer, *The Essential Gesture: Writing, Politics and Places*, ed. and with an Introduction by Stephen Clingman (London: Cape; New York: Knopf; 1988), p. 264. All of Gordimer's essays cited in this discussion to be found in this volume; all further page references given in parentheses in the text to *EG*.
2. Interview with Anthony Sampson, *Sunday Star* (Johannesburg), 5 April 1987, p. 17.
3. 'Revolution, Style and Morality: Reflections around Nadine Gordimer's *A Sport of Nature'*, *Sesame* 12 (Spring 1989), pp. 27–30.
4. 'The Deconstruction of Victory: Gordimer's *A Sport of Nature'*, *Research in African Literatures* 21 (2), pp. 91–100.
5. 'Living Legends', *New York Review of Books*, 16 July 1987, p. 9.
6. See Stephen Clingman, *The Novels of Nadine Gordimer: History from the Inside* (London: Allen & Unwin; Johannesburg: Ravan; 1986), esp. Ch. 7.
7. Nadine Gordimer, unfinished novel, c. 1951, pp. 1–84; MS in the possession of the author.
8. See 'Chief Luthuli' (1959). In *A World of Strangers* there is passing reference to 'sculptural' figures very much in the Luthuli mould; there are evidently complex recapitulations between the fictional and the non-fictional in Gordimer's work.
9. Personal interview with Nadine Gordimer, 18 March 1987.
10. Nadine Gordimer, *A Sport of Nature* (London: Jonathan Cape, 1987), p. 209. All further page references are to this edn, and are given in parentheses in the text.
11. See Weinhouse, 'Deconstruction', p. 95 on this.
12. Judith Thurman, 'Choosing a Place', *New Yorker*, 29 June 1987, p. 89.

13. This idea of understanding *through the body* – especially of the impact of apartheid – has been a constant motif in Gordimer's work. Cf., early on, Toby in *A World of Strangers* (1958; London: Jonathan Cape, 1976), p. 238, who only understands the full significance of Steven's death when it hits deep in his body: 'To my bones, I understood'.

14. On these issues see again Clingman, *Novels*, Ch. 7.

15. See John Cooke, *The Novels of Nadine Gordimer: Private Lives/Public Landscapes* (Baton Rouge and London: Louisiana State University Press, 1985), esp, pp. 14–21, which explores the impact of Gordimer's early life on some of the fundamental themes and motifs of her fiction. Also see Michael Wade's chapter in this volume; I should like to pay tribute here to the memory of Michael Wade, who did so much to open up Gordimer studies.

16. Jeremy Cronin, 'Motho Ke Motho Ka Batho Babang', in *Inside* (Johannesburg: Ravan Press, 1983), p. 18. Cronin was a political prisoner in South Africa from 1976–83.

17. See Gordimer's comments on the absence of Oedipal tensions in African literature in *The Black Interpreters* (Johannesburg: Spro-Cas/Ravan, 1973), p. 12; Cooke, *Novels*, p. 21, also draws on Gordimer's remarks.

18. The character is Cecil Rowe, in *A World of Strangers*, p. 157. Cf. also Rosa Burger's comments to Clare Terblanche in *Burger's Daughter* (London: Jonathan Cape, 1973), p. 127, which combine the biological and the political: 'They live completely different lives. Parents and children don't understand each other. . . . Some sort of natural insurance against repetition.'

19. See Cooke, *Novels*, pp. 14–21.

20. Nadine Gordimer, interview in *Sophiatown Speaks*, eds Pippa Stein and Ruth Jacobson (Johannesburg: Junction Avenue Press, 1986), p. 26. See also Gordimer's short story, 'My Father Leaves Home', *New Yorker*, 7 May 1990, pp. 40–43, which approaches the same topic through indirection.

21. Milan Kundera, *The Art of the Novel*, trans. Linda Asher (Harper & Row: New York, 1988), p. 29. Gordimer has been drawn to Kundera's fiction for some time, and quotes him in 'Living in the Interregnum', though there is no necessary question of influence here.

22. In a more politicized vein, it is clear that 'resurrection' has always been important to Gordimer. Cf., once more, the black body in *The Conservationist*, which 'rises again' to claim the land. For discussion of this and its complex historical correspondences in the early 1970s, see Clingman, *Novels of Nadine Gordimer*, Ch. 5.

23. *Weekly Mail* (Johannesburg), 23–9 May 1986, p. 8. This was at a mass funeral in Alexandra, just outside Johannesburg, held in defiance of restrictions. The whites who went into the township – also in violation of police orders – were responding to a 'call to whites' issued by the United Democratic Front.

12

My Son's Story: Drenching the Censors – the Dilemma of White Writing

SUSAN M. GREENSTEIN

Writers who accept a professional responsibility in the transformation of society are always seeking ways of doing so that their societies could not ever imagine, let alone demand: asking of themselves means that will plunge like a drill to release the great primal spout of creativity, drench the censors, cleanse the statute books of their pornography of racist and sexist laws, hose down religious differences, extinguish napalm bombs and flame-throwers, wash away pollution from land, sea and air, and bring out human beings into the occasional summer fount of naked joy. Each has his own dowsing twig, held over heart and brain.

Nadine Gordimer, *The Essential Gesture*

It is a temptation to read *My Son's Story*, Nadine Gordimer's tenth novel, as a bold new breakthrough, the novel in which she 'drenches the censors' and plunges into the welter of life in South Africa without regard to her marginal position as a white writer. Sonny, the father implicit in the title, is a mixed-race ('coloured') teacher radicalized by his students in the political upheavals of the early 1980s.[1] Much of the story is told by his son, Will, making this the first of Gordimer's novels to have its centre of gravity – narrator as well as major characters – outside the white South African world.

After years of dutiful, even ardent life within the protected circle of his profession, devoted to his students and the community, originator of 'uplift' projects, tender and temperate husband and father, Sonny enters a life of political commitment. His students point the way, staging protests in imitation of the more politically active blacks. Sonny is moved one day to support them, and makes a first gesture.

191

He picks up a red marker and corrects their misspelled and ungrammatical placards. One thing leads to another. He accompanies his students to demonstrations, soon has his name and photograph in police files, and is solicited by political organizations to make speeches. It is not long before he is dismissed from his job and barred from all teaching; in accord with a party decision, he moves his young family from their ghetto neighbourhood to a white suburb as a form of protest. Arrested and tried for political crimes, he spends two years in prison. Sonny's clandestine life is one of special passion, pursued at a pitch of high emotional arousal. Under the force of this intensity he falls in love with Hannah Plowman, a woman assigned to monitor political trials for a rights organization. In the course of her duties this young white woman corresponds with him during his imprisonment and visits his family to ascertain their needs in his absence. Their paths cross after his release. Not long after, they begin their affair.

Sonny's story is told in an antiphonal alternation of voices by his son, Will, and an unnamed narrator. The epigraph from Shakespeare's Sonnet XIII, which also furnishes the novel's punning title, alerts the reader to Gordimer's intention to tell several stories simultaneously, at the very least both a father's and a son's. Each of these stories is set in a world she has never entered so forthrightly before. She seems to have breached the barriers Stephen Clingman convincingly described as insurmountable in his 1986 study of the novels through *July's People*. Still living within a 'fractured' society, she no longer speaks from the margins, but as the 'disprivileged' subject.[2]

Her previous novels have all had white protagonists as well as white narrators although, beginning with *Burger's Daughter* (1979), they have dramatized the journey of white towards black in racially divided South Africa. Rosa Burger, self-exiled, returns to her native land after a purgative encounter with her one-time 'black brother' in London. Shocked by the revelations and invective of his middle-of-the-night phone call following their chance meeting, she vomits up the detritus of her own false consciousness. Her quest for the Other leads back to South Africa and to a prison cell, where she welcomes her sisterhood with the black women incarcerated along with her. In *July's People* (1981), Maureen Smales embarks on a similar quest against her will, driven by the outbreak of revolution to seek refuge along with her husband and two children in the desolate village of their longtime servant, July. The familiar categories of mistress and servant wither under utterly transformed conditions, and Maureen hears for the first time the authentic voice of July, whom she had always assumed she knew. Now he speaks as Mwawate, in his own language; she can only surmise his meaning. Maureen's quest is aborted by her panicked flight towards uncertain rescue.

In *A Sport of Nature* (1987) the quest is achieved, but in an imagined future. Hillela, the remarkable *lusus naturae* of the title, is a natural woman unnatural to South Africa. She is the one to change names, and learn her true name, having entered into the relation of lover, wife and trusted confidant to two black revolutionaries. She emerges as Chiemeka, mother of a daughter, Nomzamo, who is harbinger of a new relation between the races, and mother also of the nation which is birthing itself. Hillela is the new woman. Triumphantly, she lays claim to her African birthright. It is reasonable to ask whether in *My Son's Story* Gordimer does the same, writing no longer as the conservationist or even the guest of honour, but as a native South African.

The definition of 'native' is, of course, the crux of the problem. The Nigerian writer and critic Chinweizu categorically excludes people like Gordimer from the writing of African literature.[3] Gordimer's own position has evolved over the years with the awakening of her political awareness. She developed a credo which did justice to her concept of artistic and political integrity. In the period of the 'interregnum', she came to believe, the white writer must refuse to speak for blacks, must learn to 'listen', and above all must purge the self of a 'false consciousness', by 'discard[ing] a white-based value-system which it is fashionable to say "no longer" corresponds to the real entities of South African life but which in fact never did'.[4] Within the limitations imposed by such rigorously principled self-censorship, she continued to create black characters. *My Son's Story* violates these conditions. From the title to the very armature of the plot, whose congruence with *Hamlet* is underscored by the Shakespeare-steeped imaginations of both Will and Sonny, Gordimer suffuses the novel with a tradition not 'native' to South Africa. Perhaps it is only fitting, then, that it is also a miscegenation novel, reanimating once again one of the central topoi of what J. M. Coetzee has designated 'white writing'.[5] In *My Son's Story* Gordimer does not confront the censors of the state, but the internalized censors of the legitimate South African community within which she desires citizenship. Above all, by writing from within the Other, she challenges the censors of the writing self.

Not surprisingly, the novel raises in acute form the issue of authority, even though Will, as a first-person narrator, carries a certain automatic *imprimatur* of authenticity. It is also self-evident that Sonny is native to the struggle. Unlike white South Africans, he need not question his right to participate; conversely he can't remain immune. Sonny and his family, however, belong to a small educated elite not representative of any of the communities designated as 'coloured' by the South African system. Sonny is unaffectedly comfortable among his relatives and neighbours in the Benoni ghetto of his origins, but he has little to do with them. He has effectively left their world, which we merely glimpse in an occasional family gathering. The description of the house in a lower-class Afrikaner suburb to which he illegally moves his family is equally spare. A visitor notices the 'twirly wrought-iron gate' and 'plaster pelican', presumably left behind by the former owners. The smell of 'stale spiced cooking' and some Kahlil Gibran texts displayed on the walls signify the presence of the new inhabitants, along with Sonny's small collection of treasured books.[6] Similarly, the multitude of languages, dialects and registers of speech of polyglot South Africa are almost silenced in favour of the 'correct' English of the schoolmaster and his family. They speak neither the Afrikaans of the majority of the coloured population, nor the Afrikaans-influenced English of their friends and relatives in the Benoni ghetto.[7] Public events typical of the period are also brushed in lightly, amounting to little more than one student protest and a single political rally. In keeping with Gordimer's increasingly austere and poetic style, the novel offers a minimalist representation of the material, linguistic and political culture in which it is set. While some readers might be disposed to call *My Son's Story* a bold venture into new territory, others might condemn it as a travesty, a self-conscious *tour de force*, a novel written in blackface.

I WHITE/WRITING/BLACK

Gordimer has asserted that as a young woman, cloistered and bookish, she averted loneliness and entered the life of the provincial mining town that was her world through the 'Rapunzel's hair' of her sexuality.[8] In *My Son's Story* she moves along the umbilical cord, the twisted, knotted tie of family loyalty and family love, entwined and tangled with revolutionary purpose, as it was in *Burger's Daughter*.

Sonny is, by all accounts, a good man who lives by his political convictions. He is mindful of the risk and the meaning of what he has undertaken. His wife, Aila, supports his endeavours unconditionally, although she does not share his level of commitment. She encourages the children, Will and his older sister (still known as 'Baby' in recognition of her singularity as the first-born), to honour their father for his political work and sufferings.

Sonny's involvement with Hannah, though it contravenes accepted custom, is legal. The relevant provisions of the Immorality Act have been repealed; as far as the government is concerned, they can live together, make love, and pursue their affair unmolested in her borrowed cottage on a friend's estate or in a hotel at the coast. Nonetheless, this added twist to a life built on idealistic clandestinity unravels Sonny's principled existence. His family attachments shrivel under the chill of his betrayal. His comrades see Hannah, even with her loyalty to the cause, as a distraction and a disability. She is not subject to party discipline; if Sonny can align himself with Hannah, in what other ways might he diverge from the path of duty? Sonny, who dreamed of uniting the parts of his life, who hoped to connect his ardour for revolutionary work to his delight in 'needing Hannah', eventually finds himself on the outside of all these circles of love and obligation.

The son, Will, is obsessed with Sonny's secret. He discovers his father's betrayal of conjugal love and loyalty when he unexpectedly encounters Sonny and Hannah together. Cutting school in favour of an afternoon at a cinema complex in a white area, Will happens to see the pair, obviously also counting on the protection of unfamiliar haunts, as they emerge from one of the theatres. Father and son become yoked by complicity; neither wants Aila, a reserved, gentle woman devoted to the well-being of her family, to uncover this clandestine life. At an age when his own tentative sexual adventures should be Will's obsession, he becomes his father's unwilling accomplice and angry antagonist. He revels furiously in his overweening concern for his mother and wallows in racist disdain for Sonny's white mistress, punctuated by fantasies of sexual rivalry with his father. 'Love, love/hate', Will writes, 'are the most common and universal of experiences' (p. 275).

In 'Living in the Interregnum', Gordimer insisted that blacks and whites, even in their deeply divided country, could write about one another under certain circumstances (*The Essential Gesture*, p. 297). In novels prior to *My Son's Story* the known but 'never spoken' things Gordimer chose to record were those that occurred at the meeting-place of black and white. They were stories of mistress and servant, of liberal and bohemian interracial circles, of erotic adventure or love across the artificial barriers of apartheid. In this novel, the condition of the body politic drives her to the politics of the body, and above all, of the family. She probes the heart of family life and the recesses of individual personality, relying on the 'universals' of sexual desire, secrecy, betrayal – of 'Love, love/hate'.[9]

Through Will and his father Sonny, through the emotional en-tanglements of a family in disarray, Gordimer imagines her way into a world she can only have experienced tangentially. We come to know Sonny as the 'pride of the old people', the perpetual son whose nickname, retained into adulthood, represents 'not just the snobbery of the poor and uneducated, that rejoices in claiming one who has moved up out of their class. . . . The pride came from an instinct, like the water-diviner's for the pull of his twig, for Sonny's distinction. . . . Everything he was and did evidenced distinction' (pp. 5–6). He carefully draws a protective line around his young family, so that the children remain largely unaware of the barriers that prevent them at every turn from a full and decent life: 'We didn't have any particular sense of what we were – my sister and I. I mean, my father made of the circumscription of our life within the areas open to us a charmed circle' (p. 20). He keeps his distance from the 'real blacks' (pp. 22–3) and immerses himself in European literature. He resists the invitation of more radical cousins to take a stand. But one day that 'distinction between black and real black, between himself and them, fade[s] for the schoolteacher' (p. 25). He aligns himself with his students, who have 'recognize[d] the real blacks as siblings'. (p. 26). When he corrects the misspellings on their political placards Sonny makes his essential gesture.

Aila quietly accepts Sonny's decision to do political work. She sustains the rhythms and routines of family life. When the time comes, she attends his trial, decorously maintaining an unperturbed facade; for two years, she fills the five hundred words of her monthly letters to her jailed husband with family matters, closing each with a ritual expression of domestic affection. Hannah, on the contrary, touches the soul of the language-loving revolutionary. She un-selfconsciously comforts his daughter at the trial, on an occasion when Aila cannot be there. Discharging her duties, she visits him in jail, conveying information to him in a coded phrase he delights in recognizing, 'sermons in stones'. Her letters are not dutiful, but inspiring. She writes of her confidence that he will emerge 'happy for battle'. Alone in his cell, Sonny wonders, elated and nourished, how this woman comes to understand the ardour of revolutionary commitment:

> how could she, a stranger, possibly have divined that, in his quiet, schoolmaster's being, joy had come first only when he stepped out and led chanting children across the veld to face the police! . . . Happy for battle. He lay on his bed in the dark and sounded over in his mind that phrase, so simple, so loaded, audacious, such a shocking, wild glorious juxtaposition of menace and elation, flowers and blood, people sitting in the sun and bodies dismembered by car bombs; the harmonized singing coming from somewhere in the cells, and the snarl of a police dog leaping at his face, once, in a crowd. (pp. 56–7)

Part of what Gordimer knows about Sonny and his kind, then, is the euphoria of revolutionary joy.[10] Along with the refrain 'needing Hannah' which marks Sonny's desire, the word punctuates the account of their years of clandestine love: 'Joy. That was what went with it. The light of joy that illuminates long talk of ideas, not the 60-watt bulbs that shine on family matters' (p. 65). Sonny's joy is compromised, however, by the moral ambiguity of his need for Hannah in defiance of other loyalties, 'a need that clanged closed, about the two of them', like the door of a cell (p. 54).

His involvement with Hannah does more than corrode his family life; it corrupts his political will as well. He believes his commitment to Hannah and revolution reinforce one another: 'there was no conflict to taint [his desire] because in her – needing Hannah – sexual happiness and political commitment were one' (p. 125). He learns otherwise when the two of them attend a 'cleansing of the graves' for nine youths killed by the police the previous week. Sonny gives the oration, a lament for wasted lives that is also an eloquent anticipation of a better future. Hannah is present in her own right, through an organization with which she works. After the ceremony, the police, for no apparent reason, bombard the dispersing throng of blacks and sympathetic whites with tear gas, and then, in the confusion, open fire on the now-panicked crowd. Fleeing with the others, Sonny sees a man fall, wounded. His first instinct is to turn and run to the aid of a comrade, but he stays to protect Hannah. Only later, replaying the scene in his mind, does he truly see himself in that moment. Sonny temporizes, trying to convince himself that rescuing Hannah is in accord with the obligation he had intuitively assumed as a young man to live for more than himself, his children, or even the 'clan of relatives' (p. 9). But he knows better:

> She was not oneself; neither she nor the man who fell. The other – the other life, outside self – was either of them. To run or to stop: a choice between them. Who was to say which was the most valuable? But this woman whose hand was curled against his neck, wasn't she oneself, his need?
> Saved himself.
> Now he had something he would never speak, not to anyone, certainly not to her. (pp. 126–7)

With this secret, another dimension is added to the layers of Sonny's double life. What we come to know about Sonny is filtered through his experience of clandestinity, at once personal and political, and the shape it gives to the contours of his character. Like so many of Gordimer's other characters, both black and white, he is primarily vivid as an idea about life in South Africa.

II   SILENCE OF THE DAY

Nadine Gordimer has described *Burger's Daughter* as a book about commitment, not 'merely [as] a political thing', but as 'part of the whole ontological problem in life'. She has similarly observed that in *Something Out There* (1984), 'there is an obsession with betrayal. . . . political, sexual, every form'.[11] Both commitment and betrayal are important to *My Son's Story*, concerned as it is with revolutionary activity in a police state. But they are not its key words. Beginning with its enigmatic title (who is the son, who the father, who the teller of the tale, which is hidden in the other?), this novel is about clandestinity, a word that tolls like a bell throughout the narrative.

My Son's Story is obsessed with clandestinity, with secret lives lived, paradoxically, in the full glare of observation. Will may speculate on his father's whereabouts, never certain whether Sonny is attending a political meeting or spending the night in Hannah's cottage, but the ever-watchful Security Police have the answer. Though Sonny makes every attempt to sustain his usual demeanour at home, his affair is not only exposed to Will's hostile observation. It is also no secret to his favourite child, his daughter Baby. She slits her wrists in a self-dramatizing reaction to his defection from the family. Aila, too, knows without being told, nor does she tell what she knows. The family, like good revolutionaries, observe the necessary silence of the day.[12]

Will sums up Sonny's insertion of clandestinity into the heart of family life:

> He goes out, away, and when he comes back, walks in, does the things he used to (pouring himself a glass of iced water from the fridge, hanging keys on one of the hooks he put up when we first moved here, asking us what sort of day we've had) he is *acting*. Performing what he used to be. (p. 43)

The entire family is infected with duplicity, knowing the unspoken, keeping silent about the known. Elegant, decorous Aila, under cover of habitual, almost ritualized domestic behaviour, also undertakes a secret life. Not only inattentive Sonny, but also Will, who is jealously observant of his mother, misses the clues until it is too late for them to remonstrate or influence her choice – if ever they could have done so. She detaches herself from her devoted son as inexorably as she turns away without a word of reproach from her unfaithful husband. The Security Police, not blinded by familial emotions, see clearly enough to understand that she has become a revolutionary.

III MASTER/PLOTS

Such doubleness is endemic to life in South Africa, where, as Gordimer has observed, 'you just never know, really, to whom you're talking' (*Conversations*, p. 257). An inevitable result of political repression, it overshadows all relations. The duplicity that prevails in Sonny's family because of his affair, echoes the political deformation of self and community. As Will puts it, 'Everything we say to each other has a meaning other than what comes out' (p. 151).

In *My Son's Story* Gordimer chooses to explore this aspect of the South African condition through Western eyes. *Hamlet* is the paradigmatic pre-text for her study of the link between family secrets and the political dimension of life. *My Son's Story* recreates the brooding son and the triangular tensions of Shakespeare's play, and behind *Hamlet* stands its great precursor, the 'master narrative of Western literature', *Oedipus Tyrranos*.[13] Gordimer's novel traces the dis-ease of family life through an array of performances, a carnival of 'seeming', worthy of the Prince of Denmark, whose anger and disgust Will matches: 'The whole world is lying, fornicating and lying' (p. 60). Hamlet is always aware that he is surrounded by spies and false friends; Oedipus, too, never knew to whom he was talking. Like relations between Gertrude and her disaffected son, the monstrously doubled relations between Jocasta and Oedipus are a matter of state, as well as of family. Oedipus acts in both the political and personal domains without knowing it, while Hamlet's strategems craftily take the two into account. For both Oedipus and Hamlet the various arenas in which they stage their performances overlap, influencing the depths of personality as well as the personae created to mask portions of the self.

Gordimer has described immersion in the South African situation as exceptional, a deforming experience: 'One thing that happens to me and to the subjects of my stories is a distortion of sensibilities ... by living in South Africa, your personality, your perceptions, are constantly under these pressures that shape you' (*Conversations*, p. 258). In *My Son's Story* she entertains the possibility that such deformation and distortion is the human condition, although profoundly influenced by the peculiar circumstances of place and historical moment. The recognition is accompanied by a new willingness to draw on the tradition she has heretofore censored, and to use it to anatomize the intimate relation between political reality and the bent of character, the nuance of personality, the intricacies of family life and sexual love. The repugnance Will feels for the white rights-worker who is his father's lover is fed equally by his adolescent sexual rivalry with Sonny and his politically motivated (and racist-fuelled) anger:

> *She reminds me of pig. Our ancestors didn't eat pig. . . . I have terrible thoughts. About her. About my father with her. I imagine them . . . could I ever think of my mother like that! I'm sick with myself. What he's made me think about.* (pp. 93–4) [Italics here and elsewhere are Gordimer's]

Rather than an experiment in realistic representation across lines of colour and culture, *My Son's Story* is a meditation on clandestinity and the labyrinthine tangles of family life. Sonny, Will, Baby and Aila, a family with no surname, a clan whose destiny (to introduce a false etymology) is obscure and uncertain, are known to us through the archetypal figurations of the (Western) family romance.

IV   MIRROR/IMAGE

My Son's Story is also concerned with the mystery of becoming a writer, and the construction of a myth of authoring. Under the guise of writing a realistic novel, set in the immediate historical past – not an imagined place, as in *A Guest of Honor* or an anticipated future as in *July's People* and *A Sport of Nature* – Gordimer conducts her own clandestine operation, whose target is the reader.[14] In the dual narrative structure of *My Son's Story* Will's first-person account alternates with the more measured and mature voice of an unnamed third-person narrator. By the final chapter, however, if not before, we are forced to recognize that concealed within the voice of the 'not-Will' is Will himself, slightly older than the angry adolescent, and having authored his first novel. The novel is, of course, *My Son's Story*, which, he confides in its final sentence, 'I can never publish.' As disingenuous as any double agent, this Will was invisible because so obvious. Almost unforgivably, like the purloined letter in Poe's classic tale, he has been hidden before our very eyes, the perfect con-artist, the supreme double agent.

In a police state, you can never be sure to whom you are really talking. But once a clandestine identity is exposed and a trusted friend is revealed as having been all along in the employ of the state, every conversation, every gesture, is subject to revision and reinterpretation. Now the older Will's dispassionate account must be read beside and into the first-person narration. The narrative structure is not what it pretended to be. The anonymous third-person speaker – who is appreciative of Hannah's innate decency and can inscribe her consciousness, who observes the younger, wounded, angry and vindictive Will with compassionate irony, who sees Sonny's strength and dignity as well as his errors of self-delusion – is Will also. Opposed to each other in a narrative hall of mirrors, each voice endlessly reflects, refracts, incorporates, and produces the other, in infinite regression or unending dialogue.

Every conversation, every comment, every decision the reader has made about character, purpose, or motive must be rethought. Former certainties are suspect. On a first reading, the description of Sonny and Aila in town to shop on a Saturday seems unaccountably distanced and condescending. When the truth is known and the narrating voice positioned as 'Will's', the passage reads differently. It may reflect the condescension of a still-young man who will come to think better of it, or perhaps the bitter irony of someone who understands too well the seductions of a culture intended to pacify the disenfranchised with 'lounge "suites" named to bring to cramped and crumbling hovels the dimensions of palaces, "Granada" and "Versailles"' (p. 11).

Gordimer has often reiterated her conviction that 'for each idea, there's never been anything but one right way to say it. . . . If I don't find it, I can't write' (*Conversations*, p. 170). For *My Son's Story* the necessary form seems to have been a doubled and duplicitous narrative structure which destabilizes the text, thereby luring the reader into an interpretive maze. Everything must be reread, and no reading can possibly be final, but the multiple readings have the potential to generate among them the whole story. Formerly Gordimer responded to those who questioned her right to create black characters in interviews or on the lecture platform. Now her answer is implicit in the structure of the novel itself. As Will puts it:

> In our story, like all stories, I've made up what wasn't there to experience myself. . . . And so I've learned what he didn't teach me, that grammar is a system of mastering time; to write down 'he was', 'he is', 'he will be' is to grasp past, present and future. Whole; no longer bearing away.
>
> All of it, all of it.
>
> *I have that within that passeth show*. (pp. 275–6)

No single reporter, spokesperson, or vantage point, is privileged. In one narrative Hannah is a woman whose work with prisoners of conscience keeps her in 'a loving state of being'. Her spirit is enlarged by her knowledge of their profound courage, her feelings 'extended . . . in a way she would not have known possible for anyone' by the experience of 'touching the hands of the accused across the barrier [in court] while they joke about their jailers; visiting the wives, husbands, parents, children, the partners in many kinds of alliances broken by imprisonment' (p. 90). In the other, she is 'a blonde woman with the naked face and apologetic, presumptuous familiarity, in her smile, of people who come to help' (p. 14).

Within the radical indeterminacy of *My Son's Story* lies a clandestine declaration of the writer's freedom to 'grasp past, present and future. Whole.' Will confesses, 'I've imagined, out of their deception, the frustration of my absence, the pain of knowing them too well, what others would be doing, saying and feeling in the gaps between my witness' (p. 276). Oddly enough, what might be considered a post-modern 'deconstructive' fiction stakes its claim on the authority of the writer.[15]

The speaker of Sonnet XIII exhorts his auditor to memorialize himself, to look to the future, to procreate: 'And your sweet semblance to some other give. . . . /You had a father; let your son say so.' This 'son's story', therefore, is Sonny's story, the story of the father. But when Will, the image of his father, tells that story, he is also telling his own.

One portion of the story they share is their complex reaction to Hannah. After both Hannah and Aila have left Sonny, each committed to political work that takes precedence over her tie to him, he tries to imagine a scenario in which he would have been 'saved' from 'needing Hannah', saved from his desire, saved from himself:

> he found himself thinking – insanely – that if the law had still forbidden him Hannah, if that Nazi law for the 'purity' of the white race that disgustingly conceived it had still been in force, he would never have risked himself. . . . Because needing Hannah, taking the risk of going to prison for that white woman would have put at risk his only freedom, the only freedom of his kind, the freedom to go to prison again and again, if need be, for the struggle. . . . That filthy law would have saved him.
>   *Out of the shot and danger of desire.* (pp. 263–4)

The matrix in which these thoughts occur is the history of miscegenation as historical reality, as literary theme, and as occasion for fury, self-hatred, erotic stimulus, irrational recoil and fear. Ultimately, these thoughts are parts of the son's story, because their proximate author is Will, imagining his way into Sonny's mind as Gordimer must imagine her way into both. Will has created a sympathetic portrait of Hannah in the third person narration, but his younger self vents his rage on her image in the first-person account:

> Of course she is blonde. The wet dreams I have, a schoolboy who's never slept with a woman, are blonde. It's an infection brought to us by the laws that have decided what we are, and what they are – the blonde ones. It turns out that all of us are

carriers, as people may have in their bloodstreams a disease that may or may not manifest itself in them but will be passed on; it has come to him in spite of all he has emancipated himself from so admirably – oh yes, I did, I do admire my father. People talk of someone 'coming down' with a fever; he's come down with this; to this. (p. 14)

This is 'white writing' with a vengeance, in which Gordimer succeeds in 'drenching the censors' in order to turn a contaminated literary tradition to her purpose. The imagery of degeneracy and disease that is integral to the miscegenation myth comes naturally to the angry adolescent Will, but does not, in fact, infect the emotions of either his father or the older Will.[16] Within the dual narrative of *My Son's Story* the miscegenation topos serves as a form of analysis, rather than an essentializing myth debasing characters and author alike. Gordimer also dismisses the censors within, the voices that might refuse her permission to take on the subject, and writes as if she knows enough.

V   FOUND/PARADISE/LOST

My Son's Story marks the beginning of a sea-change in Nadine Gordimer's writing, perhaps as dramatic as the transformation Caroline Heilbrun finds in Virginia Woolf's late work. 'Insofar as that is possible,' Heilbrun writes, 'Virginia Woolf became another person in her fifties', by prevailing over internal censors which had prohibited her from uniting her anger with her art to 'say the unacceptable'. Like Gordimer, she had already achieved a distinguished history of courageous speech in both essays and fiction. But now she went further, to 'utter the forbidden words' that made her, as an artist, 'entirely free'.[17] For Gordimer, the 'forbidden words' not only expel the internalized censors of Black Consciousness so that she can create Will and Sonny; they also reveal the origins of her vocation in the embroilments of family and give utterance to the woman's voice formerly silenced in her writing.

It is significant that Will is not only the Other, he is a version of Nadine Gordimer, a partial portrait of the (woman) writer as a young man. Like Gordimer, Will discovers himself as a writer in the cross-currents of family life, prior to politics. When he acknowledges that 'What he did – my father – made me a writer' (p. 277), he seems to have in mind Sonny's betrayal of family, rather than his loyalty to the cause for which he is at the conclusion of the novel once again imprisoned. Less clear is the role of Aila, whose insistence that Will forgo revolutionary activity has further impelled him to write. Aila is relentlessly opaque, a mystery to both her son and her husband. She is their 'dark continent', dead centre of the novel – impenetrable, compelling, uncircumscribable even in Will's 'grammar'. Along with Baby, who recovers from her suicide attempt and rejects her father's authority by taking her marriage into her own hands, Aila remains outside the son's story and the patriarchal plot of which it is a version. She refuses her role as Hamlet's mother/desired object and Oedipus' mother/wife. Aila's story remains covered by her son's story, waiting for Gordimer to confront her remaining censors. She also figures as the 'missing term', the absent mother or enigmatic sphinx, keeper of the secrets that Will, though he is writing from the inside, cannot know. Among them is why he is a writer, while his sister and his parents risk prison.

The novel contains an indirect answer in a remarkable interlude unlike anything else Gordimer has written, a lyrical passage in which she does fulfil part of the promise to 'release the great primal spout of creativity'. Sonny experiences a visionary moment, a Words-worthian glimpse 'into the life of things' which seems outside the range of even the older Will's understanding. While talking with Hannah one afternoon in the garden surrounding her cottage, Sonny's

sense of where he was underwent a strange intensity. It was physical. He became aware on the very surface of his skin, his bare breast and arms, as well as through sight and smell, of this that was called 'the garden' hovering and pressing in upon him. . . . A tingling peace on his nerve-endings, in his ears, murmured over by some sort of birds with grey tails rustling in a fig tree. . . . the blurred rush of the chronology of living was halted for a while. The absolute of existence: an alpine pine hatched against failing light above the darkening earth, the bright tiny moths of the first stars flitting out of the hazy radiance of the sky. Clouds obscuring like shadows; the northern tree shivering at the tips of feathered branches as the heat waves of the day rose. . . . all was stayed, as before a hand held up.

Past, present and future merge. 'Grammar' folds in on itself. To Sonny the darkening landscape reveals his own alienation, but also the impermanence of this garden, the emblem of European claims to preeminence over a 'raw' landscape and its 'native' peoples.

> Over the moment he sees the foreign tree, the element like himself that doesn't belong, fall majestically, following its giant shadow that is falling across the man and woman in this garden, now. Where the saw has razed through its stout trunk the rings of its years are revealed under a powdering of sawdust.

This recognition flings Sonny out of his momentary Edenic unity with the natural world, and back into fallen time:

> What was sensuously close drew suddenly away; he was removed from it and the isolation of his presence offered its meaning. A rich white man's domain of quiet and beauty screened by green from screams of fear and chants of rage, from the filth of scrap-heap settlements and the smashed symmetry of shot bodies; he had no part in it. He did not know what he was doing there. (pp. 142–3)

Gordimer has repeatedly affirmed her responsibility as a writer to her historical situation, to the 'transformation of society', and she does not abandon it here. In Sonny's evanescent vision she forges a prophetic unity between the literary landscape of her European heritage and the terrain, physical and political, of South Africa. Sonny's experience of psychological and spiritual integration, though quickly dispelled by the shadow of South African political reality, also testifies to a new subjective quality in Gordimer's expression of desire, of loss and of possibility. Writing in an experimental visionary mode she 'washes away pollution', and dissolves the internal censors.

Along with the 'dowsing twig' as metaphor, Gordimer has fixed upon a revealing quotation from Kafka: 'A book ought to be an icepick to break up the frozen sea within us' (*Conversations*, p. 160). Like Woolf in her fifties, Gordimer in her sixties has broken through to release the waters of that frozen sea.

The novel's coda returns to the historical moment. Sonny is once again in prison, where Will sends him a poem in which a skeleton fledgling he had retrieved as a child from the burned overveld metamorphoses into a European bird, the bird of Romantic symbolism and Biblical typology, only to meet a brutal fate:

> Dove
> Sprig of olive in its beak
> Dashes in swift through the bars, breaks its neck
> Against stone walls.

In a such a world, the artist's icepick is essential.

Notes

1. Gordimer uses physical and genealogical description to identify her main characters' heritage, as well as their location within the South African system of racial terminology. However, the political realities signified by the labels imposed by a racist regime are of the essence of the story. I use the term 'coloured' here as the most efficient way to indicate those realities, and follow the narrator's practice in identifying other characters as 'white' or 'black'.

2. *The Novels of Nadine Gordimer: History from the Inside* (London: Allen & Unwin, 1986), pp. 208–10, 217).

3. See *Voices from Twentieth-Century Africa: Griots and Towncriers*, ed. Chinweizu (London: Faber and Faber, 1988), p. xxxv. Many South African writers have addressed the limitations which constrain white and black from writing about each other under current circumstances (see Clingman, p. 207 for a selection of comments.) Chinweizu's position is distinctive because it is absolute: 'communities of alien conquerors, or of their alien campfollowers, do not qualify as African, regardless of how long they have expropriated parts of the continent and settled there'.

4. 'Relevance and Commitment' (1979) and 'Living in the Interregnum' (1982) in Nadine Gordimer, *The Essential Gesture: Writing, Politics and Places*, ed. Stephen Clingman (New York: Alfred A. Knopf, 1988), pp. 138–9 and 267. Future references to the essays collected in this volume will be made in the text.

5. Coetzee describes white writing as not 'different in nature from black writing', but 'white only insofar as it is generated by the concerns of people no longer European, not yet African'. He sees 1948 and the rise to power of Afrikaner nationalists as the close of the period of 'white writing', because whites no longer saw *themselves* as colonized. Given this analysis, subsequent 'white writing' would be a belated occurrence, running counter to the majority white conviction of legitimacy in South Africa. See *White Writing: On the Culture of Letters in South Africa* (New Haven: Yale University Press, 1988), pp. 1–11.

6. Nadine Gordimer, *My Son's Story* (New York: Farrar, Straus, Giroux, 1990), pp. 90–1. Further references will be made in the text.

7. The traces of divergent English which appear in the text are sufficient, however, to set up a Bakhtinian "dialogue" between Sonny's speech and the vernacular he has abandoned.

8. *Selected Stories*, 1975; rpt (New York: Penguin, 1983), p. 11.

9. Stephen Clingman quite rightly takes issue with those critics of Gordimer who are too ready to erase the crucial distinctions that mark its historicality and praise it as 'universal' (p. 18). I think Gordimer is now affirming continuities of the human condition as part of a renewed attention to her own subjectivity as it plays out in her characters.

10. Gordimer honours the joy of revolutionary commitment in her comment on Albie Sach's book, *Running to Maputo*. In this memoir the South African lawyer and ANC activist who survived a car-bombing in 1988 describes his physical and spiritual recovery. Despite his anger and horror at the loss of an arm and the sight in one eye, let alone the profound insult to his sense of being, joy is the dominant emotion of Sach's book. Gordimer's dust-jacket comment calls attention to this 'aspect of political activism ignored or denied, that ought to be obvious to us: to risk oneself to change the world for the better is to have a capacity for the splendid tender joys of the body as well as spirit and mind'. It is interesting then, that so little of Sonny's 'joy' is convincing to the reader. Albie Sachs, *Running to Maputo* (New York: HarperCollins, 1990).

11. In *Conversations with Nadine Gordimer*, eds Nancy Topping Bazin and Marilyn Dallman Seymour (Jackson and London: University Press of Mississippi, 1990), pp. 140 and 257. Similar comments appear in several other interviews. Further references to interviews collected in this volume will be made in the text.

12. 'Clandestine' has its etymological roots in the Latin *clam*, secretly and *dies*, day.

13. I derive the term loosely from Teresa de Lauretis's discussion of the relation of narrative to the Oedipus story in Chapter 5, 'Desire in Narrative' of *Alice Doesn't: Feminism, Semiotics, Cinema* (Bloomington: Indiana University Press, 1984), pp. 103–57. De Lauretis draws on Lévi-Strauss to show that similar 'plots' serving analogous functions can, in fact, be found in non-Western mythological systems. The significance of the *Oedipus* to *My Son's Story*, however, is in its standing at the origins of Western literature, precursor to *Hamlet*, which the novel aggressively foregrounds.

14. Although political events are not filled in, the dating has been carefully worked out to indicate when the action occurs in the years of the revolutionary 1980s. The Tuesday, 14 June, on which Aila flees the country is in 1988; the characters' ages and years of birth can be figured out from this and other cues.

15. Will shares with Gordimer an address to a predominantly white audience, who, he claims, 'don't know what they're seeing when they look at us' (p. 261). He also writes, like Gordimer, to the future. *My Son's*

Story implicitly acknowledges its true audience to be outside South Africa (or in the future) by including footnotes to identify organizations such as the Black Sash.

16. See *White Writing*, Chapter 6, 'Blood, Taint, Flaw, Degeneration: The Novels of Sarah Gertrude Millin', pp. 136–62.

17. 'Virginia Woolf in her Fifties', in Carolyn G. Heilbrun, *Hamlet's Mother and Other Women* (New York: Ballantine, 1990), pp. 90–113. Woolf, of course, committed suicide not long after achieving this new voice. Heilbrun sees Woolf's taking of her own life as a clearly-reasoned choice, not a failure of nerve.

Part III
The Shorter Fiction

Part III
The Shorter Fiction
Feminism as Telling
Ambiguities in Nadine
Gordimer's Short Stories
KARIN L...

13

Feminism as 'Piffling'? Ambiguities in Nadine Gordimer's Short Stories

KAREN LAZAR

Nadine Gordimer's political trajectory is well-known. Over a period of four decades she has moved from a position of 'uneasy liberalism to a recognition of the marginality of liberalism and of its inherent hypocrisies, and finally into a "revolutionary" attitude' (Driver, 1983: p. 30). Her views on feminism, by contrast, appear to be out of synchrony with her increasingly radicalized understanding of race and class oppression. Her statements on feminism strike one as more reticent and conventional than her other political opinions. And yet, on closer reading, her views on feminism are complex and far from monolithic. I will look at some of Gordimer's short stories in the light of her multi-faceted, uneven and changing attitudes to women's oppression and feminism.

Gordimer has sometimes expressed a lack of support for feminism, and has irritated feminist critics as a result.[1] Lockett suggests, for instance, that Gordimer demonstrates a 'strong identification with patriarchy' (1990). Gordimer explains herself by claiming that in South Africa the experience of apartheid is so severe in its extent and gravity as to override the experience of women's oppression. In 1984 she comments:

> It's all based on colour, you see . . . the white man and the white woman have much more in common than the white woman and the black woman. . . . The basis of colour cuts right through the sisterhood or brotherhood of sex. . . . Thus the loyalty to your sex is secondary to the loyalty to your race. That's why Women's Liberation is, I think, a farce in South Africa. It's a bit ridiculous when you see white girls at the university campaigning for

Women's Liberation because they're kicked out of some fraternity-type club . . . who cares? A black woman has got things to
worry about much more serious than these piffling issues. White
women have the vote; no black, male or female, has. White women
have many more basic rights than black women (1984b: p. 19).

In her review of Ruth First and Ann Scott's 1979 biography of Olive
Schreiner, she claims:

> the fact is that in South Africa, now as then, feminism is regarded
> by people whose thinking on race, class and colour Schreiner
> anticipated, as a question of *no relevance to the actual problem of the
> country* . . . the woman issue withers in comparison with the issue
> of the voteless, powerless state of South African blacks, irrespec-
> tive of sex. It was bizzare then . . . as now . . . to regard a campaign
> for women's rights – black or white – as relevant . . . Schreiner
> seems not to have seen that her liberation was a secondary matter
> within her historical situation (1980b: p. 918; emphasis mine).

In spite of Gordimer's assertion that feminism is 'piffling' and that
struggles against race (and class) oppression eclipse it, she has also
made statements which suggest sympathy for feminism. For example, she comments that women are widely regarded as 'honorary
children' (1977, p. 88), and in 1981, she said: 'Well, speaking for
myself as a woman and a citizen, I've become much more radical in
my outlook' (1981: p. 291).

   The co-existence of these two views suggests that Gordimer's
views on feminism are far from clear-cut. To start with, she must be
seen within her generation: born in the twenties, she would have
reached her adulthood at a time steeped in postwar myths of frilly
femininity and female domestic satisfaction. This is not to say that
Gordimer is a typical product of her generation – there is much to
suggest that she is not.[2] However, an apparent unease in relation
to feminism is unsurprising in a woman raised in that ideological
climate.

   It is clear that in the past two decades Gordimer has undergone a
process of politicization on the question of gender (Driver, 1983;
Lazar, 1988). This movement is not a neat, continuous or linear
progression. The statement 'as a woman I've become more radical in
my outlook' occurs several years *prior* to her firm insistence that
feminism is 'piffling'. This apparent contradiction may derive from

a rethinking or erraticism on the author's part regarding questions of gender. It might also derive from a hostility to some streams within feminism and an unawareness of others.

Gordimer's antagonism to feminism in the late 1970s and early 1980s was caused by the fact that at that time she saw feminism as a trivial, white middle-class phenomenon offering nothing of benefit to black women. Her cynicism is a self-avowed response to a particular brand of feminism that arose in parts of the South African white community in the 1970s. The campaigns and goals which Gordimer cites – such as entry into 'fraternity-type clubs' – suggests a consonance between this feminism and the very liberalism that she has often criticized, particularly in the last two decades of her work: 'The laager of liberalism . . . favoured change only insofar as allowing blacks into the existing capitalist system of South Africa' (1984b: 29). Liberal feminism, in similar terms, 'seeks complete equality for women within capitalist society', and places emphasis on 'formal equality in the civil and political sphere' (Vogel, 1983: p. 3). According to Gordimer, such a feminism results in the rare and insignificant inclusion of black women, and is not noteworthy as a social phenomenon.

Gordimer has only recently recognized that there are other trends within feminism besides this 'marginal' feminism. She praises, for example, the activist feminism evident on some (mainly English-speaking) South African campuses in the 1980s, seeing it as a 'harder, more thinking feminism'. This feminism is saved from complete irrelevance because 'it doesn't see feminism as completely apart. It sees it as part of the whole issue of human rights, and it understands very well that black women have certain problems that no white female has' (1988: p. 3). In her distinction between 'piffling' and 'harder, more thinking feminism', Gordimer, perhaps unwittingly, expresses some support for materialist feminism, the latter described by Vogel as '[an assertion] that the key oppressions of sex, race and class are interrelated and that the struggles against them must be coordinated' (1983: p. 6). Such a feminism *agrees* with Gordimer that sisterhood is 'cut right through' with divisions of race and class. It shares her cautions against easy or automatic assertions of sisterhood, and opts for historically variable (as opposed to fixed or universalistic) definitions of patriarchy. A materialist feminism would depart from Gordimer on two counts. Firstly, it would argue that sexual oppression is as extensive and often as grave as other forms of oppression, and should not be trivialized when juxtaposed with these other forms. Secondly, it would stress that, although it is partially constituted in form and mediated by other types of oppression, sexual oppression has a specific and material existence that cannot be explained away as a mere facet or ancillary of other forms of oppression. This distinct and material existence calls for distinct modes of analysis and opposition.

Gordimer has only recently acknowledged such divergences within feminist thought. Her infamous labelling of feminism as 'piffling' is based on only a partial understanding (at the time when she made much statements) of what constitutes feminism. Gordimer has never set herself up as a systematic foe to feminism. There are occasions when she displays a high degree of sympathy for women and an indignation against her social position. In summary, Gordimer's approach to gender questions is highly variable, and her fluctuating sympathy with or hostility to feminism follow no neat chronological patterns. Her public statements on feminism are not reproduced in any simple, one-to-one fashion in her fiction, but some complex near-correlations are noticeable. Her variation in approach to sexual questions, makes it difficult to read her stories either as 'feminist' or as 'anti-feminist' representations, and this ambiguity of interpretation is heightened by her frequent usage of the ironical voice. Irony promotes a multiplicity of readings. As Moi puts it: 'Politically speaking, the ironist is extremely hard to assail precisely because it is virtually impossible to fix his or her text convincingly. In the ironic discourse, every discourse undercuts itself' (1985: p. 40). Gordimer's tonal slipperiness compounds the interpretive problems caused by the lack of paradigm concerning questions of gender in her work.

The three rough groupings of stories which I discuss illustrate precisely this fluidity across her work. Within single anthologies (including recent ones) there are stories in which Gordimer's portrayals of female behaviour and physique bear a disconcerting resemblance to sexist constructions of women in contemporary society. There are other stories in which race is emphatically prefaced over sex, demonstrating her assertion that gender allegiance is 'cut right through' and annulled by the stronger drives of race. Finally, there are stories in which sexual oppression is foregrounded and treated as a site of social strife in its own right.

'The Third Presence', from *Livingstone's Companions* (1972), provides an index of what Gordimer's writing is like when it potentially lays her open to charges of 'anti-feminism'. The story is about a bond between sisters, and follows a neat 'reversal-of-expectation' pattern (a frequent tactic of Gordimer's). The gorgeous, nubile sister (Naomi) eventually grows dull and matronly while the ugly, clever sister (Rose) gains attractiveness as she gets older. The 'third presence' is apparently constituted by the ugly-sister-transformed. At first glance it seems as if Gordimer is making a case against the traditional success formula for female fulfilment, namely marriage and mothering. Instead she seems to construct sympathy in favour of the working woman who finds satisfaction outside domestic concerns and within intellectual and 'public' ones. But her depiction of the two sisters is not as clear-cut as that, for the usurpation of Naomi by Rose as the successful sister does not occur *because* Rose is independent and unconventional, but because she acquires a new style of dress and has a nose-operation. The 'third presence' is thus not so much a new version of the ugly sister as a hybridization of what the two sisters represented to start off with: attractiveness and autonomy conjoined.[3] Gordimer's endorsement of Rose only occurs once she has attained sexual validity through the beauty of the body. This is a limited and compromised endorsement, and one which does not cast off sexist insistences that women be judged via 'looks'.

Gordimer frequently deploys the criterion of bodily beauty in her portrayals of favoured female protagonists. For instance, Rosa in *Burger's Daughter* (1976) and Hillela in *A Sport of Nature* (1988) are validated politically not only through their political actions but also via their status as imaginary objects of the gaze and the touch. A hero is only a hero if she is courageous and politically engaged *and* sensuous and desirable. These figures exist problematically alongside Gordimer's constructions of repugnant physicalities when she wishes to undercut the political viability of a female character, as in her merciless treatment of Clare Terreblanche in *Burger's Daughter*: 'The other girl . . . took a chair heavily. . . . At the inner starting point of each eyebrow a few hairs stood up – hackles that gave intensity to her face. She rubbed them with the voluptuousness of assuagement, the peeling eczema danced into life'(1979: pp. 118–20). Features such as this in her fiction undermine the challenges which Gordimer makes to the social position of women in other respects. One could claim that Gordimer's ubiquitous coolness and irony of voice operate as disclaimers of ideological collusion in textual instances such as the one just cited. But such an authorial tone does not obscure the fact that damaging and collusive evaluations of women are present.

Gordimer's portrayal of Joy in the 1984 novella *Something Out There* is an interesting case. Beneath her false pregnancy, the white female guerrilla is constructed as bony, austere, humourless and asexual, typical signifiers of political devalorization of a female figure on Gordimer's part. And yet although Joy may not belong in the select family of handsome revolutionary women in Gordimer's work, there is no doubt that Gordimer treats Joy's politics with respect, given that they are in line with the non-racial mode of political operation that Gordimer is endorsing by the 1980s. Joy's feminist lifestyle is treated with at least some sympathy by Gordimer. This suggests that the author is now prepared to recognize the intimate realities of women's oppression and the need for social change in that regard, and that she herself has undergone a politicization on questions of gender.

I now move to the group of stories in which Gordimer does not so much collude with sexism as question the relative urgency of sexual oppression when juxtaposed with the immediacy and force of racial oppression. Given that patriarchy has always relegated questions concerning women to secondary status relative to questions of 'greater' public urgency (such as class and race), it is small wonder that Gordimer's apparent insistence on the primacy of race has provoked the concern of some feminist critics. But on closer examination one sees that Gordimer's treatment of gender questions is far more subtle than if she had simply relegated them to second place. 'Good Climate, Friendly Inhabitants', from *Not For Publication* (1965), is a fairly early story that sets the scene for many later ones. In a form close to dramatic monologue, Gordimer constructs a first-person narrator who tells her own story and through it reveals her solitude and prejudices. Both the narrator and the 'fellow' who briefly enters her life remain unnamed – she as an anonymous member of the white petty bourgeoisie, he as an outsider and temporary havoc-raiser. It is only the black petrol attendant, finally spurned by the two other characters, but constructed by Gordimer as the moral centre of the text, who is named in full: 'Mpanza Makiwane, or Jack for those who cannot say it' (1975: p. 277). The story adumbrates the harsh realities of being an ageing woman, alone in a large city with little money. The narrator works in a petrol station office, and lives in a boarding house. Her anxiety over her waning looks is given prominence by its placement at the start of the story: 'I'm forty-nine but I could be twenty-five except for my face and legs. I've got that very fair skin and my legs have gone mottled, like Roquefort cheese'

(1975: p. 275). The woman's lack of social security expresses itself in her need for a man and her fear of not being attractive enough to gain one. Where the body is such a prominent form of social valorization, the loss of its beauty threatens women, particularly older women, with social invisibility (Keysworth: p. 1982). This woman must win her man by looking after him. The 'fellow' begins to visit her frequently at the garage, finally leaves his hotel without paying and moves into her room. He remains cagey about his movements, but lets himself into her place at will, eats her food and sleeps in her bed. To keep him, she consents. He remains a shadowy and itinerant figure throughout the story, existing mainly as an incarnation of the exploitation of women.

Gordimer's great skill manifests itself in the slow unfolding of the pain of the woman's situation. This is expressed in the unchanging, flat language of the narrator herself. Formal authorial language never interrupts the particular discourse of this monologue: a version of the speech of lower-income South African whites with its colloquialisms and Afrikaans–English hybridizations. The woman becomes increasingly aware of the man's unsavoury activities, and simultaneously starts fearing for her own physical safety. The political aspect of her relationship with him is here most clearly revealed. The fear of rape or assault is one known by women in every society, no matter what their age or background. Although usually experienced by women in isolation, sexual violence is an enactment of generic power over and control of women by men. The threat of sexual violence is the most extreme facet of the abuse that already exists in the narrator's relationship with the strange man. And yet despite her fear, she longs for the intimacy, brutal and unsatisfactory as it is, that he can give her. The relationship is for her a compound of need and fear, typical constituents of the domestic trap which so many battered women cannot escape.

The narrator's utter alone-ness, in social terms, heightens her fears: 'I sometimes wonder what'll happen to me – in some years of course – if I'm alone here, and nobody comes. Every Sunday you read in the paper about women dead alone in flats, no one discovers it for days' (1975: p. 284). Desperation finally drives her to confide in an unlikely figure: Jack, the black 'bossboy'. The narrator's relationship with him develops parallel to her relationship with the 'fellow'. Her attitudes to the black petrol attendants are deeply conditioned by ideas of racial superiority. She maintains distance by sending Jack on errands 'just to show him that he mustn't get too free with a white person' (p. 286). So much for the ideological stereotypes which inform her thinking. But immediate interaction may sometimes contradict ideology. She finds herself coming to rely on Jack for news about the stranger's appearances, and finally is forced to ask for Jack's protection and alertness. Racial ideology is thus overridden by a second political tension in her life, her nightly fear of the sexual visitor/intruder in her flat. Gordimer sets up a deeply anomalous scenario: a black man defending a white woman against a white man, stark reversal of the customary ideological pattern where white men protect 'their' women against black marauders.

Jack becomes father-figure and ally, and finally sends away the 'fellow' with the false information that the narrator has left the garage. Jack shows more compassion towards her than anyone else has done, but once she is free of fear, old guards go up again. She reasserts power over Jack through the mode most easily summoned up: racial contempt. Jack, being 'bossboy', is closer to her in class position than the other black attendants. She is an unskilled office bureaucrat, he a supervisor. Over-familiarity with him would threaten her already-tenuous class position. Thus tragically, Jack's humaneness is repaid with denigration: 'I think he fancies himself quite the educated man . . . if you take any notice of things like that with them, you begin to give them big ideas about themselves' (p. 288). In a perverse twist of misallocated blame, Jack loses his particularity in her eyes and becomes one of the 'natives' whom a woman on her own 'can't trust at night'. Memories of kindness are shorter-lived than hegemonic perceptions, Gordimer here suggests. Allegiances made on the basis of protection against sexual oppression, will invariably be overridden by the stronger drives of racism.

The telegrammatic phraseology of the title evokes the sense that the narrator's world is being appraised from a distance, as in a tourist guide-book. The appraiser could be read as the 'fellow' in the story, and the anonymity and alienation enshrouding the narrator are reinforced by this effect of distantiation. Gordimer could also be suggesting that beneath glib, de-contextualized assessments of South Africa, lies a bitter and converse truth: that (although the climate may be good!) the inhabitants are far from 'friendly', and that bonds in South Africa are beset by conflicts and cruelties. Victims turn victimizers, closeness is overrun by division. The story offers us a segment of South African life, and the bleak, sordid nature of the woman's circumstances is as much a part of that segment as are the racial tensions. Gordimer's insistence, in a dialogue with Susan

Sontag, that 'private life is penetrated by politics' (1985: p. 16), applies as much to sexual encounters between individuals as to racial ones.

In her introduction to *Selected Stories* Gordimer comments: '[T]here are some stories I have gone on writing, again and again, all my life, not so much because the themes are obsessional but because I found other ways to take hold of them' (1975: p. 10). One of the stories which she reworks in nearly every anthology is the domestic service or 'maid/madam' entanglement.[4] In *Something Out There* (1984), 'Blinder' continues this concern. The story is written in the present tense, which confers a combined effect of immediacy and continuity on to the story, confirming that this situation has long been in existence and shows no signs of letting up. The usual maid–madam duo is further complicated by the addition of a third female figure: a rural black woman, wife of the domestic servant's lover. The man is now dead, and she, made eternally dependent on him by the structure of the migrant labour system, has come to claim his pension. Many of Gordimer's stories sketch the sexual competitiveness between two women over one man.[5] Here, two women literally share one man due to force of political circumstance. Yet the differences between the two black women – the urban–rural rift which they embody, their discrepant standards of living, their sexual rivalry – are not enough to override their allegiance. The black women share an understanding that Rose (the maid) will never have with her madam in spite of their years of proximity and quasi-intimacy. We are returned to Gordimer's contention that any potential for ideological identification between women is 'cut right through' by differentials of race and class. In the invisible triangle that conceptually structures the narrative, the maid mediates gleefully between the 'lady of the house' and the bemused rural woman. In a brief moment of subversion the usually disempowered urban servant gains power through handing a lavish bunch of grapes to the visiting rural child, without asking her 'madam' for permission. Speechless, dependent on her own servant for mediation, the white woman can only watch while the maid enjoys a borrowed munificence. The white woman is uncomfortably cast into a position of temporary, atypical (and prophetic?) marginality, while the black women are drawn together in racial and economic identification.

The title 'Blinder' reverberates with multi-dimensional irony typical in Gordimer, and incorporates the many social complexities of the story. The maid's 'blinders', or drinking bouts, are a response to insecure interpersonal and political circumstance. The rural wife is figuratively blinded by dint of her isolation in a bantustan and her exclusion from her husband's urban life. The title tolls most heavily on the white madam, unnamed and interpretable as amalgam and type of the many madams we encounter in Gordimer's fiction. The madam is clearly blind to social realities, and half-blind to her own cocoonedness. South Africa is a society that engenders and thrives on such blindnesses. If, at times, Gordimer's writing has suggested that she herself is 'blind' to women's oppression, this story suggests a deepening of her understanding of the multi-sided nature of oppression, and her recognition that gender is a social determinant that plays into other determinants. Her insistence that gender commonality is 'cut right through' by stronger and more primary modes of oppression is partially demonstrated yet again in this story, but also partially diluted. The two black women in the story are not only drawn together in shared understanding of racial and economic marginality, but also in shared understanding of their exploitability as women.

We have now seen various stories which illustrate Gordimer's assertion that gender commonality is 'cut right through' by other social divides. I do not intend to suggest that these stories are 'unfeminist' but, rather, to lay bare Gordimer's naunced sense of how sexual issues are often overlaid and complicated by other political features. Because Gordimer stresses the immediacy of racial questions over sexual ones in these stories, they might provide fuel for critics wishing to 'prove' her hostility to feminism. Such readings would, however, not do justice to her complex grasp of social nexuses, and would also run the risk of ignoring her often sympathetic understanding of the position of women in South African society.

Moving on now to the third rough group of stories: there are some moments in Gordimer's work where authorial exposure of and critique of sexual oppression are explicitly clear. Often in these stories there is also a tone of oblique sanction of what Gordimer perceives as female strength and resourcefulness (such as in her treatment of the courageous wife/mother/activist/prisoner figure of Mrs Bamjee in 'A Chip of Glass Ruby' from *Not for Publication*, 1965).

'An Intruder', from the anthology *Livingstone's Companions* (1972), must belong among Gordimer's most striking stories. One of the author's persistent concerns is to depict the strange and changing bases of power in human relationships. In this story her focus is on the bizarre and grotesque in a love relationship. The South African

setting of the story, although seemingly extrinsic to the central relationship, is not unimplicated in it. The violence and rage expressed
in the obscene actions of the 'intruder', appear to be on the same
continuum of violence as the political system which manifests
paranoically in the many references to 'burglar bars' (1975: p. 386).
The story can be read as a fictionalized instance of the 'morbid
symptoms' which Gordimer, quoting Gramsci, frequently mentions:
'The old is dying, the new cannot be born; in this interregnum there
arises a great diversity of morbid symptoms' (1983: p. 21).

James, the male figure in this text, belongs to a fast-moving nightclub set with dubious habits and dubious sources of money. Into this
nocturnal world comes the unexpected figure of Marie: a passive,
petted young woman. Her mother acts as an accomplice in Marie's
lack of preparation for the seamy side of human behaviour, typify-
ing the transference of oppressive values within female lineages, as
well as the complicity of women in their own and each other's
underdevelopment. Marie's physical delicacy places her in a particular category of female figures within Gordimer's stories where
physique is metonymic of social innocence.[6] Gordimer comments
that the descriptions of these characters' physique is meant to
connote 'a dramatic contrast between the type and the size of the
experience they are going through' (1988: p. 10). Once married, the
couple move into a dingy flat which Marie assiduously tries to make
into a home. James's domain continues to be the 'nightclubs and
drinking places' where they spend their nights. Marie is constructed
as sorely incongruous at these haunts: 'She sat looking out of the rest
of the noisy party in the nightclub like a bush-baby between trees'
(1975: p. 378). In this exuberant scenario Marie is clearly the 'intruder'. But the image of the bush-baby is an immediate signal of
vulnerability rather than intrusion. Readerly responses are geared to
expect another 'intruder'.

Waking one day after a deep and unknowing sleep, Marie discovers anarchy in the flat. Gordimer spares us no ugliness: 'On each
of the three divisions of the soft cushions there was a little pile, an
offering. One was a slime of contraceptive jelly with haircombings –
hers . . . the other was toothpaste and razor blades; the third was a
mucous of half-rotted vegetable matter' (p. 385). But the 'obscene
collage' is not the work of a stranger. At this point, Marie is too
bemused for recognition, and it is only after they have moved to a
new flat that she questions how the intruder could have gained
entry. When she remembers the locked doors and the ubiquitous

burglar bars, the full horror dawns: 'and this time . . . She began to know what else he would *never remember*; something so simple that she had missed it' (p. 386).

The change in Marie, icon of lost innocence, is entire: 'she stood there wan, almost ugly, like some wretched pet monkey shivering in a cold climate' (p. 386). The monkey-image returns, but this time connotes not charm but utter wretchedness. The appeal of James's suave 'candour' is peeled away, and Marie can only ponder at what savage drives prompted him to distort 'the passionate rites of their intimacy' (p. 385). The story reverberates beyond its ending; living a Jekyll-and Hyde existence with the man whose child she is carrying, will Marie not join the train of women whom James has left (or who have left him)? Suddenly these figures can be read from a new perspective. So far we have met them only via James's voice: as 'that freckled bitch', as 'those gorgons'. Marie, with unexpected acuteness, predicts that when James tires of her he will rename her as 'that sugar-tit tart' (p. 382). All these labels arise from a harsh corner of male discourse, and construct women as hard, brittle and devouring of men. The unfolding narrative suggests another way in which 'James's women' can be seen: as a sequence of victims of his sordid sexual behaviour. Gordimer builds up a terrifying implied scenario of countless women, all facing private horror and domestic violence, but atomized to the extent that their oppression is perceived as individual. Myths of romantic fulfilment, a discourse attached to the figure of the mother in the text, do nothing to disclose such abuses. Gordimer's little Frankenstein, her character James, is only an extreme incarnation of the 'intrusions' of women's safety and peace of mind so highly present in sexist society.

Driver offers a different reading of the story. She sees the intruder as Marie's 'maddened self' (1983: p. 44) escaping from its repression and expressing rage against James. According to Driver, Gordimer thus offers a 'feminist possibility': female indignation will come out through illicit and marginal discourses. In my reading the 'maddened self' is not Marie's nocturnal 'feminist' self, but James's amnesiacal drunken one expressing sub-rational excesses of aggression against women. It is Marie's realization of these excesses which would then explain her 'wan . . . shivering' state at the end of the story. Whichever readings one takes, it is abundantly clear that Gordimer has depicted an aspect of women's oppression in an instance of particular extremity. James is a more polished and urbane version of the 'fellow' in 'Good Climate, Friendly Inhabitants', but

both are signifiers of severe exploitativeness. Both women protagonists are finally characterized by solitude. But seen together, they
belong in a family of women characters, spanning Gordimer's work,
whose sexual vulnerability is made straightforwardly clear, as opposed to the ambivalent, ironical and denigratory representations of
women and their circumstances at other points in her fiction.

A moving and vivid story is 'The Termitary' from *A Soldier's
Embrace* (1980). Its early pages are narrated as if through a child's
eyes, and the richly-evoked sights and smells of this world are
strongly suggestive of first-hand knowledge. But the story is not
simply an exercise in Proustian nostalgia. Meaning coalesces around
one narratorial 'memory' in particular, the termite-removal pro-
cedure. There are two queens in the story, the termite-queen who is
the target of the exterminator's quest, and the mother of the house
who presides over the extermination. Filtered through the figure of
the child-narrator, the process has a grotesque chivalric aura to it,
and the exterminators are akin to a ghastly breed of knights: 'Bloodied
by their lifelong medieval quest, they were ready to take it up once
more: the search for a queen' (1980a: p. 117).

The termite-queen fascinates the narrator because her endless
parturition generates a colony of white ants which are both 'subjects'
and 'progeny' (1980a: p. 117). The queen/mother convergence gives
the ant-queen eerie power, a power reflected in a spatial metaphor:
the termite's underground domain stretches as far as the house's
boundaries, making it coterminous with the domain of the 'queen'
above the floorboards. Enormous in insect-terms, the scale of the
mother's domain conversely implies confinement and radically cur-
tailed power. The two queens are tied together by this imagery of
domain, and also by the imagery of nourishment. The 'sweet creamy
stuff' exuded from the termite's body and which feeds her 'children-
subjects', is a verbal and sensory echo of the 'fragrant creamy sweetness' of the mother's cake-mixture. These imagistic parallels point to
a set of larger parallels. Despite the ant-queen's indispensable role as
progenitor and nourisher, paradoxically she is also a subject: blind,
immobile, a 'tyrannical prisoner' (1980a: p. 119). Similarly the mother
of the house is both queen and subject, simultaneously attractive and
repulsive to the family under her rule. Just as the ant-queen will
eventually be eaten by her children, she is sapped by hers; the
nourisher is also the one to be consumed.

The mother in 'The Termitary' signifies the duality of power and
impotence which women face in the conventionally defined do-

mestic realm. Her strength and will pervade the story, but the relative meagreness of her power is made clear through contiguity with her husband's daily departures into the world of political and economic power. Looking back from an adult viewpoint, the narrator wonders at the narrowness and paucity of her mother's life: 'Were those servants the sum of my mother's life?' (1980a: p. 120). The story's imagery of queenship constructs a sense of bounded dominion. This signifies power held in one area of social interaction but not in others. Questions of female exclusion and powerlessness are thus made dramatically explicit. The authorial sympathies lie squarely with the mother. Gordimer's frequent tone of cool distance is entirely absent. The final image is an especially fond one, the tone almost elegiac: 'Now she is dead and although I suppose someone else lives in her house, the secret passages, the inner chamber in which she was our queen and prisoner are sealed up, empty' (p. 120).

It is clear that Gordimer's stories cannot be neatly accommodated either under a feminist or under an anti-feminist rubric. Although many of her representations incorporate an incontestable movement away from sexist stereotypes and assumptions, there are others, occasionally even in her recent work, that retain an uncritical relationship with sexist ideology. Her statement that she has 'become more radical . . . as a woman' is exhibited in an uneven and non-linear way in her fiction. No neat chronologies, no perfect political paths can be traced. The movement of her stories in relation to feminism is a zigzagging, idiosyncratic and investigative one.

Notes

1. Gordimer is aware of the consternation she has caused to feminists; for instance, she comments in interview (Lazar, 1988: p. 7) that she was 'expecting heavy flak' from feminists over her presentation of Hillela in *A Sport of Nature* (1987).
2. In interview (Lazar: 1988) she discusses the dominating presence of strong female role-models in her early life and hints at her atypical education.
3. Gordimer's retention of female bodily beauty as a criterion of 'success' alongside the criteria of intelligence and autonomy, ironically places her in a position close to bourgeois feminism (the feminism she has so stringently dismissed) and its Superwoman ethos.
4. See Jacklyn Cock's *Maids and Madams* (1980), an excellent study of

   domestic labour and 'maid/madam' interactions in South Africa.
5.   Examples are 'The Battlefield at No. 29' from *Face to Face* (1948) and
     'Rain Queen' from *Livingstone's Companions* (1972).
6.   Two other examples of frail female figures are the central characters in
     'The Smell of Death and Flowers' and 'A Bit Of Young Life' (both from
     Six Feet of the Country).

Works Cited

Cock, J. (1980) *Maids and Madams: A Study in the Politics of Exploitation*
   (Johannesburg: Ravan Press).
Driver, D. (1983) 'Nadine Gordimer: The Politicization of Women', *English
   in Africa*, (Grahamstown, South Africa), Vol. 10, no. 2, pp. 29–54.
Gordimer, N. (1965) *Not For Publication* (London: Victor Gollancz).
_____ , (1972) *Livingstone's Companions* (London: Jonathan Cape).
_____ , (1975) *Selected Stories* (Harmondsworth: Penguin).
_____ , (1977) 'What Being a South African Means to Me', *South African
   Outlook*, June, p. 88.
_____ , (1979) *Burger's Daughter* (London: Jonathan Cape).
_____ , (1980a) *A Soldier's Embrace* (London: Jonathan Cape; Harmondsworth:
   Penguin, 1982).
_____ , (1980b) 'The Prison-House of Colonialism', *The Times Literary Supplement*, 15 August.
_____ , (1981) 'An Interview with Nadine Gordimer', Gray, Stephen, *Contemporary Literature*, Vol. 22, no. 3, pp. 263–71.
_____ , (1983) 'Living in the Interregnum', *New York Review of Books*,
   20 January.
_____ , (1984) *Something Out There* (London: Jonathan Cape).
_____ , (1984b) 'A Conversation with Nadine Gordimer', interview with
   Boyers, Robert *et al.*, *Salmagundi* no. 62, pp. 3–31.
_____ , (1985) 'Nadine Gordimer and Susan Sontag in Conversation', *The
   Listener*, 23 May.
_____ , (1987) *A Sport of Nature* (Cape Town: David Philip).
_____ , (1988) 'Interview with Nadine Gordimer', Lazar, Karen, in National
   English Literary Museum Interview Series No. 5 (Grahamstown, South
   Africa: 1992).
Keysworth, F. (1982) 'Invisible Struggles: The Politics of Ageing', in Brunt,
   R. and Rowan, C. (eds), *Feminism, Culture and Politics* (London: Lawrence
   and Wishart).
Lazar, K. (1988) Unpublished Masters dissertation: 'The personal and the
   political in some of Nadine Gordimer's short stories'. University of the
   Witwatersrand, Johannesburg.
Lockett, C. (1990) 'Feminism(s) and Writing in the South African Context', in
   Current Writing Vol. 1, no. 2, University of Natal, Durban, South Africa.
Moi, T. (1985) *Sexual/Textual: Feminist Literary Theory* (London: Methuen).
Vogel, L. (1983) *Marxism and the Oppression of Women: Towards a Unitary
   Theory* (London: Pluto Press).

14

Once More into the Burrows: Nadine Gordimer's Later Short Fiction

ALAN R. LOMBERG

In the introduction to her *Selected Stories*, Nadine Gordimer suggests that the process of composition is, for her, like burrowing into a warren 'where many burrows lead off into the same darkness but this one may debouch far distant from that' (*SS*, p. 12).[1] An instance of that is provided by the development of two stories in *A Soldier's Embrace* into the novella which is the title story of *Something Out There*.

One of the stories which provides intimations of the subsequent 'exploration' in *Something Out There* is 'Oral History'. In that, a chief, trying to protect his village from attack by reporting 'guerrillas' in it, finds that the 'arrests' that were to be made (*ASE*, p. 142) become instead an army attack which devastates the village. There is the cruel irony that he had taken his bicycle with him when he went to make his report, and that it 'would have been lost if it had been safe in the kitchen when the raids came' (*ASE*, p. 142). Gordimer drily reveals the chief's suicide through the remark 'No one knows where the chief found a rope, in the ruins of his village.' (*ASE*, p. 144) There is a notable intimation of perseverance and endurance, though, in the concluding report of the return of the surviving villagers and their gradual rebuilding of the village.

In terms of style and foreshadowing, 'A Lion on the Freeway' is a more interesting preparation for *Something Out There*. It has an aura of dreaminess, reflecting the half-sleep in which thoughts and reminiscences run through the narrator's mind. The development proceeds by association and accretion. The 'Open up!' develops threateningly into 'Open your legs' (*ASE*, p. 24) which leads to a recollection of love-making 'once . . . near the Baltic' (*ASE*, p. 25) thence to love-making 'heard . . . once through a hotel wall (*ASE*, p. 26). Parallel to that progression, and interspersed with it, is a progression related to the lion and its roar, a progression which culminates in the fusion of the sound of the lion – 'that groan straining, the rut of freedom bending the bars of the cage' (*ASE*, p. 27) – with that of a group of black strikers, 'A thick prancing black centipede with thousands of wavy legs advancing' (*ASE*, p. 27). There is a further intimation, through a device used more than once in the story – '(no spears anymore, no guns yet)' (*ASE*, p. 27) – that the strikers, like the lion, are waiting to reclaim their country.

Those earlier explorations develop into the stories in *Something Out There* which deal with the socio-political and socio-economic situation of apartheid South Africa. In 'A City of the Dead, A City of the Living', one of the protagonists (Moreke's wife) reflects on the young man they are sheltering: 'You only count the days if you are waiting to have a baby or you are in prison.' (*SOT*, p. 10) That curious combination is indicative of the circumstances by which the man has come into their lives. Were he a relative, even a distant one, they would have been obliged to give him shelter; but 'This one is in trouble' (*SOT*, p. 14), and his claims on them are only justifiable in that 'If you are not white, you are the same blood here' (*SOT*, p. 15).

While providing a detailed picture of township life with its privations and its special sense of community in the midst of poverty, together with a high rate of infant mortality (indicated by the otherwise unnecessary qualification that this is the woman's fifth 'living' baby (*SOT*, pp. 12–13)), and the unhygienic conditions and multiple uncertainties, Gordimer traces the progress of events in parallel with the woman's private thoughts and feelings about the man who is 'in trouble'. The woman's ambivalence is shown to be moving towards self-protection in a manner similar to that of the chief in 'Oral History'. The wish not to be involved is reflected in her thoughts: 'how long does it take for a beard to grow, how long. How long before he goes away' (*SOT*, p. 16). In the end, it is fear of being punished for complicity, an unuttered tendency towards self-preservation, that drives her to report the man's presence to the police. Even then, she has mixed feelings: 'I don't know why I did it. I get ready to say that to anyone who is going to ask me, but nobody in this house asks' (*SOT*, p. 26). Judgement of her action is, however, clearly provided by Ma Radebe, the shebeen-keeper, who, when she next saw the woman in the street, 'gazed at her for a moment, and spat' (*SOT*, p. 26). That terse conclusion emphasizes the fact that, however much may go unspoken, there is no question where loyalties should lie.

The ambivalence of Moreke's wife parallels the uncertainty of the chief in 'Oral History'. He had worried that his report to the army 'was not coming out as he had meant nor being understood as he had expected' (*ASE*, p. 141). Moreover, the villagers '*never saw*' but only 'heard the government say on the radio' (*ASE*, p. 142) that the strangers the chief was reporting committed atrocities to force people to connive with them. More importantly, various aspects of these stories build towards the novella, 'Something Out There', in which there is a much fuller treatment of a general anxiety about something numinous about which people hazard an identity only so that fear might be made manageable.

The 'beast' in the novella is more menacing than the 'lion' on the freeway because it is not just a threatening, misunderstood sound in the night; it has attacked, and continues to do so. The city's inhabitants have a range of suppositions about the nature of the 'beast', and there is the predictable 'embroidering' which takes place when opinion needs to be bolstered by details which will make supposition convincing. Encounters (and purported encounters) with the 'something' outline that process by which a creature or event moves from the real to the surreal, and thence into legend. While tracing that progression, Gordimer also provides cameo portraits of various social groups – from the correspondents of a Sunday newspaper who use the opportunity to air their own gripes, to a group of medical specialists out playing golf, three of whom decide the mystery creature is 'one of the black out-of-works' (*SOT*, p. 126). In all these instances Gordimer uses the sightings as a basis for some cutting social criticism, implicit in some cases, more direct in others. Mrs Naas Klopper (whose husband has rented a farm to the two white members of a four-person guerrilla group) equates accounts of the predator with 'good old stories of giant pumpkins' (*SOT*, p. 119). Important things happening in the world are considered an irritation at best, compared to the incidents of 'normal' life (*SOT*, p. 120). For the four medical specialists, their Thursday afternoon golf game is more important than their patients. A more general selfishness is reflected in the lack of concern of people in one neighbourhood when the creature no longer appears to be active there: 'So long as it attacked other people's cats and dogs, frightened other people's maids – that was other people's business' (*SOT*, p. 181). The most absurd response is that the animal 'wouldn't have had to live the life of an outlaw' if it had stuck to 'its proper station in life' (*SOT*, p. 189). That remark has obviously been transferred from its application to people who, under the apartheid system, are expected to do just that.

The remark may also be seen as applicable to the four guerrillas. In a pattern akin to that of 'A Lion on the Freeway', their story, beginning with Charles' and Joy's renting of the farm from Naas Klopper, is carefully interwoven with the reports of, and reactions to, the various attacks of the animal. An interesting reaction (and one that is typical of Gordimer's style) comes after the creature has ripped the flesh from a leg of meat hung in the window of his house by a sergeant who interrogates political detainees. The sergeant's superior says that the man's wife ought to learn to handle a gun because 'Next time it might be more than a monkey out there in the yard' (*SOT*, p. 159). That casual, reasonable remark is one of a kind that Gordimer adroitly deploys; its dramatic irony subsists in the fact that we know that there are four people out there who are planning an attack on a power plant. After the attack, there is irony as well in Mrs Klopper's providing a degree of anonymity while trying, conversely, to identify the black man she had seen at the farm: 'Just like any other black – young, wearing jeans that were a bit smart, yes, for a farm boy' (*SOT*, p. 198). There is irony of a slightly different sort in one of those small details that are inimitably part of Gordimer's style: in a police photograph of various captured weapons (some of them thrown in 'for added effect, as a piece of greenery gives the final touch to a floral arrangement'), Mrs Klopper sees 'her own biscuit tin, in which she had made the offering of rusks' (*SOT*, p. 199) to Charles and Joy.

While the stories discussed so far show an interplay of ideas and style and reflect one of Gordimer's persistent concerns – chronicling life in her country and the changes that evolve over the years – other stories reveal more strikingly her experimentation with new structures and approaches. In 'For Dear Life', the normal transitional and/or signalling phrases have been stripped away. The point of perception switches from one narrator to another so that only the form of expression and the nature of the concerns expressed are left to indicate to the reader that this is the independent narrator, the pregnant woman previously observed in the story, the father of that woman, and so on, down to the child itself ('Behind me, the torn membranes of my moorings' (*ASE*, p. 72)) emerging from the womb.

As Gordimer has herself observed, there are some stories she has 'gone on writing, again and again' (*ASE*, p. 10). Prominent among those must be Gordimer's repeated treatment of love affairs. While the primacy of the body is something she has spoken of as applying particularly to adolescence and early adulthood, she treats love relationships at many stages of life, and her heroes and heroines are usually engaged in extra-marital affairs. As with Bray in *A Guest of Honour* or Liz in *The Late Bourgeois World*, a change of partner seems to be an inevitable concomitant of developing changes in attitudes and beliefs. As in her other work, Gordimer is constantly in search of the truth about things; not, however, in an abstract manner, but as it emerges in real situations, with all their distinctive colour and flavour and (often) incongruity, paradox and irony as well. The truths that emerge in her fiction are more accurate and significant than '*the* truth' that can supposedly only emerge from non-fiction.

Truths about love relationships in these two collections range over a span from adolescence to middle-age, and arise from reminiscences as well as from more immediate events. The narrator of 'A Need for Something Sweet' looks back at an affair of his youth with an older woman who represented an adolescent fantasy lover. He harks back to it from the position of a settled middle-aged man who has just had 'a few words with the wife' (*ASE*, p. 131). It is an instance of sloughing off something considered to have been a minor aberration of one's 'salad days': 'Who would believe a clean youngster could get mixed up with a woman who would end up like that' (*ASE*, p. 131). That sort of *ex post facto* rejection takes different forms in the two parts of 'Town and Country Lovers', but reflects an important aspect of Gordimer's thinking about the way our lives develop, whether in terms of our love affairs in particular or our values and beliefs in general.

Another good pointer to Gordimer's view of love comes in 'Time Did' when the narrator speaks of the 'great confessional of our early intimacy . . . that, paradoxically, real life familiarity (in marriage, for example) seals off' (*ASE*, p. 50). She also remarks of her lover: 'your delight in the variety of my sex delighted me, too. How many men really love women?' (*ASE*, p. 50) There is a certain familiarity about this narrator which, combined with the structure of the piece, reveals Gordimer reworking aspects of a previous work. With her assertiveness, occasional hesitation, and petulant defensiveness, she reminds one of Liz in *The Late Bourgeois World*. This new venture into the 'burrows', however, has several distinct qualities. The opening, without even a 'whistle' of introduction, is cryptic: we have no idea who the narrator is, nor the person being quoted. More than with Liz, the focus here is on a dying relationship. The narrator notes that her lover is seeing in her 'the final softening of the flesh that is coming to you as a man one day, your death as a lover of women' (*ASE*, p. 53). Moreover, as 'Time' has its way, 'the schema of cosmetics . . . chalks a face that no longer exists' (*ASE*, p. 52). This 'truth' is a variation on the more general one of the various changes that take place over the course of our lives, and which everyone who is honest must acknowledge.

'A Hunting Accident' also provides a variation on the theme of love affairs. In the midst of the actual hunt – finely described by Gordimer – we become aware that Christine is engaged in her own 'hunt'; the reference to 'her' photographer in the opening line (*ASE*, p. 56) making her possessive attitude clear, a point reinforced in subsequent lines. She is later concerned that the photographer's behaving as if he were 'incredibly staid' would 'give other people the wrong impression of the kind of man she chose' (*ASE*, p. 62). The quietly affectionate quality of that relationship bears certain resemblances to that of 'Sins of the Third Age', in which the subdued tone reflects the mostly muted, nervous quality of the protagonists' responses to each other and to their situation. The only indication of their identity and why they had eventually decided to settle in a 'fifth country' (Italy) is revealed in the simple statement that he had 'a number branded on his wrist', just as the harrowing ordeals they must have experienced are intimated by the statement that her hands 'retained no mark of the grubbing – frost-cracked and bleeding – for turnips, that had once kept her alive' (*SOT*, p. 66). Like their existence, which was that of 'a well-made life' which 'did not happen; was carefully planned' (*SOT*, p. 66), 'Sins of the Third Age' is neatly arranged and subdued in tone, culminating in the toneless 'there had never been a sign of what had been found, and lost again' (*SOT*, p. 77). He had had an affair, a fact he conveyed to her by simply saying, 'I've met somebody', which remark made them 'two new people' who 'didn't know what subject they had in common' (*SOT*, p. 73). In the same matter-of-fact way, he subsequently announces the end of the affair by saying, 'I gave up that person' (*SOT*, p. 77).

Gordimer takes a very different approach in 'Crimes of Conscience', where the relationship, which seems to develop naturally from a casual acquaintance, is misunderstood. There is an echo of the effect that the man's announcement of his affair in 'Sins of the

Third Age' had on his relationship with his wife when the narrator of 'Crimes of Conscience' likens one development to that of a situation in which an 'old friend suddenly becomes something else . . . as if a face is turned to another angle.' In this case, however, on the 'next day . . . nothing's changed' (*SOT*, p. 62). Unknown to her, this new friend has not become 'something else' but has been so all along. Like Harriet in 'A Correspondence Course', this narrator appears to be one of those young whites who have been 'dumped by their elders with the deadly task of defending a life they haven't chosen for themselves' (*SOT*, p. 105). Thus, she feels she has been giving her lover 'a course in the politics of culture' (*SOT*, p. 62), whereas her attempts to reveal aspects of her earlier life (such as her time in prison) have simply been feeding him with the information he is meant to get out of her, his purpose becoming clear when he reveals, 'I've been spying on you' (*SOT*, p. 63). While the relationship is similar to others Gordimer presents – she had, for example, lived for three years 'with someone who, in the end, went back to his wife' (*SOT*, p. 61) – the difference – relative guilelessness encountering the deception of an agent of the secret police – is a reflection of the developing social and political situation in South Africa between the time of the earlier and later stories in the two collections.

'Blinder' provides an interesting contrast to relationships in other stories since the principal relationship here is between an employer and a servant. Although there is never any question of the difference in status – the usual social distance reinforced by the fact that the employer is white and the employee black – there is an aura of mutual affection and symbiosis to the relationship. The focus on the maid produces some of the acute observations that are typical of Gordimer: the human body is like the sea, 'into which no abuse could be thrown away' since it would be certain to be 'cast up again' (*SOT*, p. 83); and the maid, who regularly goes on a binge (the 'blinder' of the title) has a face 'ennobled with the bottle's mimesis of the lines and shadings of worldly wisdom' (*SOT*, p. 88). Gordimer also comments on two important aspects of the South African situation, one applicable anywhere, the other peculiar to that place: the poor are people 'to whom things happen but who don't have the resources to make things happen, don't have the means, either, to extricate themselves from what has happened' (*SOT*, p. 85) – 'black' and 'poor' being largely synonymous in this situation. The other point is that there is no resentment between Ephraim's wife and his lover, Rose, the maid; instead, there is acceptance of the fact that the socio-economic circumstances of apartheid have made it necessary for a man, far from home, to take a temporary partner.

Those circumstances are also important in the two stories which contain the fullest treatment of the development and termination of love affairs, the two parts of 'Town and Country Lovers'. The title, sounding almost like a fictional relative of *Home and Garden Magazine*, belies the outcomes of the relationships. In both cases the couple end up in court, but not because they have done anything that, in almost any other country, would have led to legal action. In the second of the two stories, the relationship between Paulus (the farmer's son) and Thebedi (the daughter of one of the black farm workers) is lovingly developed from the early exchange of gifts between them to the sexual relationship that seems as inevitable as it is natural, and – unnaturally – illegal. Gordimer chronicles the early white lies they tell to cover up the growing relationship, and Paulus' adolescent exaggerations about his life at boarding school. Part of the *dénouement* is prepared for early on when 'a boy in the kraal called Njabulo . . . said he wished he could have bought her a belt and earrings' (*ASE*, p. 87) – gifts Thebedi had received from Paulus. When Paulus eventually discovers that he is obviously the father of the baby Thebedi has borne, there is uncertainty about what Thebedi heard when Paulus went alone into the hut where the baby was. When she is first questioned, an apparent confusion of feelings leads her to claim that 'she saw the accused pouring liquid into the baby's mouth' and that he had 'threatened to shoot her' (*ASE*, p. 92). Her testimony is different when the case eventually comes to trial, and she has had another baby, by Najabulo, by then her husband. Clearly recovered from her early dumbstruck horror, Thebedi dismisses the affair as 'a thing of our childhood' (*ASE*, p. 93). The male protagonist of the first part of 'Town and Country' lovers had dismissed his affair by saying that even in his own country it was 'difficult for a person from a higher class to marry one from a lower class' (*ASE*, p. 84). The ironies here are obvious.

Thebedi's dismissive remark is important because it relates to an important aspect of Gordimer's philosophy. The remark is echoed at the conclusion of 'You Name It' when the narrator reflects on the situation of the illegitimate child she bore and which her husband still supposes is his. She observes that there must be other children 'whose real identity could be resuscitated only if their mother's youth could be brought back to life again' (*ASE*, p. 112). These remarks, together with that of the narrator in 'A Need for Something

Sweet', clearly reflect Gordimer's belief that, as we grow, we change, even to the extent that we come, in later life, to regard our youthful personalities as those of different people.

Gordimer's persistent concern to capture in words the truths of love and life involves a process of re-exploration, and of attempts to find new structures by which she can best reflect the ideas that emerge from her own examination of life. Her development as an artist, then, runs parallel with the development of her views on love and life. Common to both is that fidelity to experience results in changes without which there can be no true growth. We are not products of some form of Freudian determinism, whereby what we become in later life always has a referent in childhood experience. Instead, if we are honest, we must acknowledge that we keep changing as we grow older, and our responses to life, our attitudes and values, alter as we affirm the changes wrought by experience. Moreover, life is full of irony, paradox and incongruity, not something neat and seamless, unless we choose to ignore deliberately the details which keep disturbing the pattern and which lead to changes such as those reflected in the eventual estrangement of Thebedi and Paulus, from which point their lives will diverge and reflect little of that 'thing of [their] childhood'.

The narrator of *A Sport of Nature* puts Gordimer's position clearly: 'Only those who never grow up take childhood events unchanged and definitive, through their lives' (*ASON*, p. 17).

Note

1.   For the sake of convenience, only the initial letters have been used to indicate the work being cited.

Bibliography

Clingman, Stephen, *The Novels of Nadine Gordimer: History from the Inside* (London: Unwin Hyman, 1986).
Gordimer, Nadine, *The Essential Gesture: Writing, Politics and Places*, ed. Stephen Clingman (New York: Alfred A. Knopf, 1988).
_____ , *Selected Stories* (New York: The Viking Press, 1976).
_____ , *A Soldier's Embrace* (Markham, Ontario: Penguin, 1987).
_____ , *Something Out There* (Markham, Ontario: Penguin, 1989).
_____ , *A Sport of Nature* (New York: Alfred A. Knopf, 1987).

15

Archive of Apartheid: Nadine Gordimer's Short Fiction at the End of the Interregnum

JEANNE COLLERAN

> It is obvious that the archive of a society . . . cannot be described exhaustively . . . . on the other hand it is not possible for us to describe our own archive, since it is from these rules that we speak . . . it emerges in fragments.
>
> Michel Foucault, *Archeology of Knowledge*

All of Nadine Gordimer's fictional projects could be described as working to construct an archive of apartheid, a record which as an artist she is bound to keep, transcribing the 'consciousness of her era' (*Selected Stories*, p. 15), however much that consciousness is inevitably limited by the machinery of apartheid itself. Now after ten novels and eight collections of short stories, much can and has been said about this archive: its emphasis, primarily, on the strained sensibilities of white South Africans, its appropriation of real historical figures and events, its growing, now committed alignment with identifiable political movements, its attempt to serve instrumentally as an agent for social change. The problems confronting this archival effort have been articulated most eloquently by Gordimer herself, but whatever form these obstacles have taken – whether bannings, censorship, political disenfranchisement, or the 'split' historical position from which Gordimer must account for her word[1] – they have been met, and therefore the archive exists: a monumental task of monument-making for all those who have suffered under apartheid, struggled against it and work toward its demise.

The latest entry in the archive is a collection of short stories, *Jump*, published just as it was announced that Gordimer had received the Nobel Prize for Literature. When the announcement was made, Gordimer was out of South Africa in New York on a promotional tour for her new book. Such seems fitting, for these stories, like her earliest ones and the some two hundred in between, have appeared first before the eyes of an overseas readership; all of the pieces in *Jump*, in fact, were published previously in American magazines.[2] With their tell-tale tags of social explanation (such as the side comment in 'The Moment Before the Gun Went Off' that the Immorality Act had been repealed or the history lesson about the Cape Coloured squeezed into 'What Were You Dreaming?'), the stories take up again the 'professional responsibility' for 'the transformation of society' that Gordimer sees as the fundament of commitment for a South African writer (*The Essential Gesture*, p. 297). Like Frances Taver, her own character from the 1971 collection, *Livingstone's Companions*, Nadine Gordimer, as both writer and critic, is on the 'circuit for people who wanted to find out the truth about South Africa' (*Selected Stories*, p. 387).

'The truth about South Africa' is not the same thing as the truth about apartheid. The former, bound to history, noosed to the individual, can only be, as Foucault tells us, a fragmentary truth, part of and partial to, the times and the teller. But about apartheid, the truth is not fragmentary: it is diamond-hard, rock-solid as any nugget unearthed from a Transvaal mine. Unvarnished, it is the 'unconscious will to genocide . . . in some whites' ('Letter', p. 304); polished, it is the 'belief in the old biblical justification for apartheid' ('Letter', p. 304) or in the 'South African government's vocabulary of racist euphemisms' (*The Essential Gesture*, p. 295).

'Teraloyna', the centrepiece of the collection, tells the truth about apartheid. It unmines the history of a mythic island which was once inhabited by people 'coloured neither very dark nor very light' (p. 99) but which is now overrun by hundreds of wild cats. The story's ending relies on a metonymic slide of meaning, a technique which Gordimer frequently employs in her short fiction, particularly as a means of closure.[3] Elliptical, sparse, economic, the metonomy operates by virtue of contiguous positions and by slippage between these positions: non-causal events are aligned next to each other; public, social realities are placed alongside private, psychic obsessions. The emotional configuration underlying the one spreads to the other. The trope of metonomy thus mimics linguistically the psychological process by which events cannot be excised from their angle of refraction or stripped of their emotional overlay. In 'Teraloyna', the young white men who have 'under command and sometimes out of panic' shot schoolchildren and mourners as well as rioters, without bothering to distinguish between them, have been recruited to clear the island of the cats. This time, 'game for it', the young men need not concern themselves about making distinctions; they'll have 'abundant targets', of all colours, and they will be free to 'kill, kill them all' (pp. 106–7). Though told as fable, seemingly disqualifying itself as an historical document, the story nonetheless lays tacit claim to that power of moral authority most associated with a fable's axiomatic ending. In 'Teraloyna' the implied adage asserts that blocked desire – the desire for blood, the will to genocide – will reappear elsewhere. It will look other than what it is, this blood-thirst, perhaps take on the appearance of an environmentalist rightening the balance of the ecosystem or a young man called to respond to the 'emergency within the Emergency' (p. 106), but it will reappear and pursue its prey.

The rest of the stories in *Jump* tell the truth about South Africa. For Gordimer this task, a task similar to what Jacques Derrida has described as the 'properly reversible structure' of holding the mirror up to the law ('Laws', p. 14), is one more fraught and more fragmentary than telling the truth about apartheid. As she attempts to describe from within and as exhaustively as she can her own archive, giving at least fictional names to the 'archival record of the unnameable' (Derrida, 'Racism', p. 330), Gordimer is consummately aware of the duality of her mediating role, one which is as compromised as it is critical. In 'A Journey', Gordimer offers a story which interrogates its own presumptions as well as its subject. Through the voice of the story's first narrator, a 'lady with gray hair' in the window seat of an aeroplane (p. 149), who observes another woman across the way travelling with her newborn child and older son, Gordimer accedes that the trio exists 'only in the alternate lives I invent, the unknown of what happened to them preceding the journey and the unknown of what was going to happen at its end' (p. 145). As the narrative yields to other points of view, first the son's and then the absent father's, it signals its own partiality, and in doing so, Gordimer establishes the vocal extremes of this collection. Against the firm pitch of 'Teraloyna', the ferocious sound of moral authority, is set the tremulous uttering of the self-reflexive, self-questioning narrative of 'A Journey'. Between these, the sure voice of political commitment and the qualified voice of a narrative conscious of its own narrativity, the rest of the stories fall.

Gordimer has stated that the short story, with its 'art of the present moment' is, in important ways, more able than the novel 'to convey the quality of human life' ('Symposium', p. 459). 'Fragmented' and 'restless' in form, but absolved both of the onerous convention of the 'prolonged coherence of tone' that defines the novel and of the burden of 'cumulative' meaning, the short story is less 'false to the nature of whatever can be grasped of human reality' (p. 459). For these and other reasons, a *collection* of short stories may be the vehicle most conducive to telling whatever truths can be told about South Africa. Some of the reasons are obvious: the range and variety of voices it is possible to include within the boundaries of the collection are suggestive of the even greater multiplicity of voices, attitudes, and constituencies that comprise South African society and compete – or co-labour – to determine its future. Implicit in this multiplicity is the relentless insistence on the end of cultural monopoly, an insistence whose tacit political power derives, in this instance, from the *form* itself of the story collection.[4] Also, the brevity of the stories allows for an unsustained representation of the Other of Gordimer's South Africa.[5] The voice of the white bourgeoisie does not fill the space of this collection in the same way that it reverberates throughout Gordimer's novels, and while the clearings opened for other voices are necessarily narrow ones, the concision actually authenticates these voices, making them at once more credible and less usurped. Given that the unknowability of the Other is in South Africa the palpable result of all the legislation erected to maintain the colour bar, and not simply part of the problematics of the postmodern critique of representation *per se*, the strictures imposed by brevity seem, in fact, to be virtues. The replacement of an intensely focused penetration into one or more consciousnesses – be it that of a conservationist, an activist's daughter, or the son of a coloured schoolteacher – with an assemblage of fragmented, partial, non-cumulative narratives, invites the reader to participate in a very differently-mediated discursive journey. Rather than *critically* following those few traces inscribed to track the fluctuating sensibilities of one or two primary consciousnesses, the reader is asked to read *diacritically*, across the silences between stories, around the tacit significances of their placements or alignments, and through the implied priorities of tales told first or last or middle.

The activity of reading diacritically, at the edges of certain social sites, in the centre of others, is a corollary to the kind of political education that Gordimer deems necessary for white South Africans who must move – conceptually, physically – outside of their protected enclaves and, like Bam and Maureen Smales of *July's People*, into the homes occupied by the rest, the majority of South Africans. It is this kind of education that the white jogger of 'Keeping Fit' unwittingly acquires when, in the course of his morning run, he mistakenly crosses over past the 'outward limit' of his route, past the 'industrial buffer' between suburb and township and finds himself in the 'squatter camp which had spread to the boundary' (p. 230). The movement of the text, from a centre of hegemonic power to the edges of disenfranchisement and back again, mimics the larger epistemological excursion required both to initiate and to sustain any kind of valid critique, be it motivated by a postmodern scepticism about cultural authority and its representation or by the sheer polarities of South African society. Thus the jogger crosses boundaries that are more intellectual than physical, though it is the encounter with an unknown physical reality that initially overcomes him. The stern respectability of the black woman who pulls him out of the pathway of a mob engrossed in murderous, angry pursuit; the meagre shanty where he cowers; the gratuitousness of his recreational run; the gravity of the racing mob: these are the events and the lives which, now exposed, require radical reformulations to be made. But when he is back on the 'right side', wanting somehow to tell what has happened during his extraordinary journey between safe points – the security-system of his own home, and the temporary security he was still somehow able to claim in the black woman's shanty – the jogger knows he will never 'understand how to tell' it; he will 'never get it all straight' (p. 241).

Gordimer's stories, like the jogger in 'Keeping Fit', often end up in a place of wordlessness. The silences which settle at the end of pieces like 'The Moment Before the Gun Went Off', 'Home', and 'Some Are Born to Sweet Delight' are, however, differently sounded. For Marais Van der Vyver, the Afrikaner farmer who had accidentally shot one of his farm-hands dead, the silence is born of bewilderment and sorrow. For this labourer, whose mother was one of the black women on the farm, was not just 'the farmer's boy; he was his son' (p. 117). His conception, an illegal engendering, has been decriminalized, but the change in statute neither legitimized the boy's status nor the father's grief. And so the Afrikaner must mourn mutely, suppressing again what had once been suppressed in his name, allowing again, only, a deadly silence.[6]

In other stories, wordlessness is the only response possible to the devastating sense that life has outstripped any ability to account for it, and so the counter-counter-revolutionary of 'Jump' wordlessly considers suicide, and the husband and wife of the allegorical 'Once Upon a Time' say nothing, though the housemaid is hysterical and the gardener weeps, as they retrieve the bleeding, shredded body of their own son, caught in the razor-thorn serrations of the barbed wire fence they had themselves erected (p. 30). Some of the stories in the collection suggest events intellectually or emotionally inaccessible, either because they are horrifically inexplicable – like the young woman in 'Some Are Born to Sweet Delight' who, with her unborn child, is the victim of her terrorist/lover's aeroplane bombing – or because they recount lives lived outside a particular, impenetrable circumference. Such is the case in 'Home', where a foreigner, a Swedish ichthyologist, is married to an Indian woman. He has access to her lovely body (though this too fades) but none to those recesses of familial identification and loyalty which claim her when her mother is taken into detention. Suspecting betrayal, wondering if his wife has taken a lover during the hours she labours for her mother's release, the husband senses only that his wife has left him for 'the dark family of which he was not a member, her country to which he did not belong' (p. 140). Like many other of Gordimer's stories and novels, 'Home' is a place where intimacy and unknowability, like a couple caught in embrace, must co-habit.

Gordimer does not always score the tone of her stories in the direction of silence, though perhaps she agrees with Wittgenstein that 'in art it is hard to say anything as good as: saying nothing' (p. 23e). *Saying* nothing does not of course mean that nothing is shown, and in this sense the *collection* of stories operates in a manner which, like collage or montage, 'mounts a process in order to intervene in the world, not to reflect but to change reality' (Ulmer, p. 86). As a kind of 'intellectual montage' where real elements operate as part of the discourse, and signifiers, selected and charged, are 'remotivated within the system' of new frames, the stories in *Jump* appropriate figurally – that most obsessive image of recent South African history, the dead child. Dead children – or tortured or damaged children – haunt the collection; they are found in nearly half of the stories, and appear in each of the collection's first three pieces as, first, the child offered up as sexual reward in 'Jump'; then as the shredded little boy of 'Once Upon a Time', and next as the mal-nourished baby brother, soon surely to die, of 'The Ultimate Safari'. Their near-presence wordlessly, repeatedly insists: this is the cost, this is the cost, this is the cost.

Significantly, the stories sunk into silence are most often those about white South Africans, caught at the end of the Interregnum without an expressible sense of future or commitment. Not so the stories about black South Africans, particularly 'The Ultimate Safari' and 'Amnesty', and, as 'interventions' in the world, they speak to the last stages of apartheid's dismantling. For the small girl of 'The Ultimate Safari', a refugee from Mozambique, the future is mostly illusive – she plans to return home where she imagines her missing mother and grandfather wait for her – but it is never elusive nor hopeless. So, too, for the black woman narrator of the collection's last story, 'Amnesty', who has waited through her lover's imprisonment on Robben Island for him to return and marry her. Released, return he has, not to marry but to keep on working for the revolution. Now it is for this she waits: the revolution not of his homecoming, but of their homegoing. On this scene of waiting, waiting for home and, significantly, the birth of her child, the collection ends though the process it has begun does not: one amnesty has been given, another is still needed.

Notes

1. The phrase, 'split historical position' is Stephen Clingman's.
2. Gordimer's very first stories were published in minor literary jour-nals, and her first collection of short fiction, *Face to Face*, was published in Johannesburg in 1949; in 1950, however, she published a story, 'A Watcher of the Dead', in the *New Yorker* and acquired an American literary agent, Sidney Satenstein. She has since published most of her short fiction in the United States and in Great Britain, for reasons she gives in 'The Short Story in South Africa'. For further discussion of Gordimer's early writing career, see Haugh and Hurwitt. For a discus-sion of Gordimer's short fiction from the 1940s through the 1980s, with particular attention to her depiction of women, see Trump.
3. While there are numerous stories which end by similarly employing the kind of metonymic slippage I have described, two striking ex-amples are 'A Lion on the Freeway' in *A Soldier's Embrace* and 'The Life of the Imagination' in *Selected Stories*. In both instances, a woman's distressed state, due to a private, primarily sexual dis-

appointment, becomes associated with an image of black invasion and violence. In connection with his discussion of the ability of metaphor to shape attitudes, J. M. Coetzee examines the 'circulating power of metonomy itself' where 'one site' is 'unendingly displaced on to another' (p. 26). Coetzee's elucidation of the operation of metonomy as part of the 'sanitation syndrome' that underlies both legislation and social attitude in South Africa is an account of the 'spread of aversion' (p. 27).

4.   Paul Ricoeur's statement that the 'discovery of the plurality of cultures is never a harmless experience' is a succinct summary of the thematics of Gordimer's collection; the encounters are not always or simply, however, between white and Other, and thus the multiplicity of encounters, perspectives, or viewpoints subsumed within the boundaries of the collection are themselves a subversion of cultural monopoly (quoted in Owens, p. 57). This cultural monopoly is eroded further by those pieces which suggest, again in Ricoeur's terms, the 'dispiriting effects' of a 'recent loss of mastery' (p. 58), as these are felt by white South Africans.

5.   My valuation of the necessarily 'unsustained' and 'brief' depictions of the Other in Gordimer's short fiction is meant, simply, to acknowledge Foucault's fundamental insight about the 'indignity of speaking for others' (Owens, p. 80).

6.   While Gordimer does not obviously pair the stories, 'The Moment Before the Gun Went Off' and 'Home', she does place them next to each other in *Jump*; this placement recalls the stories Gordimer did pair in her earlier collection, *A Soldier's Embrace*. 'Town and Country Lovers' One and Two, are, like the stories in *Jump*, about an interracial couple and about an Afrikaner farmer who fathers a child by a black woman. The differences in the stories attest to the changes which occurred in the ten years separating the collections; the foreign scientist of 'Town and Country Lovers', One, must hide his relationship with the Coloured woman; the Afrikaner farmer murders his child at its birth.

Works Cited

Clingman, Stephen, *The Novels of Nadine Gordimer: History from the Inside* (London: Allen and Unwin, 1986).

Coetzee, J. M. 'The Mind of Apartheid: Geoffrey Cronje (1907–   )', *Social Dynamics*, 17.1 (1991): pp. 1–35.

Derrida, Jacques, 'The Laws of Reflection: Nelson Mandela, in Admiration', trans. Mary Ann Caws and Isabella Lorenz, in *For Nelson Mandela*, eds Jacques Derrida and Mustapha Tlili (New York: Seaver Books, 1987: pp. 13–42).

_____ , 'Racism's Last Word', trans. Peggy Kamuf, *'Race,' Writing and Difference*, ed. Henry Louis Gates, Jr (Chicago: University of Chicago Press, 1986), pp. 329–38.

Foucault, Michel, *The Archeology of Knowledge and the Discourse on Language*, trans. A. M. Sheridan Smith (New York: Pantheon, 1972).

Gordimer, Nadine, 'The Essential Gesture', *The Essential Gesture*, ed. Stephen Clingman (New York: Penguin, 1989) pp. 285–300.

_____ , *July's People* (New York: Penguin, 1981).

_____ , *Jump* (New York: Farrar, Straus, Giroux, 1991).

_____ , 'Letter from Johannesburg, 1985', *The Essential Gesture*, pp. 301–10.

_____ , *Livingstone's Companions* (New York: Viking, 1971).

_____ , *Selected Stories* (New York: Viking, 1983).

_____ , 'The Short Story in South Africa', The International Symposium on the Short Story, *Kenyon Review* XXX (1968), pp. 457–63.

_____ , *A Soldier's Embrace* (New York: Viking, 1980).

Haugh, Robert, *Nadine Gordimer* (New York: Twayne, 1974).

Hurwitt, J., 'The Art of Fiction LXXVII', *Paris Review*, 88 (Summer 1983), pp. 82–127.

Owens, Craig, 'The Discourse of Others: Feminists and Postmodernism', *The Anti-Aesthetic*, ed. Hal Foster (Washington: Bay Press, 1983).

Trump, Martin, 'The Short Fiction of Nadine Gordimer', *Research in African Literatures*, 17.3 (Fall 1986) pp. 341–69.

Ulmer, Gregory, 'The Object of Post-Criticism', *The Anti-Aesthetic*, ed. Hal Foster (Washington: Bay Press, 1983).

Wittgenstein, Ludwig, *Culture and Value*, ed. G. H. von Wright, trans. Peter Winch (Chicago: University of Chicago Press, 1984).

Index

Abrahams, Lionel 6, 17, 174, 189
Adams, Hazard 43
Adorno, Theodor 35, 43
African National Congress
    (ANC) 6, 27, 28, 72, 91, 106,
    135, 146, 147, 150, 165, 166,
    174, 176, 208
Alvarez-Péreye, Jacques 43
Arkin, Marcus 171
Atwood, Margaret 10
Auden, W. H. 103

Bakhtin, Mikhail 68, 72, 208
Barkham, John 23, 31
Bazargan, Susan 73
Bazin, Nancy Topping 58, 208
Bellow, Saul 155
Benjamin, Walter 34
Benson, Mary 138
bildungsroman 3, 156
Boyers, Robert 137, 138, 227
Bragg, Melvyn 22
Brecht, Bertolt 14, 74, 87
Bunting, Brian 71, 72

Callaway, Henry 63, 70, 95–9, 107
Chinweizu 193, 207
Christie, S. 84, 88
Clifford, James 43, 116, 120
Clingman, Stephen 7, 13, 17, 92,
    95, 101, 102, 103, 107, 114, 119,
    137, 138, 189, 190, 192, 207,
    208, 236, 243, 244
Coad, David 17
Cock, Jacklyn 226, 227
Coetzee, J. M. 69, 74, 87, 193, 207,
    209, 244
Colleran, Jeanne 71
Communist Party (South
    Africa) 6, 61, 123, 135
*Conversations with Nadine
    Gordimer* 58, 199, 200, 202,
    206, 208

Conrad, Joseph 82, 108
Cooke, John 3, 16, 87, 92, 95, 101,
    102, 106–7, 156, 171, 182, 190
Cronin, Jeremy 183, 190

de Kok, Ingrid 106
de Lauretis, Teresa 208
Derrida, Jacques 239, 244
Dostoevsky, Fyodor 186
Dowling, David 73
Driver, D. 213, 214, 224, 227

Eagleton, Terry 69, 72
Eliot, T. S. 9
Engle, Lars 5, 17, 107
Erlande-Brandenburg, Alain 138

First, Ruth 214
Fischer, Bram 28, 138, 176
Fischer, Ernst 35, 41, 42, 44
Foucault, Michel 237, 238, 244,
    245

Gardner, Susan 58
Glueck, Nelson 172
Gordimer, Nadine
    'Amnesty' 243
    'Battlefield at No. 29' 227
    'Bit of Young Life, A' 227
    Black Interpreters, The 26, 31, 190
    'Blinder' 221–2, 234
    Burger's Daughter 4, 5, 6–8, 11,
        12, 15–16, 21–2, 23, 31, 36–42,
        43, 44, 49, 57, 58, 59, 60, 61,
        63–5, 70, 71, 72, 79, 80, 120,
        121–54, 168, 176, 190, 192,
        194, 198, 217, 227
    'Chief Luthuli' 177, 189
    'Child is the Man, The' 32
    'Chip of Glass Ruby, A' 222
    'City of the Dead, A City of the
        Living, A' 229
    'Congo River, The' 177

Gordimer, Nadine – *continued*
　Conservationist, The 4, 5, 10, 11,
　　21, 29, 45, 49–55, 58, 60,
　　62–3, 70, 71, 72, 83–5, 88,
　　91–107, 156, 181, 190
　'Correspondence Course,
　　A' 234
　'Crimes of Conscience' 233–4
　'Defeated, The' 157, 159–60,
　　162, 170, 172
　Essential Gesture, The 33, 44, 72,
　　120, 138, 147, 149, 154, 177,
　　178, 189, 191, 195, 207, 236,
　　238, 245
　Face to Face 227, 243
　'For Dear Life' 231
　Friday's Footprint 160, 172
　'From Apartheid to
　　Afrocentrism' 59, 72
　'Good Climate, Friendly
　　Inhabitants' 218–20, 224
　Guest of Honour, A 3, 4, 82, 88,
　　163, 181, 182, 188, 201, 232
　'Harry's Presence' 160–2, 166,
　　169, 170
　'Home' 241, 242, 244
　'Hunting Accident, A' 233
　'Intruder, An' 222–4
　'Is There Nowhere Else Where
　　We Can Meet?' 59, 71, 72
　'Journey, A' 239
　July's People 5, 9–10, 11, 14, 22,
　　23–6, 27, 31, 49, 60, 62, 65–7,
　　70, 71, 72, 73, 83, 86, 108–20,
　　121, 122, 138, 180, 192, 201,
　　241, 245
　Jump 238–45
　'Jump' 242, 243
　'Keeping Fit' 241
　Late Bourgeois World, The 3, 7, 9,
　　12–13, 15, 35–6, 44, 47–9, 50,
　　57, 58, 79, 162, 163, 176, 180,
　　232
　'Leaving School – II' 22, 87
　'Letter from His Father' 29
　'Letter from Johannesburg' 238,
　　245
　'Life of the Imagination,
　　The' 243

'Lion on the Freeway, A' 137,
　138, 228, 231, 243
'Living in the Interregnum' 71,
　72, 109, 120, 131, 137, 138,
　173, 177–8, 188, 190, 195, 207,
　216, 227
Livingstone's Companions 172,
　227, 238, 245
Lying Days, The 21, 23, 75, 79,
　81, 87, 156, 157, 158, 159,
　166, 170
'Merci Dieu, It Changes' 177
'Moment Before the Gun Went
　Off, The' 238, 241, 244
'My Father Leaves Home' 190
My Son's Story 4, 6, 10, 13, 14,
　15, 16, 22, 29–31, 32, 67, 72,
　107, 191–209
'Need for Something Sweet,
　A' 232, 235–6
'Notes of an Expropriator' 87
Not For Publication 218, 222, 227
'Novel and the Nation in South
　Africa, The' 87
Occasion for Loving 21, 23, 31,
　45, 58, 82–3, 88, 162, 180
'Once Upon a Time' 242, 243
'One Man Living Through
　It' 177
'Oral History' 228, 229, 230
'Prison-House of Colonialism,
　The' 87, 227
'Pula' 177
'Rain Queen' 227
'Relevance and
　Commitment' 207
Selected Stories 208, 221, 227,
　228, 236, 237, 238, 243, 245
'Short Story in South Africa,
　The' 240, 243, 245
'Sins of the Third Age' 233–4
Six Feet of the Country 227
'Smell of Death and Flowers,
　The' 227
Soft Voice of the Serpent, The 72,
　156, 157, 171, 172
Soldier's Embrace, A 138, 225,
　227, 228, 230, 231, 232, 233,
　235, 236, 243, 244, 245

Gordimer, Nadine – *continued*
'Some Are Born to Sweet
  Delight' 241, 242
Some Monday for Sure 71, 72
Something Out There 58, 198,
  218, 221, 227, 228, 229–31,
  233, 234
'Something Out There' 45, 46,
  218, 228, 230, 236
'South African Childhood,
  A' 87
Sport of Nature, A 3, 4, 6, 7, 8, 9,
  10, 11, 12, 14, 15, 16, 22, 23,
  26–9, 31, 32, 36–40, 41, 42,
  43, 44, 55–7, 58, 61, 67–9, 70,
  71, 72, 80, 81, 86, 107, 137,
  138–90, 193, 217, 226, 227,
  236
'Teraloyna' 238–9
'Termitary, The' 225
'Third Presence, The' 163–4,
  172, 216–17
'Time Did' 232, 233
'Town and Country
  Lovers' 232, 235, 244
'Ultimate Safari, The' 243
'Watcher of the Dead, A' 243
'What Being a South African
  Means to Me' 227
*What Happened to 'Burger's
  Daughter'* 140, 141, 154
'What Were You
  Dreaming?' 238
World of Strangers, A 76, 78, 87,
  162, 176, 180, 189, 190
'Writer in South Africa, A' 87
'You Name It' 235
Gramsci, Antonio 60, 120, 121,
  143, 223
Gray, Stephen 59, 72, 79, 87, 227
Greenstein, Susan 120, 137, 138
Grontkowski, Christine 130, 138
Gullon, Ricardo 85, 88

Haggard, Rider 75
Hamlet 7–8, 193, 199, 200, 205, 208,
  209
Haugh, Robert 243, 245
Heart of Darkness 108, 138

Heilbrun, Caroline 204, 209
Hirson, Denis 17
Hope, Christopher 57, 85
Hurwitt, Jannika 31, 243, 245

Jacobson, Ruth 190
James, Henry 21
Johnson, Diane 175
Jonas, Hans 138
Joyce, James 107

Kafka, Franz 29, 206
Keller, Evelyn Fox 130, 138
Keysworth, F. 219, 227
Krantz, Judith 107
Kundera, Milan 184, 190

Lawrence, D. H. 26, 77, 83
Lazar, Karen 13, 214, 226, 227
Leavis, F. R. 77
Lessing, Doris 77, 87
Lévi-Strauss, Claude 59, 60, 121,
  146, 208
Liscio, Lorraine 137, 138
Lockett, C. 213, 227
Luthuli, Chief 177

Macaskill, Brian 7, 71, 72, 73
MacPherson, C. B. 34, 43, 44
Malamud, Bernard 155
Mandela, Nelson 27, 176, 186, 244
Marcuse, Herbert 35, 44
Memmi, Albert 42
Messe, Elizabeth 137, 138
Millin, Sarah Gertrude 209
Moi, Toril 216, 227
Morse, Ruth 17

Newman, Julie 35, 43, 44, 95, 137,
  138
Nkrumah, Kwame 177, 187

Oedipal 15, 161, 162, 166, 169,
  170, 183, 190, 200, 205, 208
Oedipus Tyrannos 200
Orwell, George 103
Owens, Craig 244, 245
*Oxford English Dictionary
  (OED)* 67, 68

Press, Karen 106
Proust, Marcel 26, 77

Radhakrishnan, R. 137, 139
Rich, Adrienne 125, 137, 139
Rich, Paul 87
Ricks, Christopher 29
Ricoeur, Paul 244
Rostow, W. W. 103

Sachs, Albie 91, 93, 106, 208
Salkey, Andrew 31
Sampson, Anthony 189
Sartre, Jean-Paul 33, 44
Schreiner, Olive 81, 87, 214
Scott, Ann 214
Serote, Mongane Wally 131, 148
Seymour, Marilyn Dallman 58, 208
Shakespeare, William 8, 15, 29, 31, 192, 203
Sharpeville 126, 167, 176
S. M. 57
Smith, Rowland 17
Smith, Wilbur 107
Sontag, Susan 143, 221, 227
Soweto 21, 60, 61, 123, 124, 136, 144, 147

Stein, Pippa 190
Sturgess, Charlotte 17

Taylor, Ronald 44
Thieulle, Anne 17
Thurman, Judith 189
Trump, Martin 73, 243, 245
Tutu, Desmond 147

Ulmer, Gregor 242, 245
Ulysses 107

Viola, Andre 107
Visel, Robin 137, 139
Visser, Nicholas 71, 73
Vogel, L. 215, 227

Wade, Michael 16, 17, 92, 93, 102, 106, 172, 182, 190
Ward, David 88
Wästberg, Per 43, 44
Weinhouse, Linda 174–5, 189
Wittgenstein, Ludwig 242, 245
Woolf, Virginia 204, 206, 209

Yelin, Louise 137, 139

Z. N. 57